The Master Musicians

EDITED BY
FREDERICK J. CROWEST

Schubert

The
Master Musicians

Edited by
FREDERICK J. CROWEST

LIST OF VOLUMES.

Small Crown. 3s. 6d. net per vol.

Schubert

By

Edmondstoune Duncan

With

Illustrations and Portraits

London: J. M. Dent & Sons, Ltd.
New York: E. P Dutton & Co.
1912

First Edition printed 1905
Reprinted 1912

Author's Preface

No better apology can be offered for the appearance of this little book—since it is the custom of book-writers to apologise—than that the English biographies are now mostly out of print; and those which are not out of print are out of date. For example, the English translation of Kreissle's "Schubert"[1]—the chief *life*—and Wilberforce's "Franz Schubert," not to speak of some of the popular German biographies, such as Reissmann's, being out of print, are difficult to obtain; and, in the event of a reprint, to be of any use they would need to be largely re-written. The reason of this is to be attributed to the publication by Messrs Brcitkopf & Haertel of the complete works of Schubert. For with the completion of that great undertaking, all conjecture and speculation regarding the composer's MSS. were finally disposed of. Instead of the mere mention of the names of his works—though that was valuable enough when, in 1874, Nottebohm issued the famous catalogue—the public has now before it the full and complete life-work of FRANZ SCHUBERT. By the publication referred to, Messrs Breitkopf & Haertel augmented the printed works of our composer by some one hundred and fifty songs, six symphonies, a dozen scores of operas, operettas and dramatic works, many quartets, sonatas, and a vast number of pieces of every possible

[1] By Mr A. D. Coleridge.

Author's Preface

variety and combination, beautifully set up, and edited with notable care and attention.

Writing in the *Neue Zeitschrift für Musik* for 1840, Robert Schumann remarked that "if fruitfulness is recognised as the principal sign of genius, then Schubert was of the greatest. Though he lived little more than thirty years, he has written an enormous quantity, of which only half is yet printed, while another part is now awaiting publication; and a still larger portion will probably not be published for a long time to come, if indeed ever."

About fifty years after these remarks were penned, Schubert's complete works appeared—thus offering the highest possible tribute to the memory of their illustrious author.

The wonderful vitality of his music is brought home to us the more we study it. With Schumann we may truly exclaim :—

"It carries with it the Germs of
Everlasting Youth."

E. D.

May 1, 1905.

Contents

BIOGRAPHICAL

THE MAN

Contents

List of Illustrations

Biographical

FRANZ PETER SCHUBERT was born in Vienna on Jan.
31, 1797, and, according to the zu dem Heil parish
register, was baptised in the Catholic Church on the

following day. The house where he was born—with its sign "Zum rothen Krebsen" (the Red Crab)—is situate

Birth and Parentage at No. 54 Nussdorferstrasse, though in Schubert's day it was known as No. 72 Himmelpfortgrund (Gate of Heaven), in the Lichtenthal district of the city. His father, from whom he took the name Franz, was the son of a Moravian peasant, and came from Neudorf. He would be about thirty-three when little Franz was born. He had studied and settled down in Vienna, where his integrity and ability gained the respect of all who knew him. From 1784 to 1786, he was assistant schoolmaster to his brother, who had a small educational establishment in the Leopoldstadt district of Vienna. Franz's father then obtained an appointment as head of the school, in the parish zu den heiligen 14 Nothhelfern, in the Lichtenthal district, a post which he held for some thirty-one years, indeed until he proceeded to a similar but better school-appointment in the Rossau. At the age of nineteen (about 1783) he married Elizabeth Fitz, a Silesian, who, like the mother of Beethoven, had been in service as a cook. From this union there resulted a large family, numbering no less than fourteen children, nine of whom died in infancy, and one only—Ferdinand (born in 1794)—comes with any degree of prominence into the course of this biography. It may be mentioned, however, in passing, that the first child was Ignaz (born 1784), who, like Ferdinand, became a schoolmaster, the last member being a girl named Therese. Five more children were added to the Schubert household—thus numbering nineteen—by a second wife, whom schoolmaster Franz espoused in 1812. A good account of the early years of Schubert's life is

Schubert's Birthplace

(*from a drawing by J. A. Symington*)

First Lessons

furnished by the composer's father, who outlived him some two years. "When he was five years old," says he, "I prepared him for elementary instruction, and at six I sent him to school, where he was always one of the first among his fellow-scholars. He was fond of society from early youth, and was never happier than when he could spend his hours of play in a circle of joyous comrades. When he was eight, I gave him preliminary instruction on the violin, and let him practise until he could play easy duets pretty well: after that, I sent him to attend the singing-class of Herr Michael Holzer, choirmaster in Lichtenthal. Herr Holzer often assured me, with tears in his eyes, that he had never had such a pupil. 'Whenever I want to teach him anything new,' he would say, 'I find he knows it already. The result has been I have not given him any real instruction, but have only looked on him with astonishment and silence.'" Franz's talent for music was soon discovered. His sister, Therese, states that the lad made friends with a joiner's apprentice—a namesake and relative—who used to delight in taking him to a piano-forte warehouse, where the child would try his small fingers on the fine new resonant instruments, which were in marked contrast to his father's worn-out chopping-board ("Hackbrett"). Schubert's two brothers—Ignaz and Ferdinand — had both studied the violin and piano-forte, and Franz was now receiving lessons on the latter instrument from Ignaz. He is said to have been extremely conscientious in his tuition. Young Franz, however, proved so quick to learn, and so in-dustrious in mastering difficulties, that the master was soon overtaken. Elder brothers are rarely lenient critics, yet we find Professor Ignaz confessing as follows:—"I

3

was amazed when Franz told me that he had no need of any further instruction from me, and that for the future he would make his own way. And in truth his progress in a short period was so great that I was forced to acknowledge in him a master who had completely distanced and outstripped me, and whom I despaired of overtaking." From the singing-class of Holzer and the piano lessons of brother Ignaz, Franz soon progressed to regular instruction in thorough bass, singing and piano and organ playing, under the skilled guidance of Holzer. Upon hearing his pupil extemporise on a given subject, the master exclaimed, "The lad has harmony at his fingers' ends." He began to compose at an extremely early period. Ferdinand states that Schubert's first pianoforte composition was a Fantasia for four hands,[1] written in 1810, and that in the following year he wrote the "Klagegesang der Hagar," his first song ; but Kreissle says there is no doubt that before this period he had written songs, piano-pieces, and even string-quartets, adding that with the single exception of Mozart, "we shall probably find that in none of the great musicians was the creative faculty awakened so early, or made its way with such irresistible power, as in Franz Schubert." At the age of eleven, Schubert made his first appearance in public, at the Lichtenthal parish church, where his fresh young voice and expressive, delicate manner of singing attracted much attention. Upon occasion, too, his violin was employed in the service of the church. Here it was that he gained his earliest impressions of sacred music—afterwards to bear such good fruit in his

[1] This is sometimes erroneously mentioned as "The Corpse-Fantasia"; but the latter is in reality an early setting of Schiller's song entitled "Ein Leichenfantasie."

At School

noble Masses, the *Song of Miriam, Lazarus,* and the setting of "The Lord is my Shepherd." His father now found little or no difficulty in getting the boy into the Emperor's choir, and in consequence, Schubert became a pupil of the Convict school which was attached. He had remained at home until his eleventh year. In October 1808 he was called upon to give evidence of his ability before the school authorities. The Convict was a foundation school of a kind popular in Germany. These were generally in touch with the Convent system, and supported by State, or private endowment. Franz, arrived at No. 45 in the Piaristen Gasse, Josefstadt, spectacled and clad in his light grey suit, did not escape the chaff of his fellow-competitors, who nicknamed him the miller, and pretended he must necessarily succeed. Put to the trial, before the two Court Capellmeisters, Salieri and Eybler, and singing-master Körner, the little grave-looking candidate acquitted himself so cleverly in his singing of the test-pieces that he was straightway admitted, and (to his great content) exchanged the modest miller suit for the brave gold-laced uniform of the Imperial school. Music had been in some neglect at the Convict, in common with other Viennese academies, owing to the persistent attentions of Napoleon. During the first year of Franz's pupilage, little systematic work could be expected. Vienna surrendered for a second time, on May 13, 1809, and it was not until October 14 that the treaty of peace was signed and music resumed her quiet sway. At the Convict, where Schubert was receiving a free education, there were drawbacks common enough to many of the early nineteenth century boarding establishments. The practice-rooms were cold and bare ;

Enters the Convict

5

the food was insufficient; no wonder, then, that we find young Schubert appealing to his brother for help. "I've been thinking a good long time about my position," writes he to Ferdinand on November 24, 1812,[1] "and find that it's all very well on the whole, but that in some respects it can be improved. You know from experience that one can often enjoy eating a roll ("Semmel") and an apple or two all the more after eight and a half hours' fast, with only a meagre supper to look forward to. This desire has become so pressing that willy-nilly I must make a change. The two groschen that father gave me are gone in the first few days. If, then, I rely upon you, I hope I may do so without being ashamed (see Matt. ii. 4). So also thought I. How would it be if you were to advance me a couple of kreuzers monthly? You would never miss them, whilst I could shut myself up in my cell and be quite happy. As I said, I rely on the words of the Apostle Matthew, who says: "Let him that hath two coats give one to the poor."[2] Meanwhile I trust you will listen to the voice which unceasingly appeals to you to remember your loving, hoping, poverty-stricken—and once again I repeat, poverty-stricken—brother FRANZ."

The poverty-stricken schoolboy was not the first who had quoted scripture to some purpose; and though we have no record, doubtless the tender-hearted Ferdinand sent him the couple of kreuzers for the

---

[1] In 1812 Schubert's mother died; but there is nothing remaining but the bare record of the fact, unless the "Trauermusik für Blasinstrumente" has reference to that event.

[2] Both references are misleading. "I trust in Thee: let me not be ashamed" (Psalm xxv. 2). "He that hath two coats, let him impart to him that hath none" (St Luke iii. 2).

Early Ideals

Semmel and apples. As far as Schubert was concerned, the most conspicuously useful feature of the
Convict school curriculum lay in the daily orchestral
practices held. Symphonies and overtures were in
regular rehearsal. Composers of the highest order were
drawn upon, such as Haydn, Mozart and Beethoven,
and many writers of lesser degree, as Cherubini, Méhul,
Krommer and Kozeluch. Of these, as was natural,
Schubert liked his Haydn, loved his Mozart, and
worshipped his Beethoven. The smaller men, however,
were by no means despised, for we read of the youngster
taking up cudgels in defence of Kozeluch, as against
Krommer, whose symphonies were deservedly popular
at the time of which we are writing, on account
of their tunefulness. Méhul was admired, but not
in the same manner as Mozart, whose overtures to
Figaro and the *Magic Flute*, were first favourites.
At these practices, Schubert began with a modest seat
behind the leader of the violins—Josef von Spaun.
Looking over his shoulder, at the first appearance of
young Franz, Spaun was much pleased with the clever
way in which the new recruit acquitted himself. Soon
there sprang up a great friendship between the two pupils,
though Schubert was nine years Spaun's junior. Franz
confided in him that he had already composed much,
that he could not help it, and that he should do so every
day, could he but obtain the necessary manuscript paper.
With all the generosity of a young man of twenty, Spaun
seized the enviable opportunity, and young Schubert
lacked not of music-paper for many a long day. For
this and for other kindly acts, Spaun's memory will
always be held in grateful association with Schubert's.

Schubert

Franz quickly advanced to the leadership of the orchestra, where it is said he exercised a notable influence on the *morale* of the band of youthful players.

Leader of Orchestra When the director—Ruczizka—was absent, it was Schubert who took his place. His wonderful gifts, no less than his earnest manner and frank disposition, wrought a wonderful effect on his fellow-students. The practical gain to himself was great and far-reaching. One may turn to such works as the "Unfinished" symphony or the great "C-major" symphony, and the influence of those early days may be traced in the sureness of touch, the delightful practicability which the individual players enjoy in their parts, and above all, in the supreme mastery which the composer has of the whole orchestral machine, familiar to the boy, and commanded of the man.

In the matter of general education, the subjects taught at the Convict are known to have included French, Italian, Mathematics, History, Geography, Drawing and Writing. It is noteworthy also that there were two professors of Poetry. The establishment was directed by Dr Innocenz Lang, the Curator being Count Dietrichstein, while the general staff included preachers, catechists, an inspector, and regularly ordained priests who served as visiting-lecturers. During his first year Schubert acquitted himself creditably enough, but after that his musical faculty began to assert itself so undeniably that his other studies were cast in the shade, or neglected. It is therefore more than probable that Schubert's scholarship was a negligible quantity, though his fine natural taste would carry him far beyond ordinary attainments.

"He is a Genius"

Salieri was the first to recognise Schubert's supreme gift, and he placed him with Ruczizka for lessons in composition. Before long the pupil so astonished his teacher, that he reports to his chief—Salieri—that "the lad knows everything already; he has been taught by God." Salieri himself then took Schubert in hand. The accomplished Italian was a handsome man, with an expressive eye, a quick temper, and a great reputation. He soon perceived that in " Hagars Klage " (March 30, 1811) and some string quartets, there was genius of an unusual order. "He can do everything," exclaimed he of Schubert, " he is a genius. He composes songs, masses, operas, quartets—whatever you can think of." Schubert used to go to his house in the Seilergasse, carrying a large roll of MSS. under his arm, for the master's verdict and advice. The lesson over, he would then commonly steal into a neighbouring wine-shop, where he would chat for hours over a glass with friend Doppler. These lessons extended over the five years 1813-1817, and were thus begun in the last year of Schubert's stay at the Convict, and continued long after. On Sundays and holidays, the boy commonly took part in quartets, some of which were of his own composition— "taken scarcely dry from his desk," says Kreissle. It is a pleasant picture of home life to see father Franz seated at his 'cello—earnest enough, but none too accurate—with brother Ferdinand as leader, and Ignaz taking second violin, while Franzl (in his spectacles) cleverly handles his viola, keeping a sharp eye on his father, whose slips, if recurring, would be gently pointed out with " Herr Vater, there must be a mistake somewhere." Besides the quartets, the years 1811-12 saw the

9

composition of variations, a sonata, and several choral pieces. There was also a cantata for three male voices and guitar, written for his father's birthday, Sept. 27, 1812; and finally, as the crowning effort of his school-life, a first symphony (in D), dated Oct. 28, 1813, which was performed on the birthday of Dr Lang, director of the Convict.

The theatre cast its spell on Schubert while he was yet a pupil of the Convict. Weigl's *Waisenhaus*, given December 12, 1810, was the first opera he heard. In the following year he witnessed a performance of the same composer's *Schweizerfamilie*, with Vogl and Anna Milder in the principal parts. Other operas which impressed the young musician were Spontini's *La Vestale*, Cherubini's *Medea*, Boildieu's *Jean de Paris*, Isouard's *Aschenbrödl*, and above all, Gluck's *Iphigenia in Tauris*, which he saw on April 5, 1815, when Vogl and Milder took the chief rôles. Bauernfeld states that this performance led to Schubert's carefully studying Gluck's scores : which, it may be added, had then recently been published by Trattnern of Vienna. The first-fruits of these early impressions of the theatre appeared in 1814. Josef Hüttenbrenner has left it on record that when Salieri told Schubert that he was competent to attempt an opera, the pupil stayed away from his lessons for some weeks. He then made his appearance before his astonished teacher with the full-score of a completed opera, namely, *Des Teufels Lustschloss* (a three-act piece written by Kotzebue). Kreissle explains that Schubert left two versions of this work, and that it was the second version with which Schubert astonished Salieri. The original score was carefully preserved, and came into the possession of Dr Schneider.

School Friends

The rearrangement (in its MS. form) was given to Josef Hüttenbrenner, in payment of a debt. A portion of this MS. (indeed the whole of the second act) was used by Hüttenbrenner's servants to light a fire, and thus completely destroyed (1840).

The art of making friends, and of keeping them, was no secret to Schubert. More than one friendship, formed at the Convict, lasted throughout life. Josef von Spaun, the oldest boy, when Schubert entered as a pupil, soon became one of the composer's staunchest supporters. Then there was Josef Kenner, an accomplished amateur, three of whose poems Schubert afterwards set to music. Another friend was Anton Holzapfel, a fine tenor singer and an excellent 'cellist, who afterwards took up law for his living. Nor must we forget Albert Stadler, who became a barrister by profession, and in his spare time cultivated pianoforte-playing and composition. There was also Senn, the gifted and impetuous poet, who turned misanthrope, and came to an untimely end. Randhartinger was also a contemporary scholar with Schubert, and he, like the others, maintained a life-long friendship with the composer.[1]

There is little or nothing known of Schubert's singing and vocal study with Körner during his residence at the Convict. His voice broke in 1813, and though he

---

[1] Kreissle mentions the following additional names of scholars Schubert would meet during his career at the Convict:—Leopold Ebner, Max Weisse, Franz Müllner, Josef Kleindl, Carl Rueskäfer, and J. B. Wisgrill. Those who belonged to the school orchestra were Spaun and Kleindl (first violins), Holzapfel ('cello), Senn (horn), and Randhartinger (drum).

would now be of little use to the Imperial choir for some time to come, the Convict authorities, with the direct sanction of the Emperor, it is understood, were prepared to grant him a place on the so-called Merveldt foundation, provided he submitted to examination and continued the higher classical studies. This would seem to have been utterly distasteful, and he promptly turned his back on both examination and scholarship. The decision he arrived at is said by Spaun to have been largely brought about by Theodor Körner, the soldier-poet, who chanced to be in Vienna during the years 1811-1813. Schubert had made up his mind to follow music, devoting his whole time to her. Nothing should come between him and the divine call. No man ever stepped forward to face his destiny more light-heartedly; none was ever better entitled to dream of success; and yet, the sequel will show that with a commanding genius, an ease of production never paralleled in the annals of music, and possessed of a contented spirit that could have vied with a Vicar of Wakefield, Schubert was still to go down to posterity as a man of broken fortunes—one whose ability, though it might enchant the civilised world, could not (or at least did not) succeed in keeping the wolf from the door during the thirty-one brief years of his life. Thus Schubert left the Convict. One of his friends stated that he ran away; but this was indignantly denied by Albert Stadler and other of his contemporaries. In order to qualify as a teacher, Franz now entered the normal school of St Anna, where he spent the educational term 1813-14. He had been summoned three times, says Ferdinand, for Conscription, and it was in order to escape that evil, or just possibly to please his father, who seems to have tried to break him off the habit of composing, that he now agreed to become one of the elementary teachers in his father's school. Here he passed three years of severe drudgery, for which so sensitive a nature was wofully ill-fitted; though it is greatly to his credit that the duties undertaken were faithfully discharged. His spare time was devoted to composition, which was never more prolific than during these teaching days. No less than 250 songs were composed between 1814 and 1816, while during the year 1815 alone, 146 songs found their way into existence. One is scarcely surprised to discover that our teacher's patience was severely tried. His sister Therese says that Franz was actually severe and bad-tempered with his pupils, and that "he often kept his hands in practice on the children's ears." According to one Schmidtler, it was after a smart box on the ear administered to a stupid girl, that Schubert's father was extremely indignant with his son's methods of punishment, and that the incident led to his dismissal.

Schubert was accustomed to visit a certain family named Grob. The widow was owner of a silk-factory in Vienna, and was highly cultured and well circumstanced. Her daughter, Therese, whom Schubert greatly admired, was beautiful and exceedingly accomplished as a singer, her voice being a high soprano. She often tried over his latest songs, while a "Tantum ergo" and a "Salve Regina" were specially composed for her voice. The brother, Heinrich, was a good 'cellist and pianist. In after years (in the absence of Holzer) he occasionally directed the music at the Lichtenthal parish church, in conjunction with Schubert, who would sit listening in the nave while Heinrich conducted. In this accomplished household, young Franz was as an adopted son. Here he would seek relief from the harassing cares of his daily task, and here would he often rehearse (in private) his Masses and other sacred and secular compositions.

An opportunity now arose which brought Schubert into considerable prominence. His first Mass (in F, for

First Mass

4 voices and orchestra) was to be given at the Lichtenthal parish church. The performance took place on Oct. 16, 1814, when Therese Grob sang the principal soprano part, and Mayseder acted as first violin. At its conclusion, Salieri embraced the composer, exclaiming : " Franz, you are my dear pupil, and you will bring me much honour." Ten days later, according to Ferdinand Schubert, the Mass was repeated under circumstances which gave it an air of being quite a family festival. Therese Grob again took the chief part, Ferdinand played the organ, Michael Holzer acted as Regius Chori, and Schubert himself conducted ; while friends and acquaintances filled the remaining parts. To crown all, the composer's father presented him with a new five-octave piano, which would doubtless prove a welcome exchange for the family " Hackbrett." [1]

Among the numerous compositions of 1814, were five string quartets, and many first-rate songs, such as " Gretchen am Spinnrade " (op. 2). During December of this year Schubert made the acquaintance of Mayrhofer, the census-official and tragic poet, the musician's senior by full ten years. " My acquaintance with Schubert " —says Mayrhofer in his memoirs—" was brought about by a young friend giving him my poem, ' Am See,' to

[1] See p. 3.

set to music.   The friend brought him to that very room
which, five years later, 1819, we were destined to share in
common.   It was in a dark, gloomy street.   House and
furniture were the worse for wear ; the ceiling was beginning
to bulge, the light obstructed by a huge building opposite,
and part of the furniture was an old worn-out piano and
a shabby bookstand—such was the room.   I shall never
forget it nor the hours we spent there. . . . This depth
of sentiment and mutual love for poetry and music drew
our sympathies closer and closer ; I wrote verses, he saw
what I wrote, and to these joint efforts many of his
melodies owed their beginning, end, and popularity in the
world." [1]   It will be seen that as their friendship grew,
Mayrhofer contributed poems freely, and commonly at
Schubert's instigation.   These were generally immediately
set to music.   Mayrhofer is the author of no less than 47
in the printed collection; he also wrote two operatic
librettos—*Adrast*, and *Die beiden Freunde v. Salamanka*—
which were set to music in 1815.   Seven operatic pieces
were composed during that year.   May brought forth *Die
vierjährige Posten* (words by Körner) ; another one-act
piece, *Fernando*, appeared in July, which also saw the completion of *Claudine von Villa Bella*, a three-act opera by
Goethe, which was followed by *Der Spiegelritter*, a three-
act piece (by Kotzebue) and *Der Minnesänger*.

At an early age Schubert had begun to celebrate
important occasions with specially composed music.   For
example, in 1812 he had written a little piece for the
birthday (or "name-day") of his father, which fell on Sept.
27.   There is also another work designed for a corre-

---

[1] Another account states that "the whole decorations comprised
a couple of books, a guitar, and the indispensable tobacco-pipes."

sponding occasion in 1815. Nor did he confine himself to the paternal name-day, for Louise Gosmar, Irene Kiesewetter, Vogl, and last, but not least, the Emperor Franz, were all similarly honoured at different times. A more melancholy occasion is marked by the little octet for wind-instruments, written on the death of his mother in 1812.

During the last days of December 1815, or at the latest, says Spaun, in Jan. 1816, The "Erl-king" was written. The story is given in full elsewhere (p. 138). Sung on the day of its composition, either by Holzapfel, or by Randhartinger, in the Convict practice-room, it did not appear in print until 1821, when it contributed powerfully to the making of Schubert's reputation, especially after Vogl took it up, which was soon after its performance. This wonderful song actually brought in substantial receipts, 800 copies being sold in nine months by Diabelli, who took half the profits.

Schubert was never an enthusiastic competitor for a vacant post. Early experience may have had something to do with this, or it may be that he felt himself unsuited to methodical and regular duties. He applied on a day in April 1816 for the appointment as chief teacher at the School of Music, Laibach, near Trieste. The appointment was under Government control, and carried with it the princely salary of 500 Vienna florins, or £21, a year. Schubert's application was supported by Salieri, whose half-hearted testimonial somewhat betrays him, and by Josef Spendou, who wrote a practical recommendation, as Head Superintendent of Schools. In the result, Schubert was passed over and, *on the recommendation of Salieri*, one Jacob Schaufl was accepted "as the fittest person for the position."

Refused an Appointment

Friend in Need

Schubert was now to make a valuable friend in Franz von Schober, who had met with some of the composer's songs as early as 1813, when on a visit to the Spauns at Linz. Schober had entered Vienna University as a student, and as soon as he arrived in town he sought out Schubert, whom he discovered in his father's house, surrounded with MSS. and correcting school exercises. We have already seen that Schubert had decided to go in for music, to live for it, and by it. His new friend now stepped in, and, with the consent of his own mother and of Schubert's father, young Franz was carried off to share his rooms in the "Landskrongasse." Here they lived together for six months, when Schober's brother, an Hussar officer, arrived on the scene and claimed the available room. Spaun seems then to have come to Schubert's aid. The following entry in his diary is understood to apply to this period: "Schubert, at that time poor and neglected, was for weeks and months supported by a friend at a small tavern. This friend often shared his room and bed with him." Bauernfeld states that about this time Schubert gave outside lessons in music, and that before long he gave it up altogether. The same friend who supported Schubert at the tavern, arranged for him to share rooms with Mayrhofer during the years 1819-20; but, throughout the chief part of Schubert's further career, Schober kept a room always ready for him, and when the two friends were in town, Schober's lodgings sheltered them both.

An event of importance befell on June 16, 1816, when Salieri celebrated his Jubilee. The Italian musician was a man of much influence in his day, and his fifty years, residence in Vienna, though it had never enabled him to master German, had won for him the respect of a wide circle of friends. He had come in contact with four of the great musicians of all time. Haydn he had always been on good terms with, towards Mozart, on the other hand, he had been in open antagonism: while Beethoven held him in respect, as indeed did his last pupil—Franz Schubert. Salieri was decorated with the great gold medal and chain of honour of the civic class (Civil-Ehrenmedaille), and after Mass, which was sung to some of his own music, an address was presented to him, followed by a series of compositions which had been written for the occasion by former pupils. These were given in turn, beginning with the work of the youngest, and ending with the presentation pieces of Hummel and Moscheles, who were unable to attend. Schubert was represented by a little cantata, to a simple libretto of his own composition. This is referred to in the "Diary" (see p. 96). The piece comprises a chorus ("Gütigster, Bester"), an air, and a canon for three voices, and is now to be had in published form.

Besides the piece for Salieri's jubilee, there was a cantata entitled *Prometheus*, also dated June 16, written in honour of one Heinrich Watteroth—a prominent Vienna official, words by Philip Draxler—designed for two solo voices, chorus and orchestra, a work which does not appear to have survived. The piece was given in Watteroth's garden, where were assembled the chief official people of the day. Its importance here, however, arises from Schubert having noted in his journal that it was his first money transaction. The sum he received was one hundred Vienna florins—or four pounds sterling. Schubert apparently set some store by the

Prometheus music, which was repeated at Innsbruck by Gänsbacher, and at Vienna by Sonnleitner; and other performances were in contemplation. Another cantata was produced in September of the same year, in honour of Dr Josef Spendou, chief Inspector of Schools. The piece is designed for soli, chorus and orchestra, and entitled *Expressions of Gratitude on the part of the Institute of the Widows of Teachers, at Vienna, to the Founder and Principal of the same* (Josef Spendou). It is a realistic attempt, beginning "There lies he, stricken down by death"—alluding to the dead father. Then the helplessness of the children is portrayed, the mourning of the widow, and finally there is an address to their deliverer, and a chorus of widows and orphans in praise of the Founder. The cantata is published as op. 128, with a pianoforte arrangement by Ferdinand Schubert.

Schubert's circle of friends was gradually widening. He had met Anselm Hüttenbrenner in 1815 at Salieri's. His brother Josef, with whom he was afterwards intimate, as yet he had not met. Josef Gahy was already of his circle, though it was not until later that the pair were closely associated. More important than any of these— in its bearing upon Schubert's career—was the friendship he now formed with Vogl, the Court opera-singer—a great artist and possessor of a fine tenor voice of large compass. This came about through the friendly offices of Schober and Spaun, who with some difficulty had persuaded the accomplished singer to visit the clever, but by no means famous, Franz Schubert. "The composer entered" (says Spaun) "with shuffling gait and incoherent stammering speech and received his visitor"—the successful artist, and polished man of the world. Vogl does not appear to have at first felt much impressed. He had looked through the song "Augenlied," which did not strike him, then he tried over "Ganymed"[1] and "Der Schäfers Klage," which pleased him better. On leaving he tapped Franz on the shoulder, remarking, "There is some stuff in you, but you are too little of an actor, too little of a charlatan; you squander your fine thoughts instead of properly developing them." This interview seems to have come back to his memory with redoubled force and soon he began frequently to visit Schubert. Then he studied and sang several of his songs, and before very long the two men became almost inseparable. Most remarkable is the disparity in their ages. Schubert was almost thirty years Vogl's junior; the latter, however, outlived him by fully twelve years. It became Schubert's habit to visit Vogl (in the Plaukengasse) daily—generally in the forenoon—when he would try over a song or set to work on the composition of new ones. Vogl, who was a good classical scholar of fine taste and literary judgment, now exercised considerable influence on the choice of verses which Schubert set to music. The singer would commonly declaim the poem with a passionate energy which inspired the composer to put forth his best efforts. Vogl, on the other hand, is said to have encouraged a somewhat lighter class of composition than Schubert would naturally favour, and also to have been responsible for the impracticable range of many of Schubert's songs, which were directly contrived for Vogl's own abnormal voice.

Music in Vienna meant Rossini's music, during the opera-season of 1817, when four of the successful Italian

---

[1] He had been hard to please if the exquisite "Ganymed" failed.

Rossini's Influence

composer's works were staged, and the Viennese public, with Schubert in their train, were won over to enthusiastic admiration of the bright, fresh, though light strains of *Tancredi* and *L'Italiana in Algeri*. Schubert admired the works of this brilliant writer, and Rossini's influence—passing, though it undoubtedly was—is seen in such compositions as the two overtures in the Italian style, both of which are dated 1817. A good story is told of the origin of these pieces. Returning from a performance of *Tancredi*, there was a general chorus of praise from Schubert's friends for Rossini's music—especially the Overtures. Schubert contested the point, declaring it was quite easy to write pieces in the same style, at the very shortest notice. His friends, taking him at his word, and promising him a good glass of wine, Schubert sat down there and then and dashed off a complete score of the Overture in C—a work which was followed in November by its companion Overture. But these were small efforts compared with the more serious labours which Schubert had undertaken. His activity may be measured by the fact that his finished works in 1817 at the age of twenty exceeded 500, a figure which includes Operas, Cantatas, Quartets, Sonatas, and five Symphonies, in addition to the large mass of songs.

Schubert, during the year, had parted company with Salieri. The latter did not approve of Schubert's selections of poetry, especially of Goethe and Schiller. Moreover he counselled him to adopt the "stanze" of the Italians. But another account of the rupture is given by Herr Doppler, who states that Salieri cut out and corrected all passages reminiscent of Haydn and Mozart which he discovered in Schubert's Mass in B flat. The

21

angry young composer came to Doppler's rooms, and flinging down the MS. on the table, declared that he would have nothing more to do with Salieri.

In the following summer, on the recommendation of Herr Unger—father of the great singer Caroline Unger-Sabatier—Schubert became music-teacher in the household of Count Johann Esterhazy. The change of life thus brought about was both marked and beneficial, for Franz was now living as one of the family in a fine country chateau at Zelész, Hungary, where the hours were methodical, the duties comparatively light, and above all, where (to quote his own expression) he was without anxiety of any kind. Besides the count and his lady, there were two young daughters—one of thirteen years, the other eleven—and a son of but five years old. Presumably the three children were Schubert's pupils, and the agreement entered into allowed him two gulden per lesson, while his living would, of course, be free. This was quite a novel state of things to Franz, who for some time at least appreciated the change in his circumstances. On August 3, he writes to his friend Schober to say that he is thoroughly well and happy, "and composing like a god." In the same letter he mentions his setting of Mayrhofer's "Einsamkeit," which he believes to be the best thing he has so far done.[1] Other letters exist, all showing that in his new position he was busy and full of compositions. Reports of his happy position

Music-teacher to the Esterhazys.

---

[1] This is a fine long-sustained song for Tenor and Pianoforte, dated July 1818. It is full of passionate feeling and of rare invention. The accompaniment in places suggests the manner which Wagner afterwards so grandly developed.

At Zelész

drew congratulatory letters, and in one from his brother Ignaz he is saluted in these terms: "You lucky mortal. What a thoroughly enviable lot is yours. You live in a sweet golden freedom, can give full play to your musical genius, scatter your thoughts about, just as you please; become petted, praised and idolised," etc. Such a state of things was too good to last.

Music, apart from composition and the lessons, was cultivated daily. The countess and her two daughters were fairly good singers, and the count had a good bass voice. In addition to this quartet, a regular visitor to the house—if not actually residing under the same roof, was Baron von Schönstein, a fine amateur singer who in later years shared with Vogl the honour of being the best of the Schubert singers. One of Schönstein's favourite song-cycles was the "Schöne Müllerin," dedicated to him five years after the time of which we are writing.

Whether the daily round at the chateau grew monotonous, or whether Schubert was too much attached to the gaiety of Vienna life to settle down for any length of time in the country, his letters show that he became discontented with his lot. Our quotation is from a letter to Schober, dated September 18, 1818: "No one here cares for true art, unless it be now and then the countess; so I am left alone with my beloved, and have to hide her in my room, or my piano, or my own breast. If this often makes me sad, on the other hand it often elevates me all the more. Several songs have lately come into existence, and I hope very successful ones." The description of the members of the household is highly characteristic. This lover of nature—this born son of

23

unconventionality, actually begins his description in the servants' hall. Nor are we to suppose that that was his proper place. The true explanation is simply that the humbler members of this household first awaken his interest because they appear more natural, more human than the aristocratic but frigid owners of the chateau. And so we find our sympathies for the time being entirely with the inmates of Count Esterhazy's kitchen. One cannot but smile on being informed by Schubert that "the cook is a merry fellow; the lady's-maid is thirty; the housemaid very pretty, and often pays me a visit; the nurse is somewhat ancient; the butler is my rival; the two grooms get on better with the horses than with us. The count is a little rough; the countess proud, but not without heart; the young ladies good children. I need not tell you, who know me so well, that with my natural frankness I am good friends with everybody."

Another letter which Schubert wrote from Zelész, addressed to his brother Ferdinand, concerns itself chiefly with personal and private affairs. Here is a specimen which serves to show that Schubert's step-mother had won his affection: "Tell my mother that my linen is well looked after, and that I am well off, thanks to her motherly care." Franz adds that he is looking forward to visiting Pesth, and attending a vintage at Bosezmedj. But the letter clearly indicates that the writer wishes himself back in Vienna once more. He returned at the end of the year. The compositions of this period (1818) are far from numerous. They include, however, the Mass in C, and some fifteen songs.

Schubert arriving again in his beloved Vienna, shared rooms with his friend Mayrhofer in the Wepplingerstrasse.

Back in Town

The exuberance of youth here found an outlet in sham fights and rough play, which, we may briefly note, was indulged to celebrate the composer's return to his native city. Rossini's operas still held the stage, and Schubert finds no difficulty in recognising the Italian's many merits, with a generosity as real as it is rare. *Otello*, says he in a letter to Hüttenbrenner, "is far better and more characteristic than *Tancredi*. Extraordinary genius it is impossible to deny him. His orchestration is often most original, and so is his melody; and except the usual Italian gallopades, and a few reminiscences of *Tancredi*, there is nothing to object to." This compares favourably with Beethoven's opinion, expressed about the same period, "Rossini is a good scene-painter and nothing more."[1]

Mediocrity in poetry, intolerable alike to gods and men, was no less intolerable to Schubert, when appearing in the music of the Weigls and Treitschkes, which the letter mentioned duly castigates in a good-natured manner. No wonder. These works were keeping Schubert's own operettas from the stage.[2] Finally he asks for a libretto. It seems likely that Schubert continued his music-instruction to the Esterhazys after their return to town. There is little or nothing to guide us beyond the speculations of his early biographers. Mayrhofer, with whom he was living, as a Government employé went to his office early each morning, and Schubert had the rooms to himself during the poet's absence. We read that he commonly

---

[1] See "Beethoven," by Crowest, p. 87.
[2] It is but just to add that, on the authority of Kreissle, very few poor works were given at the Kärnthnerthor theatre, the usual repertoire of which was excellent.

Schubert

slept in his spectacles to be ready for morning composition, though so supremely uncomfortable a habit would scarcely be calculated to save much time. Morning work was without doubt Schubert's settled occupation. This, in a great measure, helps to explain the extreme lucidity and healthiness of his compositions—true children of the sun, every one of them. "I compose," says he, "every morning, and when one piece is done I begin another." The most methodical person could wish for no more. This morning task was continued until the time of the mid-day meal—two o'clock, as a rule, and the remainder of the day was free for walks into the country, visits to his friends, or, as sometimes might happen, the unusual exercise of a sudden muse. Among his friends, Schubert was known by the nick-name "Kanevas," owing to his general query regarding strangers on their joining the circle of intimates—"Kann er was?"—Can he do anything? or does he know anything? One glimpse of quick work is given in the inscription on the Overture (op. 34) for pianoforte—four hands—"written in Joseph Hüttenbrenner's room at the city hospital *in the inside of three hours;* and dinner missed in consequence."[1] That little banquet, missed by the composer, is free to all who bring with them the taste for good things musical. The summer of 1819 was spent by Schubert and Vogl in a tour in Upper Austria. Their first stop was at Steyr, a well-situated town south of Linz. There they arrived at the beginning of July, and being Vogl's native place, they met with an extremely hospitable reception. The chief citizens of the town welcomed them, and Schubert's

[1] Compare the incident related in "Beethoven" by Crowest, p. 102.

Parody of the Erl-king

music, under such favourable conditions, met with rare success.

The letters of this period are all in a cheerful vein. One of July 15, 1819—addressed to his brother Ferdinand —shows that Franz was by no means insensible to feminine charms, for we read that " In the house where I am lodging there are eight young ladies, and nearly all pretty. You see one has plenty to do. Vogl and I dine every day with Herr von Koller; his daughter is uncommonly pretty, plays capitally and sings several of my songs." Schubert was enjoying the hospitality of Dr Albert Schellmann, father of five fair daughters. In the same house lived the District-collector with his three daughters. The ladies are elsewhere referred to collectively as the " eight Schellmann girls." Vogl was meanwhile quartered with Herr von Koller—a successful merchant and ironmonger, whose daughter " Pepi" could both sing and play. Mention is made of a remarkable performance of the " Erl-king," in which Mistress Pepi sang the part of the terrified child, to Schubert's impersonation of the goblin himself—Herr Vogl appearing in the character of the " fond father." As an artistic joke nothing could have been better, and the applause of "the eight Schellmann girls " would, we make no doubt, be readily forthcoming. While at Steyr, Schubert renewed acquaintance with Albert Stadler, whom he met as a pupil of the Convict. Stadler had become a Government official, but cultivated musical composition in his spare time. It was he who contributed the libretto for the cantata written in honour of Vogl's birthday. Schubert briefly mentions this work in a letter to Mayrhofer, written from Linz, about the middle of August: " We kept Vogl's birthday with a cantata, the words by Stadler, the music by me; people were thoroughly pleased." This little work is for three voices and accompaniment, and is printed as opus 158.

The most considerable townsman of Steyr was Herr Silvester Paumgartner, "deputy factor to the head guild," amateur 'cellist, and a most hospitable man. It was thanks to this estimable deputy that the melody of "Die Forelle" was employed in the slow movement of the quintet (pianoforte and strings, op. 114) composed by Schubert during this summer tour. Paumgartner was rewarded with the autograph MS., which was added to his collection. Mayrhofer's letter above-mentioned has another passing allusion to a composition of about the same date (August 1819). "There too I made acquaintance with Spaun's mother, and Ottenwald, whose 'Cradle Song' I set and sang to him." The reference is to the "Wiegenlied" (beginning "Schlumm're sanft"), a very charming little song. Though it had been originally a part of the holiday-programme to pay a visit to Salzburg, and one would have expected to find some allusion, at least, to the birth-place of Schubert's first love—Mozart—there is nothing to show that the friends proceeded further than Linz. The date of their return journey is fixed by an entry written in Schubert's hand and contained in Miss Kathi Stadler's album, as follows: "September 14, 1819.—Enjoy the present so wisely that the past may be pleasant to recollect, and the future not alarming to contemplate." An utterance as correct and sententious as any copy-book heading. Let us hope Miss Stadler duly profited by it.

Several noteworthy events had occurred in the course

First Song-performance

of the year. Foremost we may place the composition of the operetta *Die Zwillingsbrüder* (written in January), which was produced some eighteen months later. Then, on February 28th, Jaeger gave a first public performance of a Schubert song. The concert took place at the *Römische Kaiser*, Vienna, under Jäll's direction. Excepting the performance of the Mass five years previously, this was Schubert's first appeal to the public. A short critique appeared in the *Leipziger Allgemeine Musikalische Zeitung*, as follows : " Goethe's ' Schäfers Klagelied,' set to music by Herr Franz Schubert—the touching and feeling composition of this talented young man was sung by Herr Jäger in a similar spirit." During this year Schubert addressed the poet Goethe, doubtless with a view to obtaining from the great man some lines of encouragement. The three songs accompanying this letter—which has not yet been published—were as follows : " An Schwager Kronos " (1816) ; " Ueber Thal," from *Mignon* (1815) ; and " Ganymed " (1817). Most unfortunately the poet does not seem to have replied to this communication. It is still more remarkable that the six volumes of Goethe's correspondence with Zelter (who outlived Schubert by several years) contains no mention whatever of one who more than all other composers together had helped to confer immortality on the poems. It is worthy of remark that of the 603 published songs by Schubert, no less than 70 are settings of Goethe.

The first event of interest in the year 1820 was the mysterious composition of an Easter cantata or oratorio. Whether the work was completed and a portion afterwards lost, is not now easy to decide from the printed fragment. The libretto was chosen from the works of A. H.

Niemeyer, Professor of Theology at Halle, being entitled
Lazarus, or the Feast of the Resurrection. Kreissle remarks of this work that "the birth of this oratorio is a
mystery, and will probably remain so for ever, for not
even Schubert's most trusted friends, such, for instance,
as Franz von Schober, who, in the year 1820, was thrown
frequently into personal intimacy with the composer, can
give any explanation of the cause, or other external circumstances, under which the work in question was
written; but it is certain that to many of Schubert's
associates the very existence of this work remained
hidden."

It almost looks as if Schubert might have won operatic
fame if he had but secured reasonable *libretti*. Hofmann
had furnished the book for *Die Zwillingsbrüder*, which
is singularly weak and devoid of interest. Schubert's
music, on the other hand, has much to recommend it,
being light and tuneful, and at times truly dramatic. On
June 14 of this year the *Zwillingsbrüder* was brought
to a hearing at the Kärnthnerthor theatre, where it ran

Operatic Performances for six nights, and was then withdrawn.
Vogl doubled the parts of the twin-brothers,
and his share of the performance was well
received. Schubert took little interest in
the production of his work, and did not even sit out the
first performance. That he was attracting the attention
of the theatre managers is shown by the rival opera-house
—the theatre an-der-Wien—suggesting the subject for a
new work. This was the *Zauberharfe* (magic harp),
a melodrama, again by the unlucky Hofmann, who had
translated the former operatic piece. Schubert embraced
the opportunity, and, it is said, completed the music of

this three-act work in two weeks. In spite of a good Overture,[1] and among other solos a fine tenor song, and some effective descriptive choral writing, the *Zauberharfe* met with but moderate success. The piece was repeated at intervals until the close of 1820, and then allowed to fall into neglect.

A bad book generally spells failure in operatic enterprise. Not content with ridiculing the libretto, the critics of the day had the temerity to assail the music, which Schubert himself reckoned as one of his most successful works. Here is a patronising example, quoted from the *Allgemeine Musikalische Zeitung*: "The composer gives glimpses here and there of talent. There is on the whole a want of technical arrangement, which can only be gained by experi- *Glimpses of Talent* ence; the numbers generally speaking are too long and wearisome; the harmonic progressions too harsh; the instrumentation overladen; the choruses vapid and weak. The most successful numbers are the introductory Adagio of the Overture, and the Romance for the tenor; the expression in these is lovely; the simplicity is noble and the modulation delicate. An idyllic subject would be admirably adapted to the composer." The notice is curious reading to those of us who take the trouble to examine the luxurious score which Messrs Breitkopf issue. Certainly no page of Schubert, early or late, came forth without "glimpses of talent." But that his harmonies

---

[1] The Overture, a bright and rhythmical movement in C major, is now well known as the "Overture to Rosamunde," though that work has an Overture of its own (in D minor). Schubert made the change in 1828 when he published the so-called "Overture to Rosamunde" (*i.e. Zauberharfe*) for Pianoforte Duet.

were harsh, or his choruses vapid and weak, his instrumentation overladen, and the numbers generally too long
and wearisome, no serious student—present or to come—
is at all likely to admit.

Schubert most probably looked upon opera as a possible
way of gaining a living. The wonderful luck of the
gifted Rossini could not but awaken hope in the heart of
our luckless but ten times more gifted Franz. Had life
lasted there can be no manner of doubt he would have
tried again and again until through sheer persistence he
attained his object. Schubert's disappointment was
Music's gain, for stage-laurels soon fade, while "absolute"
music—comprising Symphonies, Quartets, Sonatas, etc.
—is very much more lasting ; and great songs, especially
settings of great poems, are as nearly immortal as anything of human origin can be. However much or little
of such speculation was in Schubert's mind, the dogged
determination to achieve was present in full force, and in
the autumn of 1820 he embarked upon a new stage-
venture. This was no less than a three-act opera to the
libretto of *Sakuntala*, written by P. H. Neumann.
Beyond sketching two acts of this work, the composer did
not go. The libretto was again hopelessly weak, a reason
which, coupled with the obvious lack of encouragement,
may have led to the MS. being abandoned. On December
23rd, Schubert took in hand Moses Mendelssohn's
rendering of the 23rd Psalm,—"Gott ist mein Hirt"[1]—
setting it for two Sopranos, and two Altos, with pianoforte
accompaniment. The piece was written for four young
ladies named Fröhlich (Nanette, Barbara, Josefine and

[1] Introduced to English audiences by Leslie's Choir and the
Crystal Palace Saturday Concerts.

Testimonials

Katharina), sisters, who excelled in singing, and with whom the great Austrian poet, Grillparzer, lodged the greater part of his life. The eldest sister, Nanette, was a teacher of singing at the Vienna Conservatoire for no less than thirty-five years (1819-1854), and she it was who induced Schubert to compose music for the psalm. Another work of interest which the year 1820 had seen the birth of, was the set of Variations on a French air (op. 10) for pianoforte-duet, which, it will afterwards be seen, served to introduce Schubert to Beethoven. Mention must also be made of the Fantasie in C major (op. 15) for pianoforte-solo, which is attributed to this year. The work (which introduces "The Wanderer" song) is now happily well-known, owing to the efforts of Franz Liszt, who played it with remarkable effect, and whose arrangements for piano and orchestra, and for two pianos, have helped to popularise this fine composition. It is said that Schubert himself never mastered its difficulties, the final movement being a certain stumbling-block.[1]

Soon after Schubert's birthday (January 31, 1821), three testimonials reached the composer, who may therefore have been seeking some position which such distinguished witness would help him to secure. Vogl delivered the first of these missives, which came from no less a personage than Count von Dietrichstein, the chief controller of Court-music—named of Beethoven *Hofmusikgraf*. This was couched in flattering terms, and speaks of Franz's "native genius . . . his earnest study . . . his constant labour . . . and the eloquent proofs of his deep knowledge." A second and more formal certificate

---

[1] It is perhaps fortunate that he never saw Liszt's version—with its added difficulties—of this same movement.

was forwarded by Acting-Court Secretary von Mosel. On the third of these precious documents appeared the signatures of Weigl, director of the opera ; Salieri, the old teacher ; and one Von Eichthal. It set forth that—

> " WE, the undersigned, testify that Herr Franz Schubert, on account of his famous and most promising musical talent, proved chiefly in the art of composition, has been employed by the Committee of Management of the Court Theatre, and served with great distinction to the satisfaction of everyone."

Yet, as they all led to nothing, posterity will be prone to judge that these courtiers and artists found it easier to praise than to benefit the young composer with a post or a pension, which would at least have enabled him to live in modest security, free of that anxiety which was his close companion through life, dogging his steps to the last.

True friends of Schubert were the Sonnleithners, both father and son. The latter (Leopold), Schubert had met long ago as a scholar of the Convict school. Ignaz, the father, had maintained regular musical gatherings at his house since 1815, and Schubert's songs had been freely performed, before large audiences of friends and music-lovers. A good tenor singer and an influential Imperial official named August von Gymnich, had sung the " Erl-king " with great success at the Sonnleithners' private music-gathering on December 1, 1820, and, as a result, Leopold Sonnleithner and Gymnich agreed together to secure a publisher for the song. With this aim,

Publication of Erl-king

Diabelli and Haslinger, the two leading Vienna music-printers of that time, were duly and vainly consulted. The publishing eye, so quick to detect technical difficulties, was closed to the supreme merits of this work, though to have been its original publisher would have secured lasting memory of a creditable kind.[1]

The two amateurs thereupon undertook the risk themselves and admitted a few friends to the same privilege. An appeal was made at the Sonnleithners' next concert, and all risk vanished into thin air; one hundred copies were subscribed for, there and then, a result which not only placed the transaction on a commercial footing, but eventually led to Schubert's receiving a substantial sum. Had his friends perceived that the copyright of such work would become of ever-increasing value, and influenced the composer to retain as his own property the rights connected with its publication, Schubert would, ere long, have found himself beyond the clutches of want. As it was, as soon as the publishers discovered that there was a sale for Schubert's songs, they secured the copyright themselves, in the ordinary course of business. Before this came about, the private issue of Schubert's songs had grown to twenty numbers, the list of which is as follows :—

The Erl-king

Op. 1. (issued April 1, 1821) The Erl-king.
Op. 2.   April 30,   Gretchen am Spinnrade.
Op. 3.   May 29,   Schäfers Klagelied.
                              Meeresstille.
                              Heidenröslein.
                              Jägers Abendlied.

[1] Haslinger was content to obtain this another way. See p. 149.

Schubert

Op. 4.	May 29,	Der Wanderer.
		Morgenlied.
		Wanderers Nachtlied.
Op. 5.	July 9,	Rastlose Liebe.
		Nähe des Geliebten.
		Der Fischer.
		Erste Verlust.
		Der König in Thule.
Op. 6.	Aug. 23,	Memnon.
		Antigone und Oedip.
		Am Grabe Anselmos.
Op. 7.	Nov. 27,	Die abgeblühte Linde.
		Der Flug der Zeit.
		Der Tod und das Mädchen.

It is a truly remarkable list of first publications, and especially noteworthy on account of the surviving popularity of the majority of the songs to this day. With the issue of opus 7, these private publications ceased, and Diabelli commenced operations on his own account, as is seen from opus 8, which appeared on May 9, 1822, printed as "the property of the publishers." There are indications that had Schubert at this period cultivated those in Vienna society who were disposed to be friendly with him, he might have taken a place in their circle, to which his talents entitled him, and to which he would have been welcome. Kreissle remarks on this : " He himself never expressed a wish to mix in society, where he was forced to get rid of his innate shyness, reticence and a good-natured nonchalant manner, but could not escape yielding occasionally to friendly pressure put upon him." It is surmised with some show of reason that the dedication of

Dedications

Schubert's earliest compositions would indicate his more influential friends of this date. If this be so, the following list—which shows in their order the seven dedications—deserves attention: Graf von Dietrichstein, Reichsgraf Moritz von Fries, Ignaz von Mosel, Johann Ladislaus Pyrker (Patriarch of Venice), Salieri, Vogl, and Graf Ludwig Szechenyi. With the goodwill of such influential friends Schubert seems to have remained quite content, preferring his own retirement and the company of the poets, painters and philosophers, whose simple Bohemian habits suited his taste better than the luxurious surroundings of the rich. To some extent Beethoven was of the same mind, while the life of the poet Goethe offers a contemporaneous instance in marked contrast.

In July 1821, Schubert visited Atzenbruck (near Abstetten, between Vienna and St Pölten), where the uncle of his friend Schober had a country seat. During the following month (August) Schubert sketched, but never completed, a Symphony in E, the autograph score of which passed successively through the hands of Ferdinand Schubert, Mendelssohn, Mendelssohn's brother (Paul), and thence to the keeping of the late Sir George Grove. (See p. 204.)

Whether the visit of July to Atzenbruck was extended for some weeks, or whether Schubert returned to Vienna, is not clear. In September, Schober and he are found staying at Ochsenburgh, where they enjoyed a complete change of society, and mixed with the country aristocracy, which, according to Schober, included "a princess, two countesses, and three baronesses." They were back in Vienna at the end of October, and a letter jointly composed by the friends gives a glimpse of their doings while

Schubert

holiday-making. Schober begins, "Schubert and I have returned from our visit, and look back with delight upon a happy month spent partly in the town, partly in the country. At Ochsenburgh we had plenty to do in visiting the beautiful country in the neighbourhood, and in St Pölten books and concerts absorbed our attention ; in spite of all this we both worked hard, Schubert especially— he has done nearly two acts, I am upon the last. I only wished you had been with us and witnessed the birth of those lovely melodies ; the wealth and vigorous outpour of Schubert's fancy is really extraordinary. Our room at St Pölten was exceedingly nice—two big beds, a sofa, and a good fireplace, not to mention a grand piano, gave it a very snug home appearance. Of an evening we always compared notes of what had passed during the day ; we sent for beer, smoked our pipes, and read aloud. Perhaps Sofie or Netta would join us, then we had singing. Two *Schubertiaden* were held at the Bishop's house, and one at Baron Mink's, a favourite of mine, and a princess, two countesses, and three baronesses were present, all of whom were delighted in the most approved aristocratic fashion. . . . (The postscript is Schubert's.) . . . "I must inform you that my dedications have done their duty, for the Patriarch, at the instance of Vogl, has expended twelve ducats, and Friess twenty, a fact which suits me extremely well. . . . Schober's opera has already got to the third act, and I should much like you to have been present whilst the opera was in its earliest stage of formation. We count a great deal on the work in question." The work in question was the three-act opera *Alfonso und Estrella*, the first act of which was finished on Sept. 20, 1821, and the last on Feb. 27, 1822. Though the author and com-

Visit to Beethoven

poser (Schober and Schubert) counted a great deal upon the production of the piece, it was destined not to take place during Schubert's life-time, nor indeed till long after. Domenico Barbaja had been appointed (in 1821) as manager to both the Vienna opera-houses (the an-der-Wien and the Kärnthnerthor), and, as a supporter of the Rossini school, viewed Schubert's work with distrust. So nothing was done. Hüttenbrenner, however, had the work put in rehearsal at Gratz, where, unfortunately, it was discovered that the band was unable to play the accompaniments, which it may well be believed were of an advanced type—considering the time. Again it was dropped. The score came under Weber's eye at another period, as will be seen in its place. It was reserved for Liszt—the strong man — the nineteenth-century giant among musicians—to produce this opera,[1] upon which poor Schubert had counted so much; but alas, when it came to be heard, the composer had long since gone to his grave.

Two important meetings took place during 1822, for it was in this year that Schubert first came in touch with Beethoven and Weber. There is no record of the first occasion upon which Weber and Schubert came into personal contact, beyond the barest mention by Weber's son. It is also known that Weber was in Vienna, preparing for the production of his opera—*Euryanthe*—in February and March. Statements are conflicting with regard to Schubert's first visit to Beethoven. Schindler—a good friend of both men and

Beethoven and Weber

---

[1] Liszt produced *Alfonso und Estrella* at Weimar, June 24, 1854, with many "cuts." After revising and re-writing the book, Capellmeister Johann Fuchs gave a successful revival of the work in March 1881, at Carlsruhe. Schlesinger published it the following year.

Schubert

devoted to Schubert—gives a circumstantial account which we reproduce :—

"In the year 1822, Franz Schubert set out to present in person the master he honoured so highly with his variations on a French song (op. 10). These variations he had previously dedicated to Beethoven. In spite of Diabelli accompanying him, and acting as spokesman and interpreter of Schubert's feelings, Schubert played a part in the interview which was anything but pleasant to him. His courage, which he managed to retain up to the very threshold of the house, forsook him entirely at the first glimpse he caught of the majestic artist, and when Beethoven expressed a wish that Schubert should write the answers to his questions,[1] he felt as if his hands were tied and fettered. Beethoven ran through the presentation copy, and stumbled upon some inaccuracy of harmony. He then, in the kindest manner, drew the young man's attention to the fault, adding that the fault was no deadly sin. Meantime the result of this remark, intended to be kind, was utterly to disconcert the nervous visitor. It was not until he got outside the house that Schubert recovered his equanimity and rebuked himself unsparingly. This was his first and last meeting with Beethoven, for he never again had the courage to face him."

Kreissle doubts this story and what he terms its "rather improbable details, so humiliating to Schubert." He adds that Josef Hüttenbrenner heard from Schubert's own mouth that when he called on Beethoven, the latter was not at home, and that the variations were left with the servant. Hüttenbrenner gives one interesting detail,

---

[1] Beethoven was then quite *deaf.*

Men Apart

that "Schubert subsequently heard with great pleasure
of Beethoven's enjoying these variations, and playing
them frequently and gladly with his nephew—Carl."
No doubt the reasons which prevented these two remarkable men meeting one another earlier are easily discovered.
Though both lived in Vienna, their walks in life were
widely apart : Beethoven, the eminent artist, everywhere
known as a great man—Schubert, known only to few, and
otherwise somewhat obscure. Then Beethoven's deaf-
ness, becoming daily more pronounced, left him solitary,
courting solitude and privacy, with no wish to make new
friends ; while Schubert's retiring habits, coupled with a
shyness which is scarcely paralleled among the characteristics of great men, would further tend to lead the
two composers as much apart as could any possible combination of circumstances. Hüttenbrenner may have
been led astray by Schubert himself, who would be un-
likely to give an account of the meeting with Beethoven
if it occurred as described by Schindler, and without
actually misleading him the very lack of information
might lead to Hüttenbrenner's supplementing it from
speculation or from later gossip. At any rate, Sir George
Grove accepts Schindler's account, and it ill becomes us
to doubt it. A remark of Schubert to Rochlitz—the
founder of the famous *Allgemeine musikalische Zeitung*—
shows that at this time Schubert and Beethoven had met.
It is thus given by Rochlitz himself, who was writing
from Vienna, in the summer of 1822, whither he had
gone in order to make the acquaintance of Beethoven :—
"I was just going to dinner, when a young composer,
Franz Schubert, an enthusiastic worshipper of Beethoven's,
met me. *Beethoven had spoken to him about me.* [The

41

produced with extreme rapidity, yet the music is fully matured. *Die Verschworenen* (or *Der häusliche Krieg*), the autograph of which is now in the British Museum, was completed in April 1823. The libretto had but just appeared in the Dramatic Garland, and was founded on a translation from the French, by Castelli. This one-act operetta, or Singspiel, remained unperformed until 1861, when it was produced at Vienna by Herbeck. A first English hearing was accorded the piece in 1872, at the Crystal Palace, under the title of *The Conspirators*. Returning to the year 1823, a more important work soon attracted Schubert's attention. This was the libretto of *Fierrabras*—a three-act opera-book by Josef Kupelwieser, brother to the painter, Schubert's intimate friend. The dates of the MS. illustrate that remarkable rapidity referred to above. Thus Act i., containing over 300 pages of oblong music-score, occupied no more than seven days —May 25-31. The MS. of the second act took just five days—June 1-5; and the whole work with its 1000 pages (or 537 printed pages in Breitkopf & Haertel's score), comprising an overture and twenty-three musical numbers, was completed on October 2. Although the work had been commissioned by Barbaja it was never put on the boards; the overture is, however, well known, and the full score of the opera (as mentioned above) is now available. Schubert's disappointment was as yet unknown, for it was not until early in 1824 that the MS. of *Fierrabras* returned to him. Part of the year would now be spent on the composition of the cycle of songs *Die schöne Müllerin*, which may be ascribed to the period May to October. During the last-named month Schubert came into contact with Weber, and by his imperturbable

Amantium Irae

good humour avoided what might have proved a serious quarrel. Weber had been in Vienna since September, and on October 3 began the rehearsals of his *Euryanthe*, which was to be produced for the first time at the Kärnthnerthor theatre on the 25th of that month. Musical Vienna was stirred to its depths with excitement, and Weber, by no means the most phlegmatic mortal, was naturally anxious and worried. The composition of the Overture to *Euryanthe* was put off until the last few days. No wonder then that he was in a sensitive mood. Schubert had criticised *Euryanthe* somewhat freely; its merit, said he, lay in its harmonics. He was also prepared to prove, even to Weber himself, that whereas *Der Freischütz* was genial and full of heart and of bewitching loveliness, the score of *Euryanthe* did not contain one single original melody. These severe strictures gossips duly carried to Weber, who angrily retorted, " Let the fool learn something himself before he ventures to criticise me." On receiving this challenge to combat, Schubert quietly placed the score of *Alfonso und Estrella* under his arm, and marched to the attack by boldly visiting Weber —whom he had met before—at his Vienna lodging. Schubert's score being duly examined, Weber asks for an explanation of his remarks on *Euryanthe*, which to his equal astonishment and annoyance Schubert stoutly maintains. Carl Maria then loses his temper, and shouts, " I tell you that first puppies and first operas are always drowned."[1]

Weber

[1] *Alfonso und Estrella*, written in 1821, was Schubert's twelfth dramatic attempt ; but it was the first completed three-act opera of its composer.

Franz remained unmoved. To the credit of both men the encounter was allowed to pass without further mischief. Schubert bore Weber no malice, and on his side Weber did his best to produce *Alfonso* at Dresden. Musicians' quarrels have not always ended so happily!

A third dramatic work of the year 1823 was completed in December. If we are to believe Wilhelm *Rosamunde* von Chezy (son of the librettist of *Rosamunde*) the task took but five days. After two performances, the first of which took place at the theatre an-der-Wien, December 20, the score and parts were tied up and hidden away in a dusty cupboard, there to await their deliverance at the hands of two devoted English travellers, who unearthed the treasure with all the transports of men who wrest diamonds or gold from the hidden recesses of earth—only with infinitely purer joy. The story appears in its place.

There are plain signs that Schubert's health had been *Ill-health* feeble during the past year, for in February he was confined to his house when writing to Herr von Mosel (February 28, 1823), and for a time during the hot months of the year he was placed in a hospital.

1824 brought misfortune in its train, for *Fierrabras* was rejected by Barbaja, owing, it is understood, to the badness of its libretto. In a letter addressed to his friend Kupelwieser, the painter, Schubert pours forth his distress in unmistakable terms. The artist's brother had written the opera-book for *Fierrabras*, and Schubert writes thus in the letter referred to :—

" Picture to yourself a man whose health can never be

re-established, who from sheer despair makes matters worse instead of better; picture to yourself, I say, a man whose most brilliant hopes have come to nothing, to whom the happiness of proffered love and friendship is but anguish, whose enthusiasm for the beautiful—an inspired feeling at least—threatens to vanish altogether, and then ask yourself if such a condition does not represent a miserable and unhappy man.

> ' Meine Ruh' ist hin, mein Herz ist schwer,
> Ich finde sie nimmer und nimmer mehr.' [1]

"I can repeat these lines now every day, for each night when I go to sleep, I hope never again to wake, and every morning renews afresh the wounds of yesterday. Thus joylessly and friendlessly would pass my days if Schwindt did not often look in and give me a glimpse of the old happy times. . . . Your brother's opera turns out to be impracticable, and my music is therefore wasted. . . . Thus I have composed two operas for nothing."

It was grief of no ordinary kind that brought Schubert to this pass. His natural buoyancy had quite forsaken him for the time being, and nothing now but change of scene and society would be likely to benefit him. Fortunately it befell that in May, Count Esterhazy summoned the desponding musician to accompany the family on a visit to their Hungarian home. Six months were spent at Zelész. The peacefulness of a country life in a fine bracing mountain air, no less than the regularity of a well-ordered household, helped to restore Schubert to his normal health—full of sweet dreams and quiet breathing.

[1] "My rest is gone, my heart is sore,
Never—alas—shall I find it more."
—GOETHE'S *Faust*.

Schubert

Caroline Esterhazy was now seventeen, and Franz, attracted by her beauty, and aided by the opportunities *In Love* which life in a secluded spot brings to the members of a small family party, quite naturally fell in love with her. The social gulf fixed between a young and beautiful lady of birth and position and a poor musician of little or no prospects, endowed though he was with some of Heaven's rarest gifts, was not to be bridged over by a modest and retiring man of Schubert's disposition. A Beethoven might have overcome all obstacles, but Franz's was the nature to submit to the inevitable. For such a man one way only was open, and that was to conceal his affection. Any declaration of love could but distress the gentle-hearted girl to whom he was devoted. That she knew the state of his affections no woman at least will doubt, but history gives no clue. Kreissle relates that Caroline one day inquired half-reproachfully why Franz had dedicated none of his music to her. "Why should I," said he, "when everything I ever did is dedicated to you?" This is not the language of compliment, and doubtless Bauernfeld was right in representing the love which possessed Schubert as an ideal one—that lasted to the end—not embittered or disfigured by the pettiness of jealousy or selfishness, but a pure bright flame which illuminated his compositions with the tenderness and beauty of human feeling. The only work actually dedicated to Caroline Esterhazy [1] is the Fantasia in F minor, op. 103, for pianoforte-duet, and this appeared after Schubert's death, being published in March 1829.

[1] Sixteen years after Schubert's death (namely on May 8, 1844) the Countess Caroline was married to Count Folliot von Crenneville, major in the army, and Chamberlain.

A Day's Work

Franz, while away, was not forgotten. An affectionate letter, dated July 3, 1824, from Ferdinand in Vienna, mentions having sent his brother Franz a new opera-book—*Der kurze Mantel*—and Bach's Fugues. Ferdinand also has the following curious reference to the clock —a musical curiosity—at the Ungarische Krone, Vienna —"This clock delighted me not a little, when one day at dinner for the first time I heard it play some of your waltzes. I felt so strange at the moment that I really did not know where I was ; it was not only that it pleased me, it went regularly through my heart and soul with a fearful pang and longing, which at last turned into settled melancholy." Franz replied from Zelész in no less affectionate terms. Baron Schönstein affords us a glimpse of the domestic influence in the Hungarian home bearing good fruit. He relates that at breakfast one morning in September 1824, Countess Esterhazy produced a copy of De la Motte Foqué's prayer (Gebet)—"Du Urquell"—and suggested to Schubert that he should set it to music which could be performed by the assembled family. Franz agreed, and retiring to his room, produced in the course of the day—or in less than ten hours—a completed version of the poem. In the evening, with the family gathered about the pianoforte, the new piece was tried through from the MS. Next day the composer copied out the parts, and the piece was duly performed. There were solos for the Countess and Marie Esterhazy, as well as for Baron Schönstein and the Count ; Schubert played the piano part, and perhaps we may assume that the leaves of his MS. were turned by the fair Caroline. Another work which is owing to these Zelész days is the "Divertissement à la Hongroise," op. 54, formed upon

Hungarian airs, one of which, according to Kreissle, was obtained in the following interesting manner :—" Schubert got the subject from the kitchen-maid in the Esterhazy family, who was humming it as she stood by the fireplace, and Schubert, coming home from a walk with Schönstein, heard it as he passed. He kept on humming the tune during the rest of the walk, and next winter it appeared as a subject in the ' Divertissement.' "

Life in the country, however healthy, is apt to become wearisome ; and, to so thorough a citizen as Schubert, rustication for half a year only made him turn the more eagerly towards Vienna. Now appears to have been the very crisis of his life. His operas had been rejected, his health had been assailed, and his heart had ventured a hopeless quest. "Grief sharpens the understanding and strengthens the soul," writes he in his diary. The letters of the period point to the same thing. One to his brother Ferdinand seems especially significant and has the following utterances :—" In order that these lines may not perchance mislead you to a belief that I am unwell or out of spirits, I hasten to assure you of the contrary. Certainly that happy joyous time is gone when every object seemed encircled with a halo of youthful glory, and that which has followed is the experience of a miserable reality, which I endeavour as far as possible to improve by the gifts of my imagination (for which I thank God). People are wont to think that happiness depends upon the place which witnessed our former joys, whilst in reality it only depends on ourselves, and thus I learned a sad delusion and saw a renewal of those of my experiences which I had already made at Steyr, and yet I am now much more in the way of finding peace and happiness in myself."

Happiness

The compositions of 1824 are far from numerous; they include, however, the famous Octet, for two violins, viola, 'cello, double-bass, clarinet, horn, and bassoon, a work which was composed during February, for Count Ferdinand Troyer,[1] chief of the Archduke Rudolph's household. Count Troyer was an excellent clarinet-player and assisted with his instrument in the first performance of the Octet in association with Schuppanzigh, Weiss and Linke—three of the original Rasoumowsky quartet. This Octet and the String-quartet in A minor (op. 29) were regarded by Schubert as studies for the Grand Symphony, the fulfilment of which may be seen in the C-major Symphony of 1828.

Vienna was once again the scene of Schubert's labours. Surrounded by his nearest friends, Schubert seems to have been unusually happy. Schober and Kupelwieser were both abroad, but several of the old congenial comrades were at hand. Schubert, with Jenger and Vogl, became a regular visitor at Madame Sofie Müller's. The famous actress spent the months of February and March in Vienna, and attracted to her house many of the principal artists and musicians of the town. At her gathering of March 3, 1825, she actually sang (at sight, it is said) that marvellous song " Die junge Nonne." Vogl also took part in these delightful performances, and some of the settings of Scott's poems were given for the first time. Schubert was now in his element and

---

[1] There exists a sonata—published by Haslinger—for clarinet and piano, composed for Count Troyer *by the Archduke* Rudolph —Beethoven's staunch patron. It was the same exalted personage who dedicated to Beethoven his " Forty Variations—*by his pupil.*"

supremely happy. Reviewing his past misfortunes, he might have exclaimed with Goethe :—

> " Does Fortune try thee? She had cause to do't;
> She wish'd thee abstinent ; obey, be mute."

Abstinent he certainly was in a proper sense of the word. If proof were needed apart from the tradition available, it is conclusively set forth in his works. No dissipated man ever had either the endurance or the shining purity of emotion which all Schubert's creations possess. We have only to turn to the list of his works (" Appendix D ") to perceive that he was one of the most industrious men who ever lived. Mute, or at least reticent, was he also in regard to much of his experience in life; yet he was gloriously eloquent where music was concerned. Kreissle writes that " when summer began, the two artists " (Schubert and Vogl), " like wandering minstrels, started forth on their beautiful

Minstrels country expedition, bent on making at one time a stately convent, at another a city or town, ring with their already famous lays. They made considerable halts at Linz and Gmunden, and again at the proper starting-point of their wanderings, Vogl's birthplace. Everywhere they fell in with friends and acquaintances, who received them with open arms. The still living witnesses of these days of Schubert's wanderings talk with delight of the happy hours they passed in the society of the unassuming, and, at that time, happy and cheerful Schubert." The holiday was of five months' duration, and the travellers got as far as Salzburg and Gastein. Writing to his parents from Gmunden about this time, Franz says :—" I have found my compositions all about

Descriptive Letter

Upper Austria, particularly in the monasteries of Florian and Kremsmünster, where I produced my Variations and Marches for four hands, with much success, by the help of a good pianist. I had especial luck with the variations from my new sonata, which I played alone, and which pleased very greatly." Vogl and Schubert were everywhere received with enthusiasm, and at Gastein, in the mountainous district of the Eastern Tyrol, they joined their old friend and ally—Ladislaus Pyrker, Patriarch of Venice—two of whose songs Schubert set to music.[1]

Now it was that, according to Sir George Grove (following Bauernfeld), a symphony was in active construction, if not completed. This work he christened the "Gastein" Symphony, and counted as No. 9. Unfortunately no traces of the work can be discovered, and Bauernfeld's statement that it was an especial favourite of its author may perhaps refer to one of the symphonies which are preserved to us; in any case speculation on such a subject is now useless.[2] Whether Schubert was busy with a symphony or not, we find him thoroughly enjoying his holiday. In a long descriptive letter (of September 20-1, 1825) addressed to his brother Ferdinand, Schubert gives a glowing account of his travels. "About a league from Neumarkt, the country begins to look beautiful. The Wallersee, which spreads its clear, blue green waters on the right of the road, animates this charming scene most exquisitely. The country lies very high, and from hence you descend all the way to Salzburg. The mountains grow higher and higher, the fabulous Untersberg especially rises like magic

[1] "Heimweh" and "Allmacht" (op. 79).

[2] Kreissle admits that there is much confusion on this subject.

from among the rest. The villages show traces of former wealth. The commonest peasants' houses have marble window-ledges and door-sills, often even staircases of red marble. . . . Towers and palaces appear by degrees; we drive at last by the Capuzinerberg, whose enormous wall of rock towers aloft perpendicularly close to the road, and looks terribly down on the wanderer. The Untersberg, with its satellites, is gigantic; its grandeur almost crushes us. And now through splendid alleys we drive into the town." It later appears that Schubert visited the monastery of St Peter, and saw the monument to Michael Haydn set in "an out-of-the-way corner." Though Schubert goes into much detail concerning the "heavenly valley" of Salzburg, and notes "the strangely bedecked house of Theophrastus Paracelsus," there is no word of Mozart, which is more than passing strange. Perhaps in a lost letter he had exhausted the subject. Mozart was his earliest love, and it is nearly impossible that the birthplace of such a man would pass without reference. But we must content ourselves with the few lines quoted from this excellent letter, the length of which surprised the writer himself, for he exclaims, "Heavens, this is something appalling, a book of travels I can write no more. As I shall be in Vienna the first day of October, I will give you this scribble in person, and tell you the rest by word of mouth." Vogl left for Italy, in order to obtain treatment for gout, and Schubert returned to Vienna, doing the journey thither from Linz in an *Einspänner*, in company with his friend Gahy. Outstanding expenses were then covered—including the rent of his Vienna lodging, and the repayment of a loan from his father—by the sale of his seven songs from Scott's "Lady of the Lake" (see

p. 141). One little appointment fell to his lot this year, namely that of *Ersatzmann* or substitute to the Gesellschaft der Musikfreunde, though whether it carried remuneration or not we are not informed. Among the chief compositions of the past year (1825) had been the well-known Piano Sonatas in A minor (op. 42) and in D (op. 53), and the Trauer Marsch for the Emperor Alexander of Russia —Piano Duet, op. 55. Reissmann prints a curious little pianoforte piece in F, intended to accompany a recitation of a poem by Pratobevera, which was a composition of this period.[1] Publication was now going forward with some regularity, and the same year witnessed the appearance in print of the string quartet in A minor (op. 29), an Overture (op. 34) and Sonata (op. 30) for piano-duet, and some notable songs—including the splendid setting of Craigher's "Die junge Nonne." We may pass rapidly over the year 1826, which is unimportant as regards incident, though it saw the birth of the Shakespeare songs and the Piano Sonata in G (op. 78), so highly praised of Schumann. Schubert made a fruitless attempt to obtain the Vice-capellmeistership of the Imperial Court, vacated by Eybler, who had been promoted to the full mastership, rendered vacant by the death of Salieri in 1825. Count Harrach had the duty of making the appointment, and he had to choose from eight candidates.[2]

The report of Count Harrach stated that "Schubert bases his claim on his services as court singer, confirmed by a certificate from Salieri, who taught him composition;

[1] It is the last composition in Vol. x. of B. & H.'s edition of the "Lieder," and entitled "Der Falke."

[2] The eight candidates were Schubert, Seyfried, Gyrowetz, Kreutzer, Hoffmann, Hüttenbrenner, Würfel and Glazer.

and declares that he has already composed five Masses
which have been produced in various churches." None
of Schubert's Masses had found their way to the Court
chapel, though we have his own word for it that he placed
the score of one before Eybler—the Capellmeister. All
the eight candidates were passed over, though they had
been recommended as men of merit and consideration,
and Josef Weigl, of the Court Theatre, was duly installed
by imperial edict. No better proof of Schubert's wonderful modesty and total lack of jealousy can be given than
that furnished by his comment when he found himself
passed by. The salary was fixed at 1200 florins (£120),
which would have ensured comparative independence,
and yet he simply remarks: "I should have been very
glad of this appointment, but as it has fallen to one so
worthy of it as Weigl, I must be well contented." It
has been customary to regard Schindler's statements regarding Schubert with some suspicion, but since the issue
of Thayer's "Beethoven," there is no longer just cause for
so doing. His is the authority for the scene which follows.
Herr Krebs had resigned the post of conductor at the
Kärnthnerthor theatre which, at the suggestion of Vogl,
was open to Schubert's acceptance subject to his capacity
being proved at a public trial. The candidate was to set
some operatic scenes, for which the words were provided by Duport the manager. This was of course
quickly accomplished and placed in rehearsal. Then

Scene at Rehearsal the hitch occurred. Mdlle. Schechner, the
great prima donna, called upon Schubert to
alter the principal air, by shortening it
and simplifying the accompaniment. Schubert refused,
and at the first rehearsal Mdlle. Schechner broke down.

A Gift

She sank exhausted, it is said, on a chair by the side of the proscenium. Schindler continues as follows:—"There was a dead silence throughout the house, and consternation in every face. Then Duport was seen going from one to another of the principals and discussing matters with the singer and the chief musicians present. Schubert sat through this painful scene like a marble figure, with his eyes fixed on the score before him. Then after a long interval Duport advanced to the orchestra and politely addressed the composer in these words:—'Herr Schubert, we will postpone the performance for a few days, and I must beg of you to make the necessary changes in the *aria* at least, in order to make it easier for Mdlle. Schechner.' Several of the musicians in the orchestra joined in begging him to yield. But Schubert had listened with increasing anger to the speech, and shouting out, at the top of his voice, 'I will alter nothing,' he shut the score with a loud bang, placed it under his arm, and marched home. Thus there was an end to all hope of the appointment." Kreissle doubts this story, but there is really nothing improbable in the account. Josef Hüttenbrenner affirms that Mdlle. Schechner was supremely charmed with Schubert's lovely *aria*, and that mere theatre intrigues prevented his obtaining the post. The testimony of a Professor of the Vienna Conservatoire—namely Franz Zierer—an eye-witness of the scene described, partly confirms Schindler's statement. Mdlle. Schechner's powers were on the wane, and thus, according to Zierer, the *aria* was beyond her powers. But, he adds, Schubert remained perfectly calm throughout the rehearsal, and in his opinion never really competed for the post.

A welcome gift of 100 florins (£10) was made to our

Schubert

composer on September 9, 1826, by the Musik-Verein, in recognition of his services to music. The letter con-

Gift from the Musik-Verein

veying the money speaks of his remarkable powers, and of the zeal and interest he had shown for the Society.[1]

To the bare material which the year 1826 affords us, we may add that two new publishers approached Schubert with a view to business. The first was Probst (afterwards Senff) who, on August 26, desires a selection of songs and piano pieces, not too hard, agreeable, and easy of understanding. He pronounces Schubert's works—as far as he knew them—marked by genius, but none the less strange and odd. This approach was met by Schubert in the following year, and some MSS. were despatched; Probst, however, was much too busy with Kalkbrenner's compositions at the time, and Schubert's fee of £8— eighty florins — for each composition was thought exorbitant. At the same time (or to be quite accurate on September 7) Messrs Breitkopf & Haertel proposed to issue some of the compositions subject to their author receiving a number of copies by way of remuneration. To this arrangement Schubert apparently did not agree. Little did that great publishing firm suspect that one day they would gladly undertake every scrap of the same compositions, then, as now, *beyond* price. They (at least), to their lasting credit, have made noble reparation.[2]

---

[1] In 1820 and 1822 Schubert had written two vocal concerted pieces (at the request of Fräul. Josefine Fröhlich) specially for the pupils of the Conservatoire, who frequently performed them.

[2] Dr Max Friedländer tells the following highly diverting story in the *Vierteljahresschrift für Musikwissenschaft* (1893). A MS. copy of the "Erl-king" was received by Messrs Breitkopf & Haertel

"Marie" Variations

A journey to Gratz—the Styrian capital—had been long projected. Jenger wrote to Madame Pachler on December 29, 1826, that "Friend Schubert has determined on travelling next year to Gratz; but if I do not accompany him, the plan is sure to fall through—as it has done this year." It appears that few famous artists, musicians, or actors, failed to visit the Pachlers, if they found themselves in the Gratz neighbourhood, and all were made welcome. It is of interest to note that the beautiful and highly gifted Marie Pachler had early attracted Beethoven's affectionate friendship, and it seems that he too had been meditating to stay in such congenial society. As the sequel shows, Beethoven was soon to be called away to his long home, and Schubert, later in the year, went in his place. Passing allusion may here be made to Herold's opera *Marie*, which was placed on the Vienna boards on January 18, 1827, an event which seems to have called forth Schubert's *Marie* variations for piano-duet (op. 82), which came into view

in 1817, from Franz Schubert of Vienna. This appeared puzzling, for the publishers knew only of one Franz Schubert, and he was a Royal Church composer—worthy man—of some fifty years, and resident at Dresden. To him then they applied for an explanation, which was duly furnished by the Dresden Schubert as follows:—"I beg to inform you that I received your esteemed letter of ten days ago, in which you enclosed a MS. setting of Goethe's "Erl-king," supposed to be by me. With the greatest astonishment I beg to state that this cantata has never been composed by me. I shall retain the same in my possession in order to learn if possible who sent you the stuff in such impolite manner, and to discover the person who has traded on my name. I am greatly obliged for your kindness in sending me the MS." It only remains to add that the "Erl-king" was written in 1815, and privately printed in 1821.

Schubert

the following month. A more important work, begun soon afterwards, was the "Winterreise" songs. (See page 148).

At this time all Vienna was profoundly moved at the tidings of Beethoven's mortal illness. As Schubert is in some degree concerned, a brief extract from Schindler should be of interest:—"As the disease to which Beethoven succumbed after four months of suffering made it impossible for him from the very first to exert his wonted intellectual activity, it was necessary to find some amusement suited to him. Hence it came that I put before him a collection of Schubert's songs, about sixty in all, many of them still in manuscript. This was not done merely with a view of providing him with an agreeable occupation, but also to give him a proper idea of Schubert, and enable him to form a more favourable opinion on his talent, which had been put before him by exalted admirers in a way to make him suspicious. The great master, who had not known more than five songs of Schubert's before, was astonished at their number, and would not believe that Schubert had composed more than five hundred already. But if he was surprised at their number, he was filled with the utmost astonishment by their merits. For several days he could not tear himself away from them, and he passed many hours daily over "Iphigenia," "The Bounds of Humanity," "Omnipotence," "The Young Nun," "Viola," "The Miller Songs," and others. He cried out several times with joyful enthusiasm, "Truly in Schubert there is the divine spark." . . . "If I had had this poem, I should also have set it to music." It was the same with most of the poems : he could not praise their subject and Schubert's original treatment of them too much. And he could not conceive how Schubert found leisure to exercise himself on so many poems, 'each of which contained ten others,' as he expressed himself."

More than one visit was paid by Schubert to the bed-side of the dying master. The first seems to have been in the company of Anselm Hüttenbrenner. They were announced by Schindler, who asked which of the friends was first to be admitted. "Schubert may come first," was Beethoven's reply. And afterwards, when they were together, he added, "You, Anselm, have my mind, but Franz has my soul." On another occasion, Josef Hüttenbrenner and Teltscher the painter were with him. The dying man looked fixedly at the three friends and made some signs which were wholly unintelligible, and Schubert was so overcome with emotion that he had to withdraw. At the funeral, on March 29, Schubert acted as one of the thirty-eight torch-bearers who preceded the coffin. They were dressed in full mourning, with white roses and bunches of lilies fastened to the *crêpe* on their arms. Others of Schubert's company were Lachner, Anschütz, Castelli, Carl Czerny, David, and Grillparzer.

Returning with Lachner and Randhartinger from the funeral ceremony at Währing, Schubert entered the Mehlgrube tavern and called for wine. There he drank to the memory of *Tragic Toast* the great man whom they had just seen laid in his resting-place. A second glass was then drunk to the first of the assembled friends who should follow. Alas! it was Schubert himself.

Let us pass on to more cheerful scenes. The veteran Hummel and young Ferdinand Hiller (a lad of sixteen) were in Vienna, which they visited (in March 1827) during a more extended musical tour. They had had the privilege of attending Beethoven in his last days; they had also been present at the funeral. Their meeting with Schubert has been recorded by Hiller[1] and gives a glimpse of the composer in society. The musicians were met together at a soirée given by Franz von Lascny (whose wife, *née* Buchwieser, had great repute as a vocalist), and Vogl sang Schubert's "Der blinde Knabe" (Colley Cibber's "Blind Boy," translated into German by Craigher) with the composer accompanying. Immediately after their performance, and to Schubert's great delight, Hummel gave a brilliant pianoforte extemporization founded upon the song just sung. Hiller remarks that Schubert had little technique, and Vogl but little voice, yet their interpretation was marked by so much life and feeling as to place it quite beyond all criticism; the material conditions were lost in the superb spiritual revelation. "The melodies appealed to the ear, as a vision to the eye." No wonder that master and pupil were much moved—the older man to tears, the younger to recording what he describes as the deepest musical impression he ever received. "It frequently happened," observes Kreissle, "that while the performers, instrumental and vocal, were loaded with compliments, not a thought was given to the little insignificant man who sat at the piano accompanying his own songs with an earnestness and depth of expression comparatively lost on his audience. But the unassuming artist was all the more callous to such coldness and neglect, when the applause with which his own composition was greeted was at last directed to

[1] See his "Aus dem Tonleben," second series, and "Künstlerleben," 1880, p. 49.

Parody

the composer himself. At meetings of this kind, and especially in the more refined circles, where he would sometimes, out of pure good nature, accompany his "Lieder," he was very shy and chary of talk. Whilst sitting at the piano, his face became very serious, and directly the piece ended he used to withdraw to an adjoining room. Indifferent to praise and applause, he shrank from compliments, and felt quite wretched if his friends expressed themselves satisfied with what they had heard. It was very different when he found himself free of conventional restraints. His tongue would then be loosed in the merriest humour and talk, and he would indulge in wit and practical jokes, many of which could be told by Schwindt. Amongst other strange drolleries of Schubert was his parody of the "Erl-king," which he would sing through the teeth of a comb to the amusement of his audience. If sometimes he kept quietly to himself, at others he would join in the merriment around him. His laugh was not that of ordinary mirth, it consisted of a hoarse, suppressed chuckle." On another such occasion the great bass vocalist Lablache, who with Schubert had been a torch-bearer at Beethoven's funeral, took a part (the second bass) in the male-voice quartet "Der Gondelfahrer," a poem of Mayrhofer's set by Schubert three years previously. This composition was in much request in society circles, and has been pronounced the best work of its kind which the composer has bequeathed to us.

Towards the end of July, Fräulein Anna Fröhlich (a teacher at the Vienna Conservatorium) proposed a birthday serenade, to be given in Herr Gosmar's garden at Unterdöbling, near Vienna. The occasion was in celebration of Louise Gosmar's birthday.[1] Grillparzer had composed a poem for the day, entitled "Zögernd leise in des Dunkels nächt'ger Stille," and Fräulein Fröhlich asked Schubert to set it to music, giving a solo to her sister Josefine (a mezzo-soprano), supported by female chorus. Schubert took the MS. to a window and set back his spectacles to examine it closely, and after reading it twice through exclaimed, "I have it; 'tis done already, and will go very well." A few days later, when it was produced, it was discovered that he had overlooked the ladies, and set it for alto-solo with *male* voice chorus. However, the mistake was soon rectified, and on August 11 (1827), the serenade was performed.[2]

The confirmation of the tale is seen in the published versions, both of which are given in Breitkopf's catalogue. (See op. 135 — Series xvi. No. 14, and Series xviii. No. 4.) It is said that the effect of this serenade sung in the clear moonlight and in the open air was enchanting. "Numbers of the dwellers at Döbling stood and listened at the garden-gate, though Schubert, as usual, was not present at the performance."[3]

Writing on August 30, 1827, Jenger announced to Madame Pachler that the visit to Gratz which he had long

---

[1] Louise Gosmar afterwards became Frau von Sonnleithner.

[2] Wilberforce gets into difficulties with this little story (see his "Schubert," p. 169). My authority is Kreissle (original edition, p. 474; and Coleridge's translation, vol. ii. p. 160). Wilberforce tells the anecdote of "Hark, hark, the lark" (Shakespeare's, which is described also as a "Ständchen"), and then applies it to Grillparzer's "Ständchen," which is quite another work, and of a different period.

[3] Kreissle.

Holiday-making

been planning for Schubert and himself was now actually to take place. His note is as follows:—" Next Sunday, September 2, my friend Schubert and I start by the Eilwagen at 9.30 P.M., and hope by the favour of God to be with you at Gratz on Monday evening at nine o'clock. We are already eagerly reckoning on our pleasurable visit." The Pachler family (including the seven years old son named " Faust ") were highly delighted to receive their friend and his distinguished companion, who duly arrived in his green coat and white pantaloons. Now was begun a three weeks' holiday of picnic-excursions, musical parties, dances, and a whole round of out-door and house amusements such as Schubert had probably never before enjoyed. " The visit at Gratz," says Kreissle, "was enlivened by delightful music and frequent excursions amongst the beautiful scenes in the neighbourhood. The Pachlers at that time did not invariably live in the country, and excursions from the town were often undertaken—to Wildbach, for instance, a small estate belonging to a widow lady, Madame Massegg, Dr Carl Pachler's aunt, and mother of six handsome grown-up daughters; to Hallerschlössel again, on the ' Ruckerlberg,' a favourite halting-place of the Pachlers; and Jenger and Anselm Hüttenbrenner, as well as Schubert, used to join them on these occasions. With regard to these picnics and excursions, where mirth and good humour and the society of pretty women were the order of the day, nothing further need be said than that upon every occasion a good deal of wine was consumed, and that neither Jenger nor Schubert could be called bad hands at that part of the ceremonies. Indoors there was no lack of musical entertainment, the cost of which was almost

Schubert

exclusively defrayed by the two guests of the Pachler family, for Schubert (in the absence of any singer) sang his own songs (among others the 'Wanderer an den Mond') and played pianoforte-duets with Jenger." Several memorials of this visit remain. Such are the twelve "Gratz Waltzes" and the "Gratz Galop." Then there are four songs (op. 106), including the fine "Who is Sylvia," dedicated to Madame Pachler. Nor must the little duet for Master "Faust" be forgotten. "I doubt if it will meet with your approval," says Schubert in enclosing the MS. (on October 12, 1827), "as I don't feel myself particularly well qualified for writing things in this style." One ominous line occurs in this letter, as follows:—"The pains in my head, a common disorder with me, have returned." This was written a fortnight after the two friends had reached Vienna. Here he took up (or resumed) his quarters at the Blue Hedgehog, a well-known tavern in the Tuchlauben, where his faithful friend Schober shared rooms with him. From this time forwards till almost the last thing, Schubert seems to have resided in the Tuchlauben. Indeed it is pointed out by Kreissle that, excepting the five years 1817, 1819, 1820-21, 1824 and 1825, Schubert's quarters were fixed in Schober's house, or at all events there was a room there always at his disposal.

The compositions of 1827 are neither very numerous nor important. To those already mentioned may be added the two piano trios (op. 99 and 100), and the "Nachtgesang im Walde," for four male voices and four horns. Then there was a sketch of an opera, mentioned by Bauernfeld and Lachner. The libretto is said to have been by Bauernfeld, who received assistance or advice from

Mayrhofer. But the MS. would seem to have disappeared, and is not mentioned in Breitkopf's "complete edition."

A letter from Rochlitz (poet, critic and editor) suggesting a setting of one of his poems is elsewhere dealt with, and we may now bring the record of 1827 to an end. It is satisfactory to remark that it ranks with the happiest years of Schubert's life.[1]

With the dawn of our composer's last year (1828), his powers are discovered at their best, and despite occasional complainings he was well able to *Last Year* go about his work, apparently in the full vigour of body and mind.

On January 18, he addressed Anselm Hüttenbrenner, recommending his brother Carl for the vacant post of Drawing-master at the Gratz Normal-Hauptschule. "He is a clever landscape-painter," says Schubert, "as well as a good draughtsman. . . . Bear in mind that any kindness done to my brother I look on as done to myself." The communication goes on to mention a performance of the Trio in E flat (op. 100): "Lately a Trio of mine for Pianoforte, Violin and 'Cello was played at Schuppanzigh's and pleased very much. It was exquisitely rendered by Bocklet, Schuppanzigh and Linke." This was the work of which Schumann wrote: "Some ten years since, a Trio of Schubert's, like an angry meteor, blazed forth and outshone everything in the musical atmosphere of the time; this was exactly his hundredth work, and shortly afterwards, in November 1828, he died. . . . Time, which brings to light such numberless and beautiful things, will not soon reproduce another Schubert." The Trio was set great store upon

[1] Kreissle states that the years 1825 and 1827 were "among the happiest episodes of Schubert's life and progress."

Schubert

by its composer, and it had a somewhat curious career. Written in 1827, it was commonly played in private. On the occasion with which Schubert's letter (above quoted) deals, Bocklet became so excited that on its conclusion he seized the composer's hand, and kissing it, called upon those present (in Spaun's house) to witness what a treasure they possessed in Schubert. When offered to Schott for publication, the work was returned. Probst, in a letter dated April 15, 1828, wrote: "I accept the Trio you have been so good as to offer me, at the price of twenty florins, sixty kreuzers, which you will receive by the three annexed cheques, duly noted and numbered." Having acquired this notable work for seventeen shillings and sixpence, as our currency has it, Messrs Probst proceeded to ask for a dedication. Here comes Schubert's reply—surely as characteristic an one as Beethoven himself could have contrived—"This work will be dedicated to none but those who take delight in it—that is the most profitable dedication of any."

There is but little record of Schubert's doings in 1828, apart from composition, which so fully engrossed him. He perhaps found himself driven to it by the inner consciousness that he was as yet undelivered of his best message to his fellow-men, or it may be that the creeping shadows of that long Night, which was so soon to close in on his labours, spurred him on to his most strenuous endeavours. March found him occupied with the cantata *Miriams Siegesgesang* — *Miriam's Song of Victory* — (Grillparzer's words) which curiously enough bears traces of Handel's influence, both in the first fine strophe and in the concluding powerful fugue. It seems that after Beethoven's death, Schubert was drawn to the study of

the great Saxon's oratorios, some of which—not impossibly
Beethoven's own copies of the Arnold edition—came
into Schubert's possession about this period. The month
of March also brought him the great inspiration of his
life—which found expression in the noble C-major
symphony (No. 7).[1] As soon as he had completed the
symphony, Schubert presented it to the Musik-Verein at
Vienna for performance. The parts were copied and the
work came into rehearsal, but it was then pronounced too
long and too difficult, and so, acting on the composer's
advice, his symphony No. 6 (also in C) was played in its stead.

On March 26, Schubert, with the assistance of his
friends, and owing entirely, it is said, to their initiative,
gave a private concert in the hall of the Musical Union.
The programme and other details are given in another
chapter (see p. 158). Success crowned this practical
effort to repair his fortunes, and the composer found
himself in possession of a balance of £32—a handsome
sum from his point of view. A few days later, all
Vienna was plunged into the throes of a grand agitation,
more remarkable even than that which Rossini's visit had
previously induced. Paganini had appeared, and all
classes of society came under his wonderful spell, including the dandy and the small shop-keeper. Hats, gloves,
boots, were all worn à la Paganini. Walking-sticks and
snuff-boxes bore the virtuoso's likeness; even the restaura-
teur's dishes were named after him; and all the tom-fool-
ery followed that could possibly follow in the train of a
great furore. Schubert not only attended the first of
Paganini's concerts, but found occasion to go a second
time in order to treat his friend Bauernfeld, "who had

[1] Described at p. 206.

not five farthings, while with him money was as plenty as blackberries." This flourishing state of affairs was not to last. Indeed, throughout the final period of Schubert's life, there is every indication that he was in constant need of money. Most of the prices paid him by the publishers were little short of ridiculous, and though many of their proposals were flattering enough on paper, their practical issue was trifling. "Be good enough to fix your own terms," wrote Schott & Son on Feb. 9, 1828. But by October 30, they object to pay 60 florins as "a too extravagant price" for the Quintet (op. 114), and they offer and enclose only half the sum asked—namely, 25s. We have already seen that Probst bought the splendid Trio in E flat (op. 100) for 17s. 6d., and, in this same

Songs at Tenpence a-piece

year, Franz Lachner—at Schubert's request —took half a dozen of the "Winterreise" songs to Haslinger the publisher, who purchased them at one gulden a-piece—that is tenpence each. How could the most prolific writer in the world exist on such sums?

Early in January, Jenger had been writing about the summer holidays for himself and Schwammerl (Schubert's none too elegant nickname), and in May a letter passed from Traweger (of Gmunden) quoting friendly terms for board and lodging. Then, again, in a letter of July 4, 1828, Jenger writes as follows:—

"The absence of two of my subordinates for the purpose of taking the waters at Baden, added to the not very brilliant state of the finances of my friend Schubert, who begs to send all sorts of good wishes to you, and his friend Dr Carl, will prevent us both from accepting your kind invitation to visit you at Gratz. Schubert, besides, has the project of passing a part of the summer in Gmunden and the neighbourhood, where he has received a number of invitations ; but hitherto, the pecuniary difficulties before alluded to have prevented him from carrying out his project. He is still here at present, working zealously at a new Mass," (probably the grand Mass in E flat, explains Kreissle), "and is only on the look out—come from what quarter it may—for the cash necessary to support his immediate flight to Upper Austria. Under these circumstances our excursion might possibly come off, as it did last year, at the beginning of the month of September."

All these attempts to escape from the heated city to the freedom and beauty of a country excursion were doomed to failure. On September 25, Schubert writes to Jenger—who was then awaiting his company for the trip to Gratz—" I have already handed over to Haslinger the second part of the 'Winterreise.' It's all over with my journey to Gratz for this year, for my pecuniary prospects, like those of the weather, are downright gloomy and unfavourable. I accept with pleasure the invitation of Dr Menz, as I should be very glad to hear Baron Schönstein sing. On Saturday afternoon you can meet me at Bogner's coffee-house, Singerstrasse, between four and five o'clock." In a postscript he adds that his new address is "Neue Wieden, Firmians-Gasse, No. 694, second floor, right-hand side." If, however, Schubert was prevented from taking a proper holiday by the lack of funds, he, at any rate, availed himself of the favoured surroundings of his native city. Thus, on June 3, he was at Baden, twelve miles south of Vienna, where—amid pleasant sights and sounds—lulled perhaps by the falls of Schwachat, or beside the murmuring waters of the Helenenthal, he wrote the Fugue in E minor, for four hands (op. 152)—so dry a piece of work called for romantic surroundings. He was preparing for the Mass in E flat. Work now flowed freely from his pen. July saw the completion of the 92nd Psalm, *in the Hebrew tongue*, for two baritones, soprano, alto and bass—afterwards published without the composer's knowledge, in the *Schir Zion* of the Cantor Sulzer, at Vienna. In August he set thirteen of the Schwanengesang; and September brought forth the three pianoforte sonatas, in B flat, C minor and A, which he had intended to dedicate to Hummel. The publishers (Diabelli) afterwards dedicated them to Robert Schumann. In the same month Schubert composed a little piece for chorus and wind instruments (oboes, clarinets, bassoons, horns and trumpets), entitled "Glaube, Hoffnung und Liebe" (words by F. Reil), which was performed at the consecration of a new bell at the Church of the Holy Trinity, in the Alservorstadt. During October, he wrote a new Benedictus for the Mass in C, the String Quintet in C (op. 163), and an Offertorium, "Intende voci orationis meae," for tenor solo, chorus and orchestra. The last piece of work of this kind that he set his hand to was the "Taubenpost" (words by Seidl), which fittingly appears at the end of the "Schwanengesang."

"Death with gentle but premonitory steps" (says Kreissle) "had, in the September of this year, stolen on him; and a brief time was to elapse, when, as in Mozart's case, a few quieter days had given hopes of restoration to health, and then death's relentless grasp was to carry off his victim." From Ferdinand Schubert and Franz

Sudden Illness

von Schober we learn that early in September, Schubert
took up his lodgings with his brother Ferdinand, in a
newly built house in a new street in the Wieden suburb.
Schubert, by the advice of Dr Rinna, Court physician,
came here, in order to be near the country, where he
might take plenty of air and exercise; for his sufferings
from constant giddiness and sudden rushes of blood
to the head were fast increasing. Meanwhile Schober,
as he had often done before, retained his room for him
against his return, which, however, was never to be. A
consultation of physicians was now held, and the patient
again rallied. At the beginning of October he was able
to take a short walking excursion to Unter-Waltersdorf,
and on to Eisenstadt, some twenty-five miles out from
Vienna, where in company of Ferdinand and two other
friends a visit was paid to Joseph Haydn's grave. Though
during this journey he seemed to enjoy excellent spirits,
in spite of extreme abstemiousness in his eating and
drinking, no sooner was home reached after five days'
absence, than the old trouble reasserted itself with redoubled energy. On October 31, while at dinner in the
"Zum rothen Kreuz," a favourite eating-house of his,
in the Himmelpfortgrund, after swallowing a
morsel Schubert suddenly flung down his   *Illness*
knife and fork, declaring the fish tasted like poison.
Henceforwards he took little but medicine. He was
still able to walk, and together with Carl Holz (one of
Schuppanzigh's quartet party), heard a performance of
Beethoven's Quartet in C sharp minor, which so agitated
Schubert that his friends were quite alarmed. Then,
again, early on the morning of November 3, he walked
from the Neu-Wieden to Hernals, where he heard his

brother Ferdinand's Requiem Mass (for chorus and orchestra), which proved indeed the last mortal strains vouchsafed him. For three hours, after the Requiem, he wandered about, and finally reached home much exhausted. Once more he rallied, and he and Lanz (a Vienna pianoforte teacher) called upon Sechter, the famous theorist, with a view to Schubert's receiving a course of instruction in counterpoint. It is said that everything was arranged, the text-book (Marpurg's) fixed upon, and the hour of the lesson. The project was never carried out, for Schubert's health was rapidly giving way. "The history of our composer's life," says Kreissle, "was thus robbed of one of the strangest spectacles—that of Herr Sechter and Franz Schubert absorbed in a joint musical labour."

The friends who visited Schubert in his last illness included Spaun, Bauernfeld, Lachner, and J. Hüttenbrenner. Bauernfeld mentions in his "Sketches" that Schubert spoke of a new libretto for an opera when lying on his death-bed. Lachner, who had seen him just before starting on his tour in search of artists for the Kärnthnerthor theatre, relates as follows:— "Schubert, when I visited him the last time before I left, was in full possession of all his senses, and I conversed several hours with my dearest friend and most unassuming and modest of artists. He told me of his several plans for the future, and looked forward with eager delight to his recovery that he might finish his opera *Der Graf von Gleichen*, for which Bauernfeld had written words. He had sketched out a large part of this opera." On the other hand, Ferdinand's wife, who would have every opportunity of judging, is said,

Last Letter

on the authority of Fräulein Geisler, to have stated that no one visited Schubert with the exception of Randhartinger. Schober certainly kept away, as Schubert's letter—his *last*—plainly shows.[1]

[*Nov.* 11, (?) 1828.]

DEAR SCHOBER,—I am ill, and have eaten and drunk nothing for eleven days. I have become so exhausted and shaky, that I can only get from the bed to the chair and back. Dr Rinna is attending me. If I taste anything, it at once induces sickness. In this distressed condition, kindly assist me to some reading. Of Fenimore Cooper, I have already read " The Last of the Mohicans," " The Spy," " The Pilot" and " The Pioneers." If you have anything else of his, I entreat you to leave it with Frau von Bogner, at the coffee-house. My brother, who is conscientiousness itself, will duly bring it or anything else to your friend, SCHUBERT.

Schober's answer is not now forthcoming, but doubtless the books were immediately forwarded. About this time the doctor himself fell ill, and in place of Rinna, Staff-surgeon Behring attended Schubert, during his last few days of life.

His great weakness had driven him to his bed on the 14th, but the end was not yet, as we find him sitting up and correcting the proofs of his " Winterreise " songs. The occupation was a melancholy one—Müller's gloomy poems echoed back by his own tragic muse, and set in the surroundings of death. A sick man, however, welcomes

[1] Bauernfeld quotes this letter in *Die Presse*, April 21, 1869.

any relief, and even this task might tend to cheer the lone hours. Two days later (on the Sunday) there was a consultation of doctors, who apparently did not then anticipate the worst. On the following afternoon, friend Bauernfeld had some conversation with the patient, who talked of his ardent wish for a good opera-libretto. Towards evening Schubert became delirious. Tuesday saw him in the throes of typhus. The scene of these last days is indeed a touching one. He who had sung so bravely (alike in joy and in grief) of life and of hope, was now laid low. The dread path lay before him—the bitter cup was raised; and as we tell over the brief years of his life—no more than thirty-one—the path seems bleaker and the cup more bitter. Franz, in his fever, imagined he was in a strange place and was continually trying to rise from his bed. One comforting ray there was in the gloom of this sad chamber, and it was kindled by the tenderness and loving care of his brother Ferdinand, who at this time was ministering like an angel to the wants of the poor stricken Franz. As Ferdinand bent over him, Franz whispered, "What are they doing with me?" and he replied, "Dear Franz, they are doing all they can to get you well again, and the Doctor tells us you will soon be alright, but you must do your best by staying in bed." But the invalid is not easily soothed. "I entreat you," says he, "to put me in my own room, and do not leave me in this corner under the earth. Do I not deserve a place above ground?" To this, poor Ferdinand, at his wits' end how to smooth his troubled pillow, replies, "Dear Franz, be calm and trust your own Ferdinand, whom you have always trusted, he who loves you so dearly. You are

His End

in your own room, which you have always had, and you are lying in your own bed." But " No," says Franz, "that cannot be true, for Beethoven is not here."[1] So strangely did the departed spirit of his brother-musician seem to haunt his memory in these last hours. A little later, Schubert seems to have realised that the hand of death was indeed upon him; for when the doctor came and spoke some soothing word to him, the poor dying man regarded him intently, then turned his face to the wall, and striving to grasp it with his weak hands, exclaimed in slow, broken tones, " Here, here is my end."

The end came at three that afternoon, it being Wednesday, November 19th, 1828, and the life of this man—so precious in the sight of ordinary mortals—was rendered back again to Him who gave it ; and as, with sorrowing eyes, we gaze into the gloom of that still chamber, who can doubt but that quires of angels sang him to his rest, and that his place would be with the abode of the Blessed?

Early on the morning of this last day, Schubert's father had written to his son as follows :—

" DEAR SON FERDINAND,—The days of trouble and heaviness are lowering sorely upon us. The dangerous illness of our beloved Franz weighs heavily on our souls. All that we can do in this sad time is to seek comfort from our Heavenly Father, and bear every sorrow appointed us by a wise Providence with firm submission to His holy will. The result will convince us of the wisdom and goodness of God. Be of courage then, and put your

[1] Quoted from Ferdinand Schubert's letter to his father, dated Nov. 21, 1828, 6 A.M.

trust in Him. He will strengthen you that you sink not under this sorrow; His blessing will keep a yet happy future in store for you. Take every possible precaution that our dear Franz have administered to him at once the Holy Sacraments given to the dying; and I live in a cheerful hope that the Almighty will strengthen and preserve him.

"Thy father, afflicted, and yet strengthened by trust in God, FRANZ."

Later in the day, the father had the painful duty of issuing the obituary notice as follows :—

"Yesterday afternoon, at three o'clock on Wednesday, my beloved son Franz Schubert, artist and composer, died after a short illness, and having received the Holy Sacraments of the Church. He died at the age of thirty-two. We beg to announce to our dear friends and neighbours that the body of the deceased will be taken on the 21st of this month, at half-past two in the afternoon, from the house standing No. 694 in the new street on the Neuen-Wieden, to be buried near the bishop's stall in the parish church of St Josef in Margarethen, where the holy rites will be administered."

FRANZ SCHUBERT,
School-teacher in the Rossau.

VIENNA, *November* 20, 1828.

The funeral took place on the day appointed, but the place of burial was changed almost at the last moment, in accordance with the expressed wishes (as they were interpreted by Ferdinand) of Schubert himself. "Franz"

Franz's Resting-place

(said Ferdinand) "himself induced me to think of Währing for his resting-place." Then he quotes the conversation and dying speech already given, adding, "Is not this an index, so to speak, of his heartfelt wish to rest by the side of Beethoven, whom he so deeply reverenced?" Ferdinand carried his point, and the remains were laid to rest close beside Beethoven's grave, but three places distant from it. A crowd of relations, friends and sympathisers took their last view of the body, which lay as if asleep, with face unchanged by death, dressed in the habiliments of a hermit, with a laurel-wreath round the temples. Then the coffin was borne away by students and officials, mostly young men who had been intimate wtth the composer. Schober was chief mourner, and some verses by him were sung to Schubert's "Pax Vobiscum," with an accompaniment of wind instruments, before the interment, at the parish church, where Domcapellmeister Gänsbacher conducted a funeral motet of his own composition. The funeral expenses cost Ferdinand and his father "seventy florins—a large sum" (said the former, in referring to the sad item) —"a very large sum; but very little for the honour of Franz's resting-place." The original memorial had an epitaph by Grillparzer, and was designed from a sketch by Schober, acting with an architect named Förster, and a master-mason Wasserburgher. In 1863 the body was exhumed (as was Beethoven's), and a cast and photograph of the skull were taken. After reburial, a new memorial took the place of the original one, and Grillparzer's epitaph was replaced by the simple inscription—FRANZ SCHUBERT.

On May 15, 1872, the Vienna Männergesang Verein erected a monument (a recumbent figure) in Carrara marble by Carl Kuntmann. This cost 42,000 florins,

Schubert

and is placed in the Stadt-Park. The original epitaph, which awaked much contention in its day, is as follows :—

DIE TONKUNST BEGRUB HIER EINEN REICHEN BESITZ
ABER NOCH VIEL SCHOENERE HOFFNUNGEN.
FRANZ SCHUBERT LIEGT HIER.
GEBOREN AM XXXI. JAENNER MDCCXCVII.
GESTORBEN AM XIX. NOV. MDCCCXXVIII.
XXXI JAHRE ALT.[1]

[1] Music has here entombed a rich treasure,
But still fairer hopes.
Franz Schubert lies here.
Born Jan. 31, 1797 ;
Died Nov. 19, 1828,
31 years old.

The Man

NATURE, so prodigal of her gifts of brain and heart,
seems to have given but sparingly of those personal
attractions which go so far towards reconciling genius
with the outside world. Like Mozart, Schubert was of
insignificant appearance, his stature barely reaching to five
feet one inch. Stout of figure, with rounded shoulders,
fleshy arms, and thick, short fingers—much redeemed,
however, by a picturesque head, showing a profusion of
black, vigorous hair, remarkably expressive eyes always
spectacled, an insignificant nose and fine teeth, Schubert
had but small physical aids to the battle of life.
Kreissle, his first biographer, who had the advantage of
conversing with several of the composer's intimate
friends, describes the presence and personal appearance
of Schubert as anything but attractive. "His round and
puffy face," says he, "low forehead, projecting lips, bushy

eyebrows, stumpy nose, and short curly hair, gave him that negro look which corresponds with that conveyed by the bust which is to be found at the Währing churchyard." He further observes that "however uncomely, nay, almost repulsive, his exterior, the spiritual and hidden part of the man was noble and abundantly endowed." Schubert's friend, Franz Lachner, describes the composer (almost vulgarly) as "just like a cabman." Wilhelm *Descriptions* Chezy, in his "Erinnerungen aus meinem *by Friends* Leben," 1863, speaks of "the person of the short, stumpy composer, whose exterior was like a tallow-ketch (*Talglumpen*), but whose beaming eyes nevertheless betrayed at first glance the depth of the fire therein concealed." The broad, almost massive, lower jaw bespeaks purpose, determination, if not obstinacy. The lips slightly protrude, while the features generally are naturally mobile, in repose uninteresting perhaps, but upon due occasion capable of considerable expression. The eyes, so commonly an index of the soul, were clear and peculiarly bright and penetrating. From quite early youth Schubert wore spectacles. Spaun says that the composer sometimes spent the night at his house, that he slept in his spectacles, and, in the morning, while but half dressed, would go to the pianoforte and improvise.

The most successful portraits include an engraving by Passini, founded on a sketch by Wilhelm Rieder; a *Portraits* lithograph by Clarot, also from a drawing by Rieder; a painted miniature originally in the possession of Spaun; a drawing by Leopold Kupelwieser (found in 1862) which is dated 1821; and some small plaster casts sold by Haslinger.

Passini's engraving, which is reproduced in our frontispiece, was made from a replica dated 1840, now in the Musik-Verein, Vienna. The original of this favourite portrait is a half-length, three-quarter-face, done in water-colours in 1825, and purchased by Dr Granitsch in 1881 for £120. Kupelwieser's head of Schubert is an un-attractive presentment, which may be seen prefixed to Kreissle's biography. The bust on the tomb is pronounced by Grove to be "a very prosaic version of his features."

Reserve was Schubert's most prominent characteristic. He could certainly have said with Beethoven—"no mortal man hath lifted my veil." The inner life of Franz Schubert was screened from all inquisitive eyes. That it was extremely simple, there is everything to show; while whatever of complex thought or emotion arose in the mind of this remarkable being was duly translated into song, and transferred to paper, at white heat and with lightning rapidity. Then for the most part the mood was dismissed. "I compose every morning," says he, "and when one piece is finished I begin another." Occasions, however, there were, when his thoughts did not so lightly return to their normal channel; as, for example, on the completion of the "Winterreise" songs, when he announced to his friends: "You will soon learn the reasons of my growing despondency. I will sing for you, at Schober's, some awfully gloomy songs; they have had a great effect on me." [1]

Generous beyond belief, Schubert had not the least taint of malice or meanness in his nature. He could have stood for the exemplar of Landor's utterance—

"I strove with none,
For none was worthy of my strife."

[1] Spaun's "Memoirs."

Schubert

It was only in later life that he came to know Beethoven personally, and it was only then that he could possibly have appreciated him as a man. Once known, he was ever afterwards revered. The greatness of that solitary life seems to have come upon Schubert as a revelation, and he had him constantly in mind towards the end. The increased seriousness and deeper import of Schubert's later works must be attributed to the influence of the master-mind of the older composer, not to speak of those last sad scenes in which Schubert bore a part.

Modesty—that universally appreciated gift, so rarely bestowed by the gods on the children of song—was Schubert's undoubted heritage. He could leave out self from all estimates of others and their works. If he failed to obtain a post—as indeed he invariably did—the winner was sure of a good word. He could admire the genius of Rossini—not an easy task for a Vienna composer of Schubert's day. He could cheerfully pay (at a high rate) for admission for himself and Bauernfeld to hear Paganini. Nor was he short of courage; for though he fled in haste from Beethoven, who had conveyed some gentle censure with marked courtesy and consideration, he still dared to face Weber over a principle. The incident has already been given (p. 45). Schubert's absolute dislike of praise is another marked characteristic of the man. Any mention of his own merit seems to have had the effect of making him shrink into himself, if indeed he did not turn his back on the offender. "That man likes everything I do," said he, in open ridicule of Josef Hüttenbrenner, thereby earning for himself the nickname of "the tyrant." His diary for June 13, 1816, quoted later, contains a remarkable

Religion

instance of modesty, where in mentioning a performance of his own setting of " Rastlose Liebe," he adds that "much of the applause must be attributed to Goethe." On the occasion of a party at Princess Kinsky's, where a number of Schubert's songs were sung, " with not a thought for the little insignificant man at the piano," the hostess—vexed with her guests' behaviour, said some kind words in their excuse to the composer; Schubert replied that she need not trouble herself about the matter; he was used to it, and was more at his ease if he might remain unnoticed.

His philosophy of life does not seem to have been fixed by any very hard and fast rule. *Religion* Creation of music was his first and last care, and to this everything had to give way. Given that, he was in the full exercise of his splendid faculties, he was doing the right. Nothing else mattered. This is the simple explanation of his conduct, as it appears to us. Of his religion little or nothing is known. Certainly the Masses breathe forth a piety and deep feeling which none but a good man could offer. Pure, lofty, beautiful sentiment informs these works as certainly as it does the sacred compositions of Bach, Beethoven or Handel. But while admitting so much, we are no nearer to an accurate declaration of Schubert's religion. He was baptised in the Catholic Church—so much is learned from his birth-certificate. It is also seen from his father's announcement of the musician's death, that he had received the last Sacraments from his mother Church. The Viennese were chiefly Catholic, possessing, however, a large Jewish community and a comparatively small sprinkling of Protestants, at the time of which we are writing. It is worthy of note that Schubert (with true artistic impartiality) contributed a setting of the Hebrew version of the 92nd Psalm, which was duly produced by Sulzer at the Vienna Synagogue.

In early boyhood Schubert had the reputation of being both quick and intelligent. He was fond of his home and family; while outside, his frankness won him friends at every step. He soon became a favourite alike with his teachers and school-mates. Holzer (his first teacher outside the home-circle) recalled with tears in his eyes, young Franzl's initial efforts in organ-playing and the pride and joy with which he witnessed his first attempts at extemporisation. At the Convict School, Spaun (the leader of the boys' orchestra) was immediately struck by the clever manner in which the lad handled his violin, and the acquaintance thus formed ripened into a life-long friendship. It was during these days at the Convict that Schubert first became attracted by the music and personality of Beethoven, some of whose symphonies and overtures were in regular practice at the school. A glimpse of the man himself came to Schubert through his fellow-students. The band, it appears, had been ordered to Schönbrunn, where were Beethoven and Teyber (the music-master of the Archduke Rudolf), and its youthful members had enjoyed the privilege of playing in the master's presence. This little incident, however, had happened a short time before Schubert's arrival, and he had therefore to content himself with the story of his companions' visit—which he took great delight in hearing repeated. The lad was not without his day-dreams at this period, for we find him, after a performance of some settings of Klopstock's poems, asking of a fellow-

Convict School

pupil present, if he really thought he could hope to accomplish anything of worth. "You have already done some first-rate work," answered his young friend; to which Schubert replied, "I too sometimes think so; but who can ever hope to do anything after Beethoven?"

The Convict authorities did not pamper their charges. Schubert's first letter (quoted at p. 6) shows that they were sparing of food; the following passage quoted from a treatise by Kenner, further proves that they were, if possible, still more economical in the matter of fuel. "In the instrumental practice-room" (says Kenner), "during leisure hours after dinner, Albert Stadler, a composer, and Anton Holzapfel, his form-fellow, used to play Beethoven's and Zumsteeg's works, and on such occasions I represented the audience. The room was never heated, and the cold fearful. Occasionally Spaun joined the party, and Schubert also, after he left the Convict. Stadler played the pianoforte, Holzapfel sang; occasionally Schubert sat down to the piano. Leopold Ebner did not become intimately acquainted with Schubert until after the latter had left the Convict; for Schubert, off and on, for a couple of years, used to visit his friends at the institute, and run through with them his latest songs and pianoforte works."

Josef Spaun—himself one of the truest and most disinterested of friends—brought about most of *Schubert's* Schubert's principal friendships. He it was *Friends* who introduced the young musician to Theodor Körner, who is understood to have persuaded Schubert to take the course he did in quitting the Convict in order to devote himself wholly to music. Franz von Schober came to know Schubert through Spaun. But of all the friends with whom Schubert came in contact, Vogl was the one who influenced Schubert most in his music. The composer had long admired the great singer at the opera-house, and it was due to Spaun and Schober that the two men were brought together. A scarcely less powerful friend was, at a later period, discovered in Baron Schönstein, whom Schubert met at Count Esterhazy's country seat at Zelész, in Hungary. The Baron was not only an enthusiastic admirer, but an active and capable performer of Schubert's songs. So late as 1838 (ten years after Schubert's death), Liszt heard Schönstein, and wrote of him in the *Gazette Musicale* as follows:—" Dans les salons j'entends avec un plaisir très-vif, et souvent une émotion qui allait jusqu'aux larmes, un amateur le Baron Schönstein dire les Lieder de Schubert. La traduction française ne nous donne qu'une idée très-imparfaite de ce qu'est l'union de ces poésies presque toutes extrême-ment belles avec la musique de Schubert, le musicien le plus poète qui fut jamais. La langue allemande est admirable dans l'ordre du sentiment, peut-être aussi n'y-a-t-il qu'un Allemand qui sache bien comprendre la naïveté et la fantaisie de plusieurs de ses compositions, leur charme capricieux, leur abandon mélancolique. Le Baron Schönstein les déclame avec la science d'un grand artiste, et les chante avec la sensibilité simple d'un amateur qui se laisse aller à ses émotions sans se préoccuper du public." [1]

[1] " In the *Salons* here I have often heard Schubert's songs given by the Baron Schönstein, always with the liveliest pleasure, and often with an emotion which moved me to tears. The French version gives but a very poor idea of the manner in which Schubert, the most poetical musician that ever lived, has united his music to the

The Sonnleithners

Schubert's growing reputation brought him in touch with music-lovers of all ranks in life, some members of which were of good social standing in Vienna. He cannot be said to have always felt drawn to the representatives of rank and wealth, and he certainly did not share Beethoven's (humorously described) gift of " imposing on the aristocracy." Conspicuous among the best class of Schubert's acquaintances was Dr Ignaz von Sonnleithner, at whose house a number of artists and amateurs foregathered periodically, for the practice of music. During the years 1815-1824, songs, chamber and choral music were practised every Friday in the summer months, and fortnightly during the winter. Schubert's music was in constant demand, and such works were produced as the cantata *Prometheus*, the " Gesang der Geister über den Wassern," and the 23rd Psalm. Here too the "Erl-king" was sung (Dec. 1, 1820) by August von Gymnich, with brilliant success. The meetings were first held in the Gundelhof, where was accommodation for some 120 people. To the Sonnleithners belongs the credit of bringing the "Erl-king" to successful publication. Leopold von Sonnleithner (advocate and accomplished amateur), nephew of Dr Ignaz, was no less a valuable patron of Schubert, who met at his house the sisters Fröhlich, Grillparzer the poet, Schwindt the painter,

---

words of these poems, which are often extremely beautiful. The German language is admirable for sentiment, and it is all but impossible for anyone not a German to enter into the naïveté and fancy of many of these compositions, their capricious charm, their depth of melancholy. The Baron gives them with the declamatory science of a great artist, and the simple feeling of an amateur who thinks only of his own emotions and forgets the public."

Schubert

and others with whom he was intimate. Leopold Sonnleithner also took great pains to preserve Schubert's
songs, many of which he collected in their original form.
From a letter dated March 26, 1821, it is seen that Sonnleithner had no little difficulty in prevailing upon Schubert
to attend the rehearsals of his own works. "I beg you,"
writes he to Josef Hüttenbrenner, "to take particular
care, and see that Schubert comes to-morrow to Frl.
Linhardt, to rehearse with her 'Der Jüngling,' which she
sings with me; and afterwards that Schubert comes to me
on Wednesday at half-past twelve o clock, to try over his
'Geisterchor.' I count on your good services to get
Schubert to be certain and attend these rehearsals. I
must honestly confess my surprise that he never comes
near me, as I am very anxious to speak to him about
his 'Erl-king' and other matters."

Schubert used also to visit Matthias von Collin—
brother of the poet—at whose house he met many distinguished people, such as Hammer-Purgstall the Orientalist,
Count Moritz Dietrichstein, Caroline Pichler the authoress,
and Ladislaus Pyrker, Patriarch of Venice and a recognised
poet. Meetings also took place every week at Frau von
André's, where it is said "music was made until past
midnight," the sociable company including the brothers
Carl and Josef Czerny, Linke the 'cellist, the elder and
younger Giuliani, the two tenors Barth and Binder, and
Rauscher the opera-baritone. Here too came Schubert and
Umlauff, one of the male-voice party which introduced much
of the composer's concerted vocal music to the public.[1]

[1] The Schubert singers were twelve; their names were as follows:
—Tieze, Barth, Umlauff, Götz, Nejebse, Weinkopf, Frühwald,
Heitzinger, Rauscher, Ruprecht, Seipelt, and Johann Nestroy.

Umlauff

Of Umlauff some further particulars may be given, as he preserves an interesting anecdote concerning the subject of this biography. Carl Umlauff, an Austrian officer of justice, resident in Vienna during the years 1818-1822, was an enthusiastic member of the Schubert male-voice party, for which several important pieces were composed by Schubert, such as the original version of the " Gesang der Geister über den Wassern." In 1822, Umlauff was summoned on official duty in the eastern provinces, where besides following his profession in the Buko-wina, "he sang" (says Kreissle) " to Bojaren, who had fled thither out of Turkey, the earliest of Schubert's songs." Umlauff used to visit Schubert in the morning before office hours, and usually found him jotting down his music as he lay in his bed, or seated at his desk. He would often sing to the composer his latest songs, accompanying himself on a guitar. His son (who relates the story) adds that " he ventured to argue the propriety of the musical expression given to single words; but Schubert, who was very tenacious of his own views, would never lend himself to an alteration of what was once written down. Of my father's stories " (continues young Umlauff) " I remember only one controversy he had with Schubert, on the subject of the question in the ' Wanderer ' —' O Land, wo bist du ? ' Schubert insisted on emphasis-ing the word *bist*, Umlauff the word *du*. Schubert stuck to his opinion, and the line was published in this form."

Allusion has already been made to the surprising fact of Beethoven and Schubert living for a quarter of a century in the same city without becoming acquainted. What an opportunity for an ideal friendship was thus lost. Had the two men learned to know one another the annals

Schubert

of music might have matched those of poetry; and by the side of the famous friendships of Virgil and Horace, of Goethe and Schiller, of Metastasio and Farinelli, there would have appeared those of Beethoven and Schubert. Schindler's account of the meeting of the composers in 1822 has already been quoted. The evidence of Ferdinand Schubert does not add materially to our scanty record of the relations of the two men, for when asked as to his brother's relationship with Beethoven, his answer was merely that "they very seldom came together." Another scrap of information is afforded by William Lenz (a biographer of Beethoven), who states that "Franz Schubert knew Beethoven only a short time. People had misrepresented to Schubert the noble spirit of Beethoven, and purposely kept him away from Beethoven." Kreissle adds that "Beethoven, as is well known, was often to be met with at the 'Fuchshöle' in the Paternostergässchen, kept by Herr Steiner, *and there Schubert often fell in with him.*" The words italicised probably mean no more than that the two men occasionally took their meals at the same eating-house. Schubert had a thorough knowledge of Beethoven's principal works, such as the Symphonies, which he had heard at public concerts, and was accustomed to play as piano-duets with Gahy, the Hüttenbrenners, or Jenger. On the other hand, Beethoven knew only a few insignificant songs of Schubert, and had taken little or no trouble about Schubert's performances.

Prominent among the mutual friends of the two men were Carl Pinterics, Anselm and Josef Hüttenbrenner, and Schindler, and (in a lesser degree) Count Dietrichstein, Count Troyer, Grillparzer the poet, Teltscher the painter, the quartet-players Schuppanzigh and Linke, and

Schubertiaden

Leidesdorf the picture-dealer and music-seller. Beethoven's old friends, the Pachlers, Schubert only became acquainted with when the great master had passed away. Carl Pinterics, an accomplished pianoforte-player, and private secretary to Count Pallfy, lived at the "Zuckerbäckhaus," where Schubert, Vogl, Schober, Gahy and other of their friends frequently visited him. Pinterics was a particular friend of Beethoven, with whom he often went to the "Blumenstöckl." The secretary found time to make a collection of 505 of Schubert's songs, the value of which was unfortunately much reduced owing to his miserable habit of making alterations in the text—a trick which Vogl also resorted to. Josef Hüttenbrenner, for the greater part of his life, worked in Schubert's interest; but whether through lack of influence or inadequate tact, he met with quite disproportionate success. The two visits to Beethoven in 1827 (already described) show that Schubert visited the dying man in company with Anselm Hüttenbrenner and Schindler, and afterwards (on the final occasion) with Josef Hüttenbrenner and Teltscher.

Mention has already been made of many of Schubert's friends and acquaintances; some of these, with the addition of a group of young men drawn from official circles, the arts, and philosophy—all men of an intellectual turn and possessing aspirations—banded together in a kind of social union, which became known by the name of *Schubertiaden*. Games were played, *Schubertiaden.* dancing and speech-making were cultivated, while the heart of the whole entertainment was discovered in the performance of Schubert's latest songs, and other of his compositions.

Schubert

These doings were by no means confined to Vienna, but were carried to such places as Linz, St Pölten, the castle of Ochsenburg, and Atzenbruck—in the neighbourhood of Abtetten. A three days' festival was held annually at the last named place, to which a large number of ladies and gentlemen were invited. One of these scenes we are enabled to reproduce from a sketch, dated 1821, preserved by Heinrich von Dobloff, showing the representation of an allegory, with Schober, Kupelwieser and several young ladies taking part; while seated in the foreground is Schubert, easily recognised in his spectacles, looking intently at the performers. Among the regular attendants on these occasions were Schwindt, Bauernfeld, and Anton Dobloff, and of course Schubert himself, who, it is said, "paid for his salt with marches, schottisches and waltzes—some of which appear under the title "Atzenbrucken Tänze." Franz von Schober has left it on record that "the intellectual enjoyments of these scenes, no participator can ever forget as long as he lives." Besides the regular Schubertiaden, parties and excursions in the country were organised, and on these Schubert must perforce put in an attendance, if only to please his companions. Occasionally, at some of these merry-makings, it is whispered that the wine-cup circulated too freely, and the midnight hour passed by unregarded.

In striking contrast to the gaiety of these Schubertiaden, are the grave and thoughtful utterances contained in the

Diary

few leaves preserved from his diary, which, in point of time, dates back to the year 1816. Aloys Fuchs recovered the fragment from an autograph-collector in Vienna. The vendor had been parting with the leaves separately, and thus the greater part had been

94

At Atzenbruck

(From the "Musical Times" of January 1897, by permission of Messrs Novello & Co., Ltd.)

Immortal Mozart!

irrecoverably lost before Herr Fuchs appeared on the scene.

June 13, 1816.—"I shall remember this clear, bright, beautiful day for the rest of my life. Softly, as if from afar, the magic tones of Mozart's music echo in my ears. Schlesinger's masterly playing impressed them deep on my heart, so powerfully and yet so tenderly. In such wise doth beauty impress the soul—immune from time— to work for our good. In life's darkest day there is thus a shining horizon of hope. O Mozart! immortal Mozart! what countless images of a brighter and better world hast thou stamped on our souls. This quintet, among the smaller works, may be described as one of the greatest. Upon this occasion I too was moved to introduce myself. I played Beethoven's variations, and sang Göthe's 'Rastlose Liebe' and Schiller's 'Amalia.' The first won applause, the second but scant praise. Yet I believe my 'Rastlose Liebe' to be more successful than 'Amalia'; but much of the applause must be attributed to the genius of Göthe. On the same occasion I made the acquaintance of Mdlle. Jenny, a pianist with extraordinary powers of execution, though I found her lacking in the subtleties of expression."

The remarks which follow were jotted down on Schubert's returning from Salieri's jubilee festival.

June 16, 1816.—"It cannot but be pleasing and stimulating to the artist to have all his pupils gathered about him, each striving his best, in honour of the master's jubilee-fête; to hear in their compositions a simple and natural expression, free of all that *bizarrerie* which in most of the compositions of our time is the prevailing element, for which we have chiefly to thank one of our greatest German artists ; free, I say, of all this, which links the tragic with the comic, the pleasing with the disagreeable, the heroic with the puling, the most sacred subjects with the profane—all without discrimination, so that men become mad or frantic instead of being moved, and stirred to laughter rather than raised towards heaven. That all this miserable confusion should be under ban and ignored by the circle of his pupils, so that they may face Nature in her purity, must be a source of the liveliest pleasure to the artist, who, with Gluck for his forerunner, has studied Nature, and has clung to her despite the evil influences of our day.

"Herr Salieri celebrated his jubilee, having been fifty years in Vienna, and an almost equal period in the Emperor's service. His Majesty presented him with a gold medal ; and many of his pupils, male and female, were invited to the ceremony. The pupils' compositions, specially written for the occasion, were produced in order, according to the date of admission of each pupil. The music ended with a chorus from Salieri's oratorio *Jesu al Limbo* (Christ in Hades). The oratorio is designed in the true Gluck style. Everyone was pleased with the entertainment.

"To-day I composed for money for the first time—the work was a cantata (*Prometheus*) for the name-day festival of Herr Professor Watteroth von Dräxler. The honorarium was 100 florins, Viennese currency.[1]

"Man is like a ball tossed 'twixt chance and passion. I have often heard it said by literary men that 'the world is like a stage, where every man plays his part. Praise and blame follow in the other world.' Still, every man has a

[1] 100 florins Viennese = 40 florins Austrian = £4 sterling.

part assigned him—'tis *given* to him—and who shall say whether he has played it well or ill? He is a bad theatrical manager who distributes among his players parts unsuited to their capacities. Carelessness in such a matter is not to be thought of. There is no instance of an actor being dismissed for bad declamation. Give him a part for which he is adapted, he will play it well enough. The applause rests with a capricious public. In the other world, praise or blame depends upon the grand Manager of the globe. Blame, therefore, is put in the balance.

"Natural disposition and education determine the mind and heart of man. The heart is ruler; the mind should be.

"Take men as they are, not as they ought to be.

"Happy he who finds a true friend; happier he who finds a true friend in his wife. To a free man, marriage has become a fearsome thought; he is lost between dulness and sensuality.

"Man bears misfortune without complaint, and thus it pains him the more. Why did heaven give us these tender sympathies? Light tongue, light heart; a light tongue oft hides a heavy heart. Urbanity is a barrier between men of integrity."

The two journeys to Zelész, in Hungary, were the longest, as they were also the most fortunate, which Schubert ever undertook. He was actively teaching the Esterhazy family, and so *Country Visits* earning a definite salary, while the mountain air and methodical household habits were both of undoubted benefit. Both visits have already been described. It is however interesting to note that Baron Schönstein, whom Schubert met at Zelész, had been devoted exclusively to Italian music. He no sooner made the young Viennese composer's acquaintance than he became a convert—like Vogl before him—to the German "Lied," as represented by Schubert's songs. With the Esterhazys Schubert became an established favourite. It is curious to read a list of the works practised by this accomplished family when Schubert first came to stay with them in 1818; it included Hadyn's *Creation* and *Seasons* Mozart's "Requiem," and Anselm Hüttenbrenner's "Der Abend," which was much admired by Schubert. In the course of time many pieces of Schubert's were added to this repertory; and, in at least one case, the work was the exclusive possession of Countess Esterhazy, who set great store by the MS., and could scarcely be induced to part with it for publication. On the occasion of Schubert's first visit to Zelész, Caroline Esterhazy was a mere child (she was born in 1806); but six years later, Schubert found his pupil grown into a handsome young lady of irresistible charm. Kreissle (his first biographer) is at such pains to prove that Schubert had a love-affair, and that he never "proposed," that he almost contradicts himself. "Schubert" (says he) "very often made himself merry at the expense of any friends of his who fell in love. He too was by no means proof against the tender passion, but never seriously compromised himself. Nothing is known of any lasting passion, and he seems never to have thought seriously about matrimony; but he certainly coquetted with love, and was no stranger to the deeper and truer affections. Soon after his entering into the Esterhazy family, he had a flirtation with one of the servants, which soon paled before a more romantic passion, which consumed the inflammatory Schubert. This was

Devout Lover

for the Countess's younger daughter, Caroline. The flame was not extinguished before his death. Caroline esteemed him, and appreciated his genius, but did not return his love, and probably never guessed its extent and fervency. His feelings towards her must have been clear enough, by Schubert's own declaration." He then quotes the remark about everything being dedicated to Caroline, which has already been given. The following lines by Bauernfeld are supposed to have reference to this episode in Schubert's life :—

> "Verliebt war Schubert ; der Schülerin
> Galt's, einer der jungen Comtessen,
> Doch gab er sich einer ganz andern hin,
> Um—die andere zu vergessen."[1]

However beneficial the Hungarian air—and Schubert confesses himself to be a new man—one thing is quite clear—he is heartily glad to get back to Vienna.

It is not to be wondered at that Vienna, long the head of the musical world, should have such a remarkable fascination for Schubert. Robert Schumann felt its subtle magic when, some years later, he penned the following lines :—" It is true this Vienna, with its tower of St Stephen's, its lovely women, its pageantry, and the way it spreads over the smiling plain, that gradually rises into ever loftier hills, enwound by the Danube with countless bands : this Vienna, with all its memories of the greatest German masters, must be a fruitful field for the

[1] "In love with a Countess of youthful grace,
  —A worthy pupil—: in desperate case
  Young Schubert surrenders himself to another,
  And fain would avoid such affectionate pother."

musician's fancy. Often when I gazed at it from the mountain-tops, it came into my mind how frequently Beethoven's eyes must have wandered restlessly to that distant chain of Alps; how Mozart may oft have followed dreamily the course of the Danube, which always seems to swim in wood and forest; and how father Haydn may have looked up at the tower of St Stephen's—shaking his head at such a giddy height. The pictures of the Danube, the tower of St Stephen's, and the distant Alpine summits, put in one frame, and breathed upon with a faint odour of Catholic incense— that is a picture of Vienna; and with that charming landscape living before you, you feel that chords are touched within you which would otherwise never have vibrated. At the touch of Schubert's symphony, and the clear, blossoming, romantic life in it, the town rises more clearly than ever before me, and again I see most plainly that it is just in such a neighbourhood that such works can be born."

Schubert's daily habits were simple, and almost mono-
Habits   tonous in their regularity. He was an early
riser, and it was his custom to begin the day with composition—pursued half-dressed or even in bed, it was a matter of indifference—or with experimental extempore playing on the pianoforte of ideas which were afterwards to be jotted down. This exercise continued till the breakfast hour, after which work was resumed, and briskly carried forward until two o'clock in the afternoon. Then he would repair to a restaurant, usually the Gasthaus, where he could dine for a Zwanziger ($8\frac{1}{2}$d.)—a sum not always at his command. Dinner over, he was free for the rest of the day, which would

Vienna, looking across the Glacis

(from an old engraving)

commonly be spent in walking in the delightful surroundings of the city. In Schubert's later years he was to be found at Bogner's coffee-house from 5 to 7, smoking a pipe and enjoying the conversation of friends. The evening was sometimes devoted to the theatre, after which there would be supper at the Gasthaus, and perhaps a final visit to Bogner's café. Not an infrequent alternative to such a programme would lead to an afternoon call on Fräulein Anna Milder, or Madame Lacsny-Buchwieser : the Esterhazys, with whom he was on friendly terms without regard to music : or to the rooms of Madame Sofie Müller (the great actress), who had the courage on one of these occasions to sing " Die junge Nonne" *at sight*. A fine summer evening would take precedence of any town appointment, and Schubert and his friends would stray at their own sweet will, regardless of everything but the enjoyment of the hour.

Tavern-life in Vienna was a mere commonplace to a bachelor, who would naturally resort to such places, just as in London a man would repair *Taverns* to his club. Beethoven, surrounded by his friends, might any day be seen at the Gasthaus, where he often dined, and where, no doubt, Schubert looked on him with an interest and regard of which the great man was perfectly oblivious. Schubert had, of course, at various times other favourite tavern-haunts, such as the " zur Ungarischen Krone," in the Himmelpfortgasse, where he and his companions were wont to foregather,[1] or the "Zum rothen Kreuz," where his brother Ferdinand joined him at dinner. Ferdinand did not mix with the troop of friends

[1] Writing to Spaun in 1822, Schober remarks with surprise, "We found ' Die Krone' completely deserted."

Schubert

which commonly surrounded the composer; his younger
brother Carl (the painter), on the contrary, often frequented
the round table of intimates which was wont to assemble
of an evening. Poets and painters have brought many
a modest and obscure little inn into notoriety, surround-
ing them with a fragrant memory, which speaks en-
chantment to succeeding generations. It is doubtful
if any such place before 1826 ever witnessed the birth
of so beautiful a work of art as the setting of " Hark!
hark the lark," which the Währing beer-garden saw brought
to light. One Sunday in July, Schubert, Doppler and
others were returning to Vienna from Pötzleinsdorf, and
strolling through the village of Währing, they espied there
a friend, Tieze, seated at one of the tables of the "Zum
Biersack." They agreed to call a halt, and Schubert sat
down beside Tieze, and began to turn over the leaves of
his book that was lying open on the table. Suddenly he
stopped and, pointing to some verses, exclaimed, "Such
a lovely melody has come into my head; if I had but
a sheet of music-paper with me." The resourceful
Doppler drew some lines on the back of a bill of
fare and, then and there, in the midst of all the
attendant noise of fiddlers and skittle-players, of waiters
running here and there in different directions with
orders, in the full hubbub of a holiday crowd, Schubert
wrote that lovely song—truly "a wonderful sweet air,
with admirable rich words to it." Beer-gardens deserve
better of mankind in consequence. There is another
view of the tavern-life of our hero which is not so
pleasant to contemplate. The authority for the succeeding remarks is found in W. Chezy's " Recollections
of my Life" (vol. ii. p. 292). Schubert became over-

fond of good wine. He even took a curious pride in the accidents which resulted from over-indulgence. When the juice of the grape flowed in his veins, he would retire to a solitary corner, and there nurse himself comfortably into a passion. Chezy assures us that "he became a laughing tyrant"—whatever that may be —"and would destroy everything he could, without making a noise—glasses, plates, cups, etc.—and sit simpering and screwing up his eyes into the smallest possible compass." When the Kellner came for the reckoning, the guest placed his hand quietly underneath the table, and the number of fingers he held up indicated the number of measures consumed. It is also said that his illness was aggravated by carelessness in these tavern matters.

The occasional poetical exercises of our musician have already been mentioned. He began early, with a composition for his father's birthday *Poet* fête, acting as his own librettist. Salieri's jubilee called forth a "harmless libretto of his own rhymes," and there are others, a small specimen of which may be seen in the two following sets of verses, which Ferdinand Schubert published in the *Leipziger Musikzeitung* of 1838. The first piece is dated September 1820.

> "Lasst sie nur in ihrem Wahn,"
> Spricht der Geist der Welt,
> "Er ist's, der im schwanken Kahn
> So sie mir erhält."

> "Leave them to their self-deceit,"
> Thus the world may say;
> "He who rules the waves that beat,
> Holdeth us in sway."

Schubert

Lasst sie rennen ; jagen nur
Hin nach einem fernen Ziel,
Glauben viel, beweisen viel
Auf der dunkeln Spur.

Nichts ist wahr von alledem,
Doch ist's kein Verlust,
Menschlich ist ihr Weltsystem,
Göttlich bin ich's mir bewusst.

Let them hurry wildly on
Towards the distant goal,
Much have they to trust upon ;
Vague is Time's dull scroll.

Truth eludes their weaker grasp,
Fails their beck or nod ;
Dust and ashes would they clasp ;
Man, trust thou in God.

Schumann remarked of the two little poems that, though
they betray an unpractised hand, they still show a poetical
aptitude and bias which Schubert's friends well knew him
to possess.

The second poem, entitled "My Prayer," has been
thought to have reference to the theological differences in
the Schubert family. Franz took little part in these, but
his brother Ignaz seems to have been considerably exercised, to the point of open rebellion from his father's
creed, which was of the orthodox pattern.

"My Prayer"

MEIN GEBET.

Tiefer Sehnsucht heil'ges Bangen
Will in schön're Welten langen ;
   Möchte füllen dunklen Raum
   Mit allmächt'gem Liebestraum.

Grosser Vater ! reich' dem Sohne,
Tiefer Schmerzen nun zum Lohne,
   Endlich als Erlösungsmahl
   Deiner Liebe ew'gen Strahl.

Sieh, vernichtet liegt im Staube,
Unerhörtem Gram zum Raube,
   Meines Lebens Martergang
   Nahend ew'gem Untergang.

Tödt' es und mich selber tödte,
Stürz' nur Alles in die Lethe,
   Und ein reines kräft'ges Sein
   Lass', O Grosser ! dann gedeih'n.

Longings of the heart so tearful,
Fain would yield to thoughts more cheerful,
   Quitting gloom, to rise above
   Clouds of doubt, to realms of love.

Mighty Father, let Thy giving
Be of sorrow, for the living ;
   Sorrow changing into bliss,
   When redeem'd are things amiss.

Lo, defiled in dust a-lying,
—Grief and pain and heavy crying—
   Life yields all—a flickering spark ;
   Soon 'tis snuff'd in endless dark.

Strike, nor spare not my poor being ;
Hurl beyond the reach of seeing ;
   Then in mercy pure and blest,
   Grant, O God, eternal rest.

Schubert

The poet's adage, "haud facile emergunt quorum virtutibus obstat Res angusta domi,"[1] found eloquent illustration in Schubert's case. As a boy he had scarce food enough; he was short of music-paper to write upon; for years he had no rooms of his own; he was unable to take proper holidays owing to lack of means; and last thing of all, there was not sufficient estate to pay for his funeral. Being unable to wait, he was obliged to accept any offer from music-publishers; and his trans-

Poor Business-man

actions, in which his modesty was usually taken full advantage of by the grasping publishers, are, with few exceptions, hopelessly foolish. That he was a bad businessman goes without saying. Surrounded as he was by clever men whose advice at the very least should have been sought, Schubert in a weak moment, when no doubt short of money, allowed Diabelli to persuade him to part with the copyright of the first twelve books of his songs for 800 florins. A portion of these works (op. 1-7), as we have seen, was published by the efforts of the Sonnleithners as Schubert's own property. It is further to be noted that 800 copies of (op. 1) the "Erl-king" had been sold in nine months; while the set of twenty songs (*i.e.* op. 1-7) brought in the sum of 2000 Gulden, which (allowing 10d. per Gulder) amounts to £83, 6s. 8d. Here is a list of some of Schubert's known transactions—not put forward to encourage other composers, who manage this part of their business better nowadays, but rather to show that Mayrhofer's view, quoted below, was a reasonable one.

[1] " Slow rises worth by poverty depressed."—JUVENAL.

Vera pro Gratis

1816.	Cantata for Herr Watteroth ("the first time I composed for money")	£4	0	0
1822.	Profit on twenty songs during one year's sale, 2000 Gulden (half of which went to the publisher), £83, 6s. 8d., less 50% .	£41	13	4
1822.	Sold the plates and copyright of the above (besides entering into some foolish agreements respecting future works) to Diabelli .	70	0	0
1825.	Seven Scott songs sold to Artaria .	20	0	0
1825.	Sonata (op. 53), Divertissement (op. 54), Artaria, 300 Vienna florins	12	0	0
1828.	Impromptus and five-part songs for male voices, sold to Schott, 200 silver Gulden . . .	2	10	0
1828.	Quintet, 30 florins, Schott .	1	5	0
1828.	Six songs from the "Winterreise," per F. Lachner, sold to Haslinger (6 Gulden) . . .	0	5	0

(After the above remarkable transaction Schubert wrote "It's all over with my journey to Gratz this year; I have already handed over to Haslinger the second part of the "Winterreise.")

1828.	Trio in E flat (op. 100), sold to Probst for 20 florins, 60 kreutzers .	£0	17	6

A few further items may be set down :—

1822.	The dedication of op. 2. ("Gretchen am Spinnrade") to Count Moritz Friess was rewarded with twenty ducats (? gold) . .	10	0	0

Dedication of op. 4. (three songs,
including "The Wanderer") to
the Patriarch Ladislaus Pyrker,
twelve ducats (? gold). . . £6 0 0

1826. Gift of the Musik-Verein in recognition of his services to Music . 10 0 0

1828. Schubert's concert realised a clear
profit of . . . 32 0 0

At the composer's death a large
number of MSS. were valued in
the official inventory at . 0 8 6

In 1872 the Männergesang-Verein (Vienna) erected a
monument to Schubert's memory which cost 42,000
florins, or £1700.

One is strongly reminded of old Sam Wesley's lines,
intended for another occasion it is true, but none the less
applicable :—

> " See him when starved to death and turned to dust,
>   Presented with a monumental bust.
>   The poet's fate is here in emblem shown,
>   He asked for bread and he received a stone."

A comparison of the sums other musicians were receiving in Schubert's day shows that Beethoven in 1801
obtained £10 a-piece for the septet, the first symphony,
a sonata (in B flat, op. 22) and a concerto (No. 1).
Rossini drew £32 per opera, and contrived to write four
per annum. Hünten received 2000 francs for each
pianoforte piece, of eight or ten pages (i.e. £83, 6s. 8d.).[1]

It may be added that Probst (the publisher) intimated
to Schubert that he thought his price, quoted at eighty

[1] On the authority of Weitzmann.

Saving Grace

florins (£3, 6s. 8d.) per piece, *too much*, and mentions with great pride that he is busy with "the complete works of Kalkbrenner"!

There is little doubt that Schubert conducted his affairs without reference to his friends, who were genuinely sorry that his transactions were so fruitless. "When I consider the illnesses and pecuniary embarrassments of my poor friend" (says Mayrhofer), "it invariably occurs to me that he failed particularly in two things which might have grounded his financial position and made him entirely independent. Contrary to a well-digested scheme, and one actually in the course of operation, he disposed of the copyright in these and other works that followed, and neglected a favourable combination of circumstances for obtaining a good musical appointment, with a regular salary attached. A love of enjoyment, confirmed by deprivations in early life, and ignorance of the world, may have led him to commit such errors. In later times (1827 and 1828), he always made modest offers to the publishers, which they thought exorbitant."

It is certain that Schubert did not lack a sense of humour, for when rid of conventional restraint he would indulge himself to the top of his bent in merriment and practical jokes. His favourite *Humour* drollery, when in this vein, was a performance of the "Erlking" through the teeth of a comb, a feat which always drew the laughter and applause of his audience. His own laugh, we are told by Kreissle, was no ordinary mirthful performance; "it consisted of a hoarse, suppressed chuckle." Schubert did not dance, but he was ever ready to extemporise by the hour for those who desired to trip it lightly. He is said to have turned some of these fleeting fancies to practical account by repeating such strains as pleased him until he was able to carry them in his memory. They were afterwards written down. No doubt the "Grätzer Galopp," and the "Grätzer Walzer," preserve ideas which sprang to his fingers as he sat playing on such occasions. Then there are the "Erste Walzer," which Schumann's picturesque pen cleverly characterises as "Little fairies, hovering over the earth, no taller than a flower, how I love the 'Sehnsuchtswalzer' steeped in a hundred virgin thoughts. How I dislike the three last, which, as æsthetic errors in the main, I can't forgive the composer."

When living with Mayrhofer (in 1819) the composer and poet seem to have amused themselves with

> "Jest and youthful jollity,
> Quips, and cranks, . . ."

of many sorts, "for whilst we were together" (says Mayrhofer) "many a curious thing happened. Both of us were of the right temperament and opportunities there were in plenty for droll amusements. We used to tease each other and exchange pleasantries and epigrams for our mutual benefit. A favourite joke with Mayrhofer was to charge at Schubert with a sword-stick with a bayonet fastened at the point, shouting out the while in an Austrian dialect, "Was halt mich denn ab, du kloaner Raker?" to which Schubert, while thrusting him back, would reply, "Waldl, wilder Verfasser." This little scene is testified to by Gahy, who witnessed it more than once. Mayrhofer adds that his friend's "free, open-hearted, cheerful manner, and my retired nature came into sharp contrast, and gave us an opportunity of nicknaming each

other appropriately as though we were playing certain
parts assigned us. Alas, it was the only rôle I ever
played." The mention of nicknames reminds us that
Schubert enjoyed a full share of these friendly soubriquets.
As a boy it was the "Miller"; then it became the
"Tyrant"; later (as we have seen) he was called "Kanevas"; and finally he was widely known among friends—
not excepting the ladies—by the atrociously vulgar name
of "Schwammerl."[1] A few of his acquaintance with
better taste preferred to call him "Bertl."

No one who studies the biography of Franz Schubert
can fail to observe that he (if anyone ever did) lived a
dual life. His outward demeanour was that of an ordinary
mortal—shy, awkward and retiring; his inner habitation
was with the immortals. Heaven was in his mind. "In
ordinary life" (says Franz Schober) "the opportunity was
only offered to a select few, and only to those on the rarest
occasions, of convincing themselves of Schubert's entire
nobility of soul, and this they arrived at through scenes and
conversations which cannot easily be repeated or described."
With such a man all documents privately written are likely
to be so many confidences, which, as is observed by
Schober (above-quoted), were rarely vouchsafed to his
dearest friends. The following narrative, entitled "My
Dream," is dated July 3, 1822; but though we can tell
the dream, we cannot show the interpretation, which must
therefore be left to the reader.

July 3, 1822.—"I was one of a number of brothers
and sisters. Our father and mother were
worthy people, and I was deeply attached   *My Dream*
to the whole circle. One day my father took us to a

[1] Bauernfeld addresses him in a letter as the "fattest of friends."

Schubert

favourite spot, on a party of pleasure. My brothers were in high glee, but I was wretched. Then my father came to me and bade me enjoy the good things set before me; but I could not. Whereupon, in a rage, my father banished me from his presence. I turned away my steps, and with a heart full of boundless love for those who despised it, I betook me into a distant land. During long years I felt myself preyed upon alternately by the greatest pain and the most fervent love. Then it was that the news of my mother's death came to me. I hastened to see her, and my father, softened by affliction, did not then stay my going. So I gazed on the dead body of my mother. My eyes were blinded by tears. Like the dear old departed days, to which my mother had once thought we should be able to look back, even as she had looked back, she was lying dead before me. And we followed her bier in mourning and woe and the coffin sank into the earth. My father once more took me into his favourite garden; he asked me if I liked it. But the garden had grown hateful to me and I dared not speak. My father, whose anger was kindling a second time, asked me if I liked the garden. I trembled and said "No." Then my father struck me and I fled. So a second time my steps were turned away and with a heart overflowing with love for those who scorned it. For many long, long years I sang my songs. If I were fain to sing of love, it turned to pain; if I would sing of pain, it turned to love. Thus was I divided between love and sorrow. It came about that I was told of a pious maiden who had just died. A crowd gathered about her tomb, and in the midst of that crowd were many youths and old men who wandered on and on, as though in great joy.

Diary

They spoke gently, as though fearing to awaken the maiden. Heavenly thoughts seemed, like sparks of fire, to be for ever darting on the youths upwards from the maiden's sepulchre, and a quiet rustling noise was heard. I felt afraid to walk there. "By miracle only is it that you are come to this place," said the people. And I advanced to the grave with slow steps and concentrated gaze, but before I could have imagined it possible, I found myself in a circle from which there arose spontaneously a most wonderful strain of music, and I felt the bliss of eternity concentrated as it were into a single moment. There too did I see my father, who was reconciled and loving towards me. He clasped me in his arms and wept. But I wept more sorely than he."

Sir George Grove observes of the foregoing narrative, that it is hard to guess what events or circumstances Schubert had in his mind. "It may not improbably have been occasioned by some dispute on religious subjects of the nature of those hinted at in his brother Ignaz's letter of October 12, 1818. At any rate it is deeply pathetic and poetical."

Perhaps the most convincing proof that Schober and others were right, when they characterised Schubert as a man of reticence and reserve, is to be found in the small surviving fragment of the diary for 1824. In his entry for March 27, Schubert confesses the solitariness which most thoughtful men experience, and apparently none more so than men of an acutely sensitive temperament. A homily might be written upon each of the reflections quoted below. It is a high courage that dictates such an expression as "Grief sharpens the understanding and strengthens the soul." This was no idle echo of ancient wisdom, to a man who had survived the fiery ordeals which Schubert had undergone. Nor will anyone be inclined to doubt the diarist's remark concerning his own music, which our English poet—contemporary with Schubert, and endowed like him with but brief span of life—had expressed so beautifully : [1]—

> "We look before and after,
> We pine for what is not :
> Our sincerest laughter
> With some pain is fraught ;
> Our sweetest songs are those that tell of saddest thought."

"Grief sharpens the understanding and strengthens the soul, whereas joy seldom troubles itself about the former, and makes the latter effeminate or frivolous."

"I hate from my inmost heart the narrow, one-sided view of things which makes so many wretched people imagine that what they alone pursue is the only good, and that all else is worthless. One great ideal should possess a man through life, it is true, but the light of this enthusiasm should illumine all else."

March 27.—"No one understands the grief or joy of others. We always imagine we are approaching each other, whereas we travel in parallel lines. Oh, the misery of him who experiences this !"

"My compositions in music are the product of my mind and spring from my sorrow ; those only that were born of grief give the greatest delight to the outside world."

"The sublime is but a step removed from the ridicu-

[1] Solomon uttered the same thought : "Even in laughter the heart is sorrowful."—PROVERBS xiv. 13.

lous, just as wisdom is a near neighbour of crass
folly."

"Man enters the world in faith, which is far ahead of
reason and knowledge ; for to understand anything he
must first have faith. It is the higher basis upon which
the weak understanding rears its first pillars of proof.
Reason is nothing but belief analysed."

March 29.—"Oh Fancy, thou inscrutable fount, from
which artists and learned men do drink. Abide with us,
though known and honoured of few; abide, and safe-
guard us against so-called wisdom, that skeleton without
flesh or blood."

Friedrich Johann Rochlitz—critic and founder of the
Leipsic *Allgemeine musikalische Zeitung*—comes into
brief and unenviable prominence through his extraordinary
persistence in attempting to obtain a worthy setting of
one of his own poems. He had made the acquaintance
of Schubert in 1822 when he visited Vienna to confer
with Beethoven regarding a proposed setting of Goethe's
"Faust." Five years later (on Nov. 7, 1827) Rochlitz
wrote to Schubert, who had meanwhile set three of his
songs (as op. 81), in the following terms :—"Herr
Haslinger has told you how grateful I am for your
settings of my three songs, and how I wish that you
would illustrate by your lovely music some longer work
of mine. . . . The poem I have in mind is "Der
erste Ton," which you will find in the fifth volume of
my collected works. . . . And here I will give you my
ideas of what would be appropriate music. . . . Overture
—a short sharp chord; FF to begin with, and then
possibly a long sustained passage for clarinet or horn,
with pauses. Then, opening calmly and gradually,

clothed in music becoming gloomier as it proceeds, and more intricate in character, treated harmonically rather than melodiously—a sort of chaos, which only by degrees develops and becomes brighter." Rochlitz's amusing directions to the composer (of which our quotation is a fair sample) may be matched by Dryden's instruction to Purcell, which appears as follows in the adaptation of the "Tempest":—"A Symphony of Musick, like trumpets, to which four Tritons dance." Rochlitz's poem had been set by Weber as early as 1808, but the poet was not satisfied and thought the result far from good. He then tried to induce Beethoven to set the poem; the master, however, suspected that such a work might recall Haydn's *Creation*—a dire imputation to be avoided at all costs. Schubert, when it came to his turn to be solicited, viewed "Der erste Ton" with no less diffidence; and so it came about that the "short sharp chord, FF to begin with, and then possibly a long sustained passage for clarinet or horn, with pauses," was never written.

Schubert's taste in literature is not easily gauged, either from his selection of words for songs,[1]

Literary Tastes

or judging from the references in his letters; for the one is altogether too catholic, and the other too meagre to afford solid grounds for an opinion. In the last letter he wrote, there is mention of four of Fenimore Cooper's works, one of which—"The Last of the Mohicans"—Schubert must have read as soon as the translation was published, for the book itself did not appear until 1826. In this connection too

[1] A complete list of the poets drawn upon in Schubert's songs will be found on pp. 134-137.

Sharing Rooms

may be noted the formation of a social union which had for its object the reading and study of the classics. These meetings were usually held at Schober's or Bruchmann's, when one of the two friends acted as *reader*. Homer was one of the authors studied. The only reference Schubert makes to this Society is in his letter to Kupelwieser, dated March 31, 1824. "Our Society, as you will have heard by this time, came to an end, owing to the increase of undesirable members, given to beer-drinking and sausage-eating; its dissolution followed in two days. I had, however, given up attending immediately after your departure."

A proposal was made on September 13, 1826, by Bauernfeld, on behalf of Schwindt and himself, to share rooms in common with Schubert. "Moritz Schwindt and I propose to you to join us in sharing a common lodging-house for all three, if you are content. Do say yes; we should so like to join forces." Schubert replied a few days later: "As regards our joint occupation, I should like the thing very much, but knowing as I well do what comes of such student association, I should not like to be left at last to stumble between two stools." Bauernfeld describes in the Vienna *Presse* of April 17, 1869, the working of this arrangement. It was disastrous to poor Schubert from any sensible point of view. Both Schwindt and Bauernfeld were much younger men, and on Schubert fell the whole responsibility of providing for all three. His slender income from the sale of his compositions, scarcely enough for one, was hopelessly inadequate to meet the expenses incurred by the friends, who rarely stinted themselves when funds were available. One occasion is recorded

Schubert

when Bauernfeld and Schubert met by chance at a coffee-house near the Kärnthnerthor theatre, and discovered each other in the act of ordering a *café au lait* and biscuits, because neither had the requisite Zwanziger (8½d.) for dinner. Not only did the three share their rooms in common, but the arrangement actually extended to hats, coats, boots and cravats. The evenings were spent at the Gasthaus, after which the company would wander forth in the city and its environs until daylight drove them home to their separate quarters, or to the room of one, where the whole party commonly put up.

I cannot do better than close this part of my account by quoting Schindler's summary of Schubert's life, and adding the official inventory of the composer's goods and chattels. "It is true" (says Schindler) "that there was neither hill nor valley in Schubert's life, nothing but a level plain, over which he moved at an even pace. His frame of mind was also tranquil and clear as a mirror, difficult to be irritated by external things, and in perfect harmony with the essence of his character. His days passed as befitted the offspring of a humble sphere, who had been born poor and remained poor. He lived at home till his tenth year; from thence to his seventeenth year a singer in the imperial Convict and on the benches of the gymnasium; three years usher with his father in the Lichtenthal school; finally, a pianoforte-player, and an admirable one, as well as a composer, writing what he chose, and remaining free and independent, as his publisher gave him fifteen florins for a sheet of songs, and fifteen florins for a pianoforte composition. His early poverty had guarded him against the temptation

Schindler's Summary

of the high demands and desires which we meet with in other musicians. Family wants and cares, dating from an early and imprudent marriage, did not hamper his genius; for he stood alone in his magic circle, not disturbed by the prose of domestic life. During the last eight years of his life he had given up the office of musical teacher, which was also the source of much labour and ingratitude. He made no journeys worthy of the name, excepting a few short trips to Upper Austria. One reason of the obscurity to which Schubert's talent was condemned during his life-time lay in a certain obstinacy, an unbending habit, which, without detracting from his declared independence, made him absolutely deaf to good and practical counsels on the part of well-meaning friends. This characteristic often appeared in social intercourse as well as in musical matters, but it is not to be attributed to an excessive self-esteem, or overweening self-confidence. The devotion shown by Schubert on all occasions for the great musicians, his unwearied endeavours to improve himself, show that there is no ground for such an accusation. Schubert did not know the feelings of jealousy and thirst for fame which do so much to stimulate some artists to activity; his love of retirement, and his quiet life, bear witness to the purity of his ambition. He was quick to detect flattery, however cautiously it was administered, and he was positively indifferent to praise; the utmost applause bestowed on any of his works did not produce a change of countenance."

Schubert died intestate. In the official inventory the possessions of the musician and composer (" Tonkunstler und Compositeur") are mentioned as follows:—

3 dress coats;
3 walking coats;
10 pairs of trousers;
9 waistcoats;   37 florins

1 hat;
5 pairs of shoes;
2 pairs of boots;   2 florins

4 shirts;
9 cravats; and pocket-
    handkerchiefs;
13 pairs of socks;
1 towel; 1 sheet; 2
    bed-cases;   8 florins

1 mattress;
1 bolster;
1 quilt;   6 florins
A quantity of old
    music;[1]   10 florins
                            _____

        Total   63 florins (about £2, 10s.)

[1] The item of old music is understood to have included a vast store
of MSS., among which was the great C-major symphony.

The Musician

A family-quartet grows into an orchestra—Feats in musical composition—
Revisions and corrections—Song-writing—Zumsteeg and Schubert—
"King of Thule"—Poets set by Schubert—Breitkopf & Haertel's
edition of the songs—"The Erl-king"—English songs—"Die schöne
Müllerin"—"Winterreise"—"Schwanengesang"—Opera—Why
Schubert failed—Librettists—Schubert gives a concert—Sacred
music—An oratorio written in secret—Music in chalk—Mass in E
flat—Schubert as a pianist and composer for the pianoforte—He
breaks down in his own piece—Pianist's point of view—The theorists
—G-major sonata—Opus 53—Sonata in A minor—String quartets—
Schubert's music in England—Treasure trove—Schubert's combinations—The symphonies—L'envoi.

THE musician in Schubert was chiefly manifested in
his works, for though a gifted singer and violinist in his
school-days, and a passable pianist in later life, neither
as performer or conductor, nor in any branch of executive
art, did he achieve any measure of fame. He gave up
singing when his voice broke in 1813, and never again
returned to it, excepting as an amusement for others,
when no other voice was available. To his violin he
was faithful for many years, not only at the Convict, to
which as a past student he always had ready admission,
but also in the family circle, where string quartet-playing
(as we have already seen) was in regular cultivation.
This quartet — which originally included Ferdinand
Schubert, Ignaz, Franz and his father, was destined to

Schubert

play an important part in Franz's education, inasmuch as it formed the nucleus from whence sprang a complete orchestra. Among the earliest recruits were Herr Josef Doppler (bassoon), Ferdinand Bogner (flute), the two 'cello-players Kamauf and Willmann, and Reidlpacher the double-bass-player. The elder Schubert's house was soon found too small for this growing Society, and a move was consequently made to a house in the Dorotheengasse. Before the winter of 1815, it was possible to play small symphonies, such as the lesser works of Haydn, Mozart, Pleyel and Rosetti. The gatherings now began to attract attention, and rarely went without a numerous audience of friends and acquaintances. Again the quarters proved inadequate, and the orchestra migrated to Schottenhofer, the residence of Otto Hatwig (once a member of the Burg theatre). On the removal of Hatwig, the orchestra followed to his new house in the Gundelhof. Many first-rate players were attracted by the Society's performances, the repertory of which became more imposing as the years advanced. The larger symphonies of Haydn, Mozart, Krommer and Romberg, and the two first symphonies of Beethoven were now within its reach. Then there were overtures by Cherubini, Câtel, Spontini, Boieldieu, Méhul, Winter and Weigl. Even the bare list of composers is instructive, inasmuch as it casts some light on the musical doings of young Vienna in the early part of the nineteenth century. The importance of the Society to Schubert now becomes apparent; here he would gain experience not only as an executant (for like Beethoven and Mozart he played the viola), but also in writing and conducting his earlier symphonies and overtures. Those he specially wrote

Clairvoyance

for the Society were the two symphonies (No. 4. in C minor, and No. 5 in B flat) and two overtures (one in B flat, and the other known as "in the Italian style"). The concerts—or open practices—for no admission fee was charged—were not confined to instrumental music ; for we read of first-rate singers such as Tieze and von Gymnich taking occasional part. The gatherings continued until the autumn of 1820, at which time the place of meeting was in the Bauermarkt, when, having to find fresh quarters, and seeing no feasible plan by which the members could be accommodated without paying for a concert-room, the whole scheme was allowed to fall through.

Schubert's extraordinary facility in transferring to paper the long and imaginative creations of his brain astonished his friends, whose close *Fertility* observation merely served to increase their wonder. Vogl, the singer, attributed the composer's marvellous and ever-ready command of invention to a state of *clairvoyance*, and appears to have regarded other methods as those of mere mechanical manufacture. His remarks are worth quoting :—" If the subject be that of manufacturing, producing, or creating, I don't care, I won't have anything to do with it, especially since I have learnt, by my experience of Schubert, that there are two kinds of composition ; one which, as with Schubert, comes forth to the world in a state of clairvoyance or somnambulism, without any freewill on the part of the composer, the forced product of a higher power and inspiration— one may well be astonished and charmed at such a work, but not criticise it ; the other is the reflected." [1]

[1] From a letter of Vogl, dated November 15, 1831, addressed to A. Stadler.

Schubert

Both Schober and Schönstein agreed with Vogl in this matter. The remarkable success of Beethoven's laborious methods sufficiently rebuts the idea that the clairvoyance system (if any such thing existed) was the only one. The attempt of Schubert's friends to explain the marvellous by the aid of the supernatural at least serves to show how great was the impression produced by the musician's feats of composition. He himself refers to his settings of Goethe as coming "unsought and uncalled for; suggested by truth and actuality, they are grounded and rooted therein." Speed, of itself, is of no avail in art; yet if a masterpiece result, and inspiration is discernible in a work set down with all the ready despatch of a copyist, one can readily appreciate Vogl's point of view, and become tempted to subscribe to his theory of clairvoyance. The setting of Matt. von Collin's ballad—"Der Zwerg"—is a case in point; Schubert, pressed by his publisher for "a song written off-hand," literally carried out the suggestion. Without preparation, and conversing the while with Randhartinger, who was waiting to take him for a walk, Schubert wrote down this long and highly dramatic piece as if it had been mere child's play. The work bears no traces of haste; the accompaniment is of comparatively simple design, it is true; but, as a whole, the music is a fine earnest piece of work which would be of credit to any composer of the immortal group. Another well-authenticated story tells how the musician, when lying ill in the Vienna hospital, was yet able to rise above bodily weakness and produce several of the "Müllerlieder" and "Der Einsame," (dated 1825). Sudden inspiration bearing remarkable fruits has already been instanced in the composition of "Hark! hark, the lark"—born in a

MS. Corrections

Währing beer-garden—the solo and chorus for Fräulein Fröhlich, or the "Italian Overture" written in a fit of bravado, after returning from the theatre. Here is an anecdote that will please musicians. At the request of a friend, with whom the composer was intimate during his stay at Steyr, Schubert employed the melody of "Die Forelle"[1] for the theme and variations of the pianoforte quintet (op. 114). The movement was done very hurriedly, and there was no time to write out a score; so the string parts were set straight down on paper, and the composer carried in his head the piano part, which was only written out after the performance. Mozart had performed a similar feat when (at the Burg theatre, Vienna), in 1784,[2] Madame Strinasacchi played his new sonata in B flat (Köchel, 454) from the violin part, while the composer trusted to his memory for pianoforte-accompaniment.

Schubert as a general rule did not make many corrections, nor did he believe in alterations and revisions. Once set down on paper his rule was to place the MS. in a drawer, turn the key, *Revisions* and think little more about it. Vogl relates that, having copied and transposed a certain song of Schubert's

[1] Schubert wrote the following letter to Josef Hüttenbrenner, Feb. 21, 1818:—"Dearest Friend,—I am overjoyed to find that my songs please you. As a proof of my sincere friendship, I send you herewith another ("Die Forelle"), which I wrote at midnight for Anselm. But what mischief! Instead of the box of blotting-sand, I seize the ink-bottle. I hope, over a glass of punch at Vienna, to become better acquainted with you. *Vale*." (Schubert.)

[2] Mozart afterwards filled in the part for piano, using, by chance, an ink of a slightly different colour. The MS., which was in the possession of Mr F. G. Kurtz (of Liverpool), clearly showed the addition.

(the original of which had found its way to the locked drawer), after an interval of about a fortnight the copy was put before the composer, who, when Vogl sang, exclaimed with some enthusiasm—"H'm : pretty good song ; pray whose is it ? " But although much of his work was done without revision, there is a not inconsiderable portion which proves the composer could take infinite pains to improve upon his first draughts. This is well seen in Breitkopf & Haertel's edition of the songs, which gives all the original copies (obtainable) of each song. Thus there are four "Erl-kings," each differing from the other, and the last and originally published copy proving much the best. Goethe's "Sehnsucht"[1] was set six times over. Several of the songs—and some of the same being among the longest—are provided with new endings. A glance at our *facsimile* of a page from the score of the symphony in C major[2] will show that

---

[1] Beethoven set the same poem four times.

[2] " It seems that Schubert's friends used to lecture him a great deal on the diffuseness and want of consideration which they discovered in his works, and were continually forcing Beethoven's laborious processes of composition down his throat. This often made him angry, and when repeated evening after evening he would say, so you're going to set upon me to-day; go it—I beg you. But for all his annoyance the remonstrances appear to have had some effect, and after Beethoven's death he asked Schindler to show him the MS. of *Fidelio*. He took it to the piano and poured over it a long time, making out the passages as they had been, and comparing them with what they were ; but it would not do, and at last he broke out and declared that for such drudgery he could see no reason under any circumstances ; that he thought the music at first just as good as at last, and that for his part he had really no time for such corrections.' —Grove's Dictionary, iii. 349.

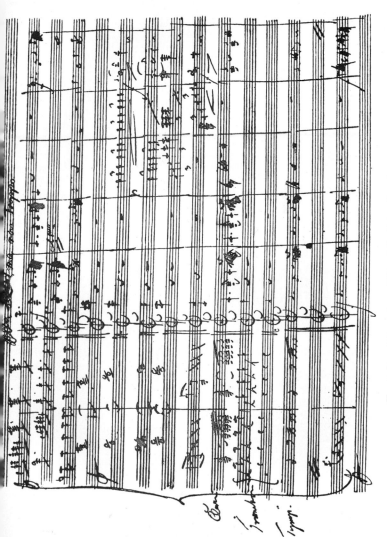

Facsimile of Page from MS. of C Major Symphony

(from the "Musical Times" of January 1897, by permission of Messrs Novello & Co., Ltd.)

Song-writing

Schubert had the courage to alter even a *first subject*, after completing a full-score — a proceeding which necessitates a large number of alterations, inasmuch as the subject in the course of development often reappears. Another instance of revising his work was noted by Randhartinger, who was present at the first trial of Schubert's string-quartet in D minor, when the composer made a series of revisions, writing them on the freshly-copied parts which the players had used. Such instances might be further multiplied, but enough has been said to prove that Schubert often made important revisions in his works.

When Schubert, as a boy of fourteen, began (in 1811) to compose songs, he was entering into competition with Zumsteeg, Reichardt, Schulz, Zelter and Himmel. The song-form, as it then existed, had no doubt been influenced to some extent by Bach, Mozart and Haydn, but the time was ripe for an original mind to mould and develop the capabilities of lyrical expression to a new and higher order of things. Schubert—not unlike an inventor dealing in mechanics—rediscovered for himself much that had gone before, and reproduced at an early age ballads of more significance, if not of greater finish, than the best of Zumsteeg's. A few comparisons will serve to illustrate these remarks. For this very purpose Messrs Breitkopf & Haertel print three of Zumsteeg's ballads, which will be found in the appendix of volume iii. of Schubert's "Lieder." "Hagars Klage"—as set by Zumsteeg—is long, well-knit, melodious and melancholy; Schubert's setting of the same words (dated 1811), at times highly dramatic, breathing a fine atmosphere, often Mozartean,

is in part quite individual, as for example in the ending.[1]
Its faults are obvious. The composition halts too often ;
Zumsteeg managed better in that respect. In the second
of the songs quoted in the volume mentioned—Schiller's
" Die Erwartung "—Zumsteeg is seen in a graceful and
melodious vein. His setting is refined and on the whole
consistent, though it ends in a *bizarre* manner. It
cannot, however, compare with Schubert's version of
the same ballad (dated 1815), which is fresh, interesting,
and full of invention. One can understand Vogl exclaiming that the composer squanders his ideas, or
Beethoven's remarking that such a song contains ten
others. A third example will suffice to dismiss the
comparison. Zumsteeg's " Ritter Toggenburg " offers
a string of little movements, somewhat weak in invention,
but vocal and pleasing. The composition (which in
this respect foreshadows many of Schubert's) begins in
one key (C) and ends in another (A flat). Schubert's
version (dated 1816) is superior in both melody and

---

[1] " Hagars Klage " is the first song in vol. i. of B. & H.'s edition.
The time indications of this one song are as follows :—

Largo			C minor				3-4
Allegro			D minor				C
Largo			B flat				3-4
Geschwind			C minor				C
Adagio			D flat major				C
Largo			E				C
Allegro			C major				C
Allegretto			G major				2-4
Allegro			G minor				6-8
Andante			C minor				C
Largo			F minor				2-4
Adagio			A flat major				3-4

construction, though not otherwise remarkable. Like Zumsteeg, he is not content with one key; for after beginning in F major, the ballad ends in B flat minor. We need not stay to consider whether Schubert could have found better models from which to work; there were many scattered pieces in the German treasury of song;[1] and in England such a work as "From Rosy Bowers"[2] — far superior to anything of Zumsteeg's — had made its appearance more than a century before.

The song-form of Schulz, Reichardt and Zelter (if not also of Himmel) was practically identical with the folk-song. For his shorter pieces Schubert makes free use of this strophical form, and even in his earliest productions shows a desire to widen the musical possibilities of so simple a style, by enriching the pianoforte-accompaniment, or by the introduction of novel modulations, and perhaps above all by an emotional reproduction of the words, unknown to all his predecessors—including the great masters.

Zelter's setting of "The King of Thule" (from Goethe's verses, written in 1774)—known to have been the poet's favourite one—appeared in 1812. Schubert set the same ballad four years afterwards. A comparison is interesting, because it shows as nothing else can the actual steps the young composer had to take in gaining a lead on the foremost of his contemporaries.

[1] Mozart's "Das Veilchen" is a favourable specimen of the forty-one "Lieder" attributed to him, and is further noteworthy as his only setting of Goethe. Bach, Handel, Haydn and Beethoven all leave a few specimens of their powers in the writing of "Lieder."

[2] By Purcell.

Schubert

Slow.

SCHUBERT, Op. 5, No. 5.

Es war ein Kö-nig in Thu-le.

Schubert has the advantage in colour and richness of harmony, while there is more of freshness and variety in his melody. He wisely groups two stanzas of the words as one, and thus is enabled to produce a melody of double the length of Zelter's.

ZELTER, "Lieder-Schatz," Peters, i. 43.

Es war ein Kö-nig in Thu-le.

The older musician has certainly the advantage of a swinging rhythm—if indeed that was wanted; and there is a fine manly tone in his air, which is sufficient to account both for its preservation and Goethe's admiration. Both the settings are in plain chords with all the straightforward character of folk-song. It is tempting to further compare the exquisite musical conceit of Berlioz (wedded to the same words), in which his perverse genius offers a *feminine* version of the rugged old ballad.

A still earlier song of Goethe's—"Heidenröslein"—dating from 1773, allows of our placing Reichardt and Schubert side by side. Reichardt's composition is a primitive but expressive tune, written in 1793. It is in most popular German song-collections and a few bars will serve to identify it.

REICHARDT.

Sah ein Knab' ein Rös-lein stehn, Röslein auf der Hei-den.

"Schäfers Klagelied"

In 1815—the year of the "Erl-king"—Schubert was moved to re-set the same verses. This he accomplished with surprising ease and spontaneity.

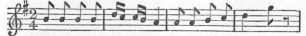

Sah ein Knab' ein Rös - lein stehn, Röslein auf der Hei - den.

Here is the very charm of Mozart, in all its daintiness and youthful grace. One can quite believe the delicate strain rose to Schubert's lips as he read over the verses. It was quite beyond the art of Reichardt; but certainly Mozart could have matched it.

Another of Goethe's songs—the well-known " Schäfers Klagelied "—a poem of 1802, has the good fortune to obtain sympathetic treatment at the hands of all three composers. Reichardt was first in the field with his setting of 1809.

REICHARDT.

Da dro - ben auf je - nem Ber - ge.

This is a grave and well-minted melody, capable, in clever hands, of considerable expression. The prolonging of the final bars prove that Reichardt had a soul above the cut-and-dried lengths which the mere imitators of folk-song prescribed.

Zelter's vigorous little melody came to light in the following year (1810).

ZELTER.

Da dro - ben auf je - - nem Ber - ge.

Schubert

One cannot but admire the strength of its outline, and the simple unity attained in this composition of eight bars. It is, of course, directly modelled on the style of the old folk-song, and it has the advantage of simplicity, and the disadvantage of monotony. But Franz Schubert was undeterred by these excellent settings, and in 1814 (when he was eighteen), he cast the poem in another mould of quite new significance.

Mässig. SCHUBERT, Op. 3, No. 1.

Da dro - ben auf je - nem Ber - ge.

He begins with an expressive strain of eight bars (in C minor), then there is a second portion of some length, which passes through the keys of E flat, G minor, A flat, A flat minor, and C flat, the mood always following or reproducing that of the poem. A part of this material (bars 11-19) is repeated (at 39-46); and so back to the original eight-bar phrase of the opening, which is now extended to twelve bars. The ballad is a decided advance on the meagre settings of Reichardt and Zelter.

In 1840, some 300 of Schubert's songs had reached publication; in 1865 this number had been increased to 360; the complete edition of Messrs Breitkopf & Haertel[1] includes 603[2] songs—at which number (in all probability) they will remain, in spite of Wurbach's " Biographical Lexicon " (vol. xxxii. p. 94) making

---

[1] Announced in 1884 and completed in 1897.
[2] Thirteen of these 603 are fragmentary.

Ballad of " Edward "

mention of 634 poems. Schubert, in his earlier days, was attracted by the sentimental and tender verses of Hölty, Matthisson, Kosegarten, Salis, etc., which were popular at the time, and were often to be found in the hands of his school-fellows, who would naturally enough bring them to his notice. In his later selections, the composer had the advice and guidance of Mayrhofer and Schober, and especially of Vogl, who is responsible for a large number of the verses chosen. Appended is a list of the poets drawn upon by the musician, showing the number of poems set, and giving a reference to the particular volume (in Breitkopf & Haertel's edition) where the settings may be found. A glance at our list will show that no less than seventy of Goethe's poems are included. Curiously enough, Zelter eclipsed the number of settings of verses by this particular poet, actually accomplishing a round hundred. Schubert composed music for forty-two of Schiller's poems, and forty-seven by Mayrhofer. English poets will be referred to in their place ; it is sufficient here to point out that they are well represented (though in translations); the settings number thirteen, several ranking with the best work the composer ever accomplished. The Ossian poems (nine in all), translated by Harold, will also make a special appeal to those of us who are acquainted with the originals. Finally it is noteworthy that Herder's translation of the Old Scottish Ballad " Edward " so fascinated Schubert, that he set and reset the poem to music—a brief but weird-sounding melody.

Schubert

A LIST showing the authors' names, and the number of
their poems set to music by Schubert. The No. of
each vol. (in B. & H.'s edition) is indicated above
the names. The figures, in line with each name,
show how many poems were set.

B. & H.'s edition, Vol.	I.	II.	III.	IV.	V.	VI.	VII.	VIII.	IX.	X.	Total
Bauernfeld	...	...	...	...	...	...	...	...	I	...	I
Baumberg	...	...	5	...	...	...	...	...	...	...	5
Bernard	...	I	...	...	...	...	...	...	...	...	I
Bertrand	...	2	...	...	...	...	...	...	...	...	2
Bruchmann	...	...	...	...	...	...	5	...	...	...	5
Castelli	...	...	...	...	...	...	...	I	...	...	I
Claudius	...	...	...	8	3	...	...	...	...	...	11
Collin	...	...	...	2	...	...	2	I	...	I	6
Craigher	...	...	...	...	...	...	...	2	...	...	2
Colley Cibber (Translation by Craigher)	...	...	...	...	...	...	...	I	...	...	I
Dante	...	...	...	...	I	...	...	...	...	...	I
Deinhardtstein	...	...	I	I	...	...	...	...	...	...	2
Erlich	...	I	...	...	...	...	...	...	...	...	I
Ermin	...	I	I	...	...	...	...	...	...	...	2
Fellinger	...	2	I	...	...	...	...	...	...	...	3
Fouqué (De la Motte)	3	...	...	I	I	...	...	...	...	...	5
Goethe	6	10	20	9	2	9	5	4	...	5	70
Goldoni	...	...	...	...	...	...	...	...	...	I	I
Gotter	...	...	...	...	...	...	...	...	...	I	I
Grillparzer	...	...	...	...	...	I	...	...	...	...	I
Hardenberg (See "Novalis")	...	...	...	...	...	...	...	...	...	...	...
Heine	...	...	...	...	...	...	...	...	6	...	6

134

Poets set by Schubert

B. & H.'s edition,	Vol. I.	II.	III.	IV.	V.	VI.	VII.	VIII.	IX.	X.	Total
Hell	...	...	...	1	...	...	...	...	...	...	1
Herder	...	...	...	...	...	...	...	1	...	...	1
Hölty	1	9	...	12	...	...	...	...	...	...	22
Hüttenbrenner (H. A.)	...	...	...	...	...	1	...	...	...	...	1
Jacobi	...	...	...	6	1	...	...	...	...	...	7
Kalchberg	...	...	1	1	...	...	...	...	...	...	2
Kenner	...	3	...	...	...	...	...	...	...	...	3
Kind	...	...	...	...	1	...	...	...	...	...	1
Klenke	...	...	...	...	...	...	...	...	1	...	1
Klopstock	...	...	9	4	...	...	...	...	...	...	13
Köpken	...	...	...	1	...	...	...	...	...	...	1
Körner	...	10	2	...	1	...	...	...	...	...	13
Kosegarten	...	13	7	1	...	...	...	...	...	...	21
Kuffner	...	...	...	...	...	...	...	1	...	...	1
Lappe	...	...	...	...	...	...	...	2	...	...	2
Leitner	...	...	...	...	...	...	1	...	7	...	8
Leon	...	...	...	...	1	...	...	...	...	...	1
Lübeck	...	...	...	1	...	...	...	...	...	...	1
Lubi	1	...	...	...	...	...	...	...	...	...	1
Mailath	...	...	...	...	...	1	...	...	...	...	1
Matthisson	14	3	1	7	...	...	...	...	...	1	26
Mayrhofer	1	...	2	10	16	10	3	4	...	1	47
Metastasio	...	...	...	...	...	...	...	...	...	11	11
Müller	...	...	...	...	...	...	20	...	24	1	45
"Novalis" (Hardenberg)	...	...	...	...	...	6	...	...	...	...	6
Ossian	...	2	3	2	1	...	...	...	...	1	9
Ottenwalt	...	...	...	...	1	...	...	...	...	...	1
Petrarch	...	...	...	...	2	...	...	...	...	...	2
Pichler	...	...	...	2	...	1	...	...	...	...	3
Platen	...	...	...	...	...	...	2	...	...	...	2
Platner	...	...	...	...	1	...	...	...	...	...	1

Schubert

B. & H.'s edition,	Vol. I.	II.	III.	IV.	V.	VI.	VII.	VIII.	IX.	X.	Total
Pope (Herder)	I	...	...	...	...	...	...	...	...	...	I
Prandstetter	...	...	I	...	...	...	...	...	...	...	I
Pratobevera	...	...	...	...	...	...	...	...	I	...	I
Pyrker	...	...	...	...	...	...	...	2	...	...	2
Reil	...	...	...	...	...	...	...	...	I	...	I
Reissig	...	...	I	...	...	...	...	...	...	...	I
Rellstab	...	...	...	...	...	...	...	...	7	3	10
Rochlitz	I	...	...	2	...	...	...	...	...	...	3
Roos	...	...	...	...	...	...	I	...	...	...	I
Rückert	...	...	...	...	...	I	...	4	...	...	5
Salis	...	...	I	II	3	I	...	...	...	...	16
Sauter	...	...	...	...	...	...	I	...	...	...	I
Schiller	8	5	10	6	5	4	2	I	...	I	42
Schlecta	...	I	...	...	...	I	...	3	I	...	6
Schlegel (Fr.)	...	...	2	3	3	11	I	I	...	...	21
Schlegel (A. W.)	...	...	...	...	...	...	...	2	...	...	2
Schober	...	...	I	I	3	...	5	2	...	...	12
Schopenhauer	...	...	...	...	...	...	...	I	...	...	I
Schreiber	...	...	...	...	4	...	...	...	...	...	4
Schubart	...	...	...	2	2	...	...	...	...	...	4
Schubert	...	...	...	...	...	...	...	...	I	...	I
Schulze	...	...	...	...	...	...	...	9	...	...	9
Schütz	...	...	...	...	...	...	...	2	...	...	2
Schücking	I	...	...	...	...	...	...	...	...	...	I
Scott (Sir Walter) (Trans. Storck)	...	...	...	...	...	...	...	6	2	...	8
Seidl	...	...	...	...	...	...	...	10	I	...	11
Senn	...	...	...	...	...	...	2	...	...	...	2
Shakespeare (Translations into German by Mayrhofer, A. W. Schlegel and Bauernfeld)	...	...	...	...	...	...	...	3	...	...	3
Silbert	...	...	...	...	...	...	2	...	...	...	2
Spaun	...	...	...	...	I	...	...	...	...	...	I
Stadler	...	I	...	...	...	...	...	...	...	I	2

B. & H.'s edition,	Vol. I.	II.	III.	IV.	V.	VI.	VII.	VIII.	IX.	X.	Total
Stolberg	...	...	2	2	...	...	2	...	...	...	6
Stoll	...	...	3	...	...	...	...	...	...	...	3
Széchényi	...	...	...	...	2	...	...	...	...	...	2
Uhland	...	...	...	...	...	1	...	...	...	...	1
Uz	...	...	...	4	...	...	...	...	...	...	4
Werner	...	...	...	1	1	1	...	...	...	...	3
Zettler	...	1	...	...	...	...	...	...	...	...	1
Anonymous	1	1	4	5	5	...	...	1	...	6	23

Total   603

Some interesting notes are furnished by Herr Mandy-czewski, who edits the ten volumes of songs in the edition of Breitkopf & Haertel. Four hundred and fifteen autographs were referred to in the course of publication. These MSS. were for the most part beautifully written. Schubert—like Zumsteeg—wrote his directions for performance in German. His marks of expression were confined to the pianoforte part, the singer having the poet's text to guide him. Musicians will note with interest that the first published copies of the songs were not uncommonly transpositions from difficult to easy keys. All such departures from the composer's original intention may easily be detected by referring to the edition under notice. The progress of the composer in song-writing may be traced in regular steps, for the volumes give the various pieces in the order of their composition.[1] Thus the years 1811-1814 are covered by volume i., which contains the first thirty-eight songs, beginning with "Hagars Klage," and further including

[1] The plan of Nottebohn's Thematic Catalogue is thus followed.

the "Corpse-fantasia"—Schiller's poem set for tenor and pianoforte. The great song-year was, of course, 1815, which brought forth 146 songs, groups of which were sometimes written down and composed during the same day. It is a cynical reflection that Schubert might easily have earned a better living as a copyist, owing to the extreme rapidity of his pen. "Schubert" (says Dr Hugo Riemann) "was the real creator of the modern "Lied"; his importance in the history of music, is analogous to that of Goethe as lyricist in the history of poetry." Liszt did not hesitate to pronounce him "le musicien le plus poète qui fut jamais"—the most poetical musician that ever was. "He ought to have been alive now (says Schumann) "to know how he is praised; now when he has long been at rest, let us carefully collect, and heed-fully examine, what he has left us. Few authors have impressed the seal of individuality so clearly on their works as he has done on his."

Accounts differ as to the original production of the "Erl-king," and the honour of its first per-*The "Erl-king"* formance is severally claimed. Spaun says Schubert himself sang it. But I will give the story as it stands in Kreissle :—Schubert wrote this song one afternoon (late in December 1815) in his room at his father's house in the Himmelpfortgrund, where Spaun called, and found him hard at work. He had twice read the poem of the "Erl-king" in a state bordering on frenzy. As the splendour of the ballad awoke his imagination, he was dashing the music down on paper, in the form of a sketch, which needed little but mechanical detail to render it a finished production. In the evening of the same day the song was brought to the Convict, where

Startling Discord

Schubert first (and after him Holzapfel) sang it to an audience of friends and pupils. The audience made wry faces and smiled incredulously at the passage, "Mein Vater, jetzt fasst er mich an." Ruczizka—the teacher of

Mein Va - ter, mein Va - ter.

theory and composition—thereupon undertook to explain the mystery of the discords, which are now reckoned so harmless in our music. Vogl soon after this became intimate with Schubert, and he immediately monopolised this song, which served so well to display his extra-ordinary powers. He sang it commonly in private society, and in 1821 produced it for the first time in public at the Royal opera-house.

"In Schubert's Biography," says Mr Albert B. Bach ("The Art-ballad," p. 107), "the court opera-singer Vogl is always mentioned as having been the first to sing the 'Erl-king' in public. Randhartinger, however, told me the following facts:—'I was still at school at the "Stadtconvikt" of Vienna, when one day Schubert, who was quite excited, brought me the MS. of the "Erl-king" and asked me, then a boy of fourteen, to sing

Schubert

it. Like lightning the news flashed through the institution that Franzl (so they called Schubert) was there and had brought a new composition. In a trice the concert-room of the institution was filled with the students and teachers, and Randhartinger was chosen to sing for the first time Schubert's grand composition, accompanied by the young composer himself. The beautiful playing of Schubert, and the spirited singing of Randhartinger, inspired the whole audience, and the "Erl-king" had to be repeated. Schubert, who was very modest, said, "Benedictus, the song pleases me too, if only it were not so very difficult to play." The second time Schubert omitted the triplets and replaced them by quavers. Some of the teachers asked him why he omitted the triplets. Schubert replied, "They are too difficult for me; a virtuoso may play them." The second time Randhartinger sang with more expression and animation, and there followed quite a storm of applause. "Of all good things there are three," shouted the students, and poor Schubert and Randhartinger had to perform the "Erl-king" for the third time."

Schubert was rewarded with gifts of MS. music-paper, while Randhartinger received no less than the original MS. of the "Erl-king." Randhartinger gave the autograph of this splendid composition to Madame Schumann, whose husband had so timely gone to the rescue of Schubert's unpublished works—especially the great Symphony in C, which he brought to Mendelssohn's notice, and thereby secured its initial performance.

It may be not uninteresting to observe that in ancient German mythology the "Erl-king" has no place. Moreover, the very name is mistakenly derived. Herder first introduced it in his "Stimmen der Volker" (1778), where it is used in a rendering of the "Elf-king's Daughter," out of the Danish. It is pointed out that "Elbkönig," or "Elbenkönig," would have been a true German equivalent. In modern literature the Erl-king is represented as a gigantic bearded man, with a golden crown and trailing garments, who carries off children to that remote and undiscovered country which he inhabits. Loewe, in an interview with Goethe, remarked that he considered the "Erl-king" to be the best of German ballads—for this reason, that the characters represented in it were all introduced in dialogue. "There you are right," said the poet. The earliest composer to set Goethe's ballad to music was Reichardt (1752-1814), whom Schubert is known to have thought well of, and admired of Mendelssohn. It has been since treated by no fewer than thirty-eight composers, Schubert and Loewe being included in that number. The best known translations are those of Lewis and Sir Walter Scott.

Schubert's MS. of the "Erl-king," preserved in the Berlin Library, was reproduced in *facsimile* by Espagne, and published by Müller of Berlin, of which we give a specimen. Another autograph score has been already alluded to as in the possession of Madame Schumann.

Englishmen cannot but view with especial pride and satisfaction those of Schubert's songs which *English* were called into being through the actual *Songs* agency of their own poets. A medium was employed, it is true, for Schubert knew nothing of the English tongue. He nevertheless hoped the songs would reach this country. To this end, we find him writing (in a letter to his parents, under date July 25, 1825, from Linz), apropos of some settings of Scott's songs:—

Schubert

"I intend to have some other arrangement as to the publication of these songs, the present one inviting so little attention. They must have the illustrious name of Scott on the title-page, and thus make people more curious; with the addition of the English text they might help to make me better known in England, if only once I could make some fair terms with publishers; but in that matter the wise and beneficent management of the Government has taken care that the artist shall remain for ever the slave of miserable hucksters." Wonderful to relate, the sale of the seven songs from Scott's "Lady of the Lake" was one of the best bargains the composer ever struck. They were sold on October 29 (1825) to Artaria for the sum of 200 silver Gulden, or £20 sterling, an unusually generous amount compared with most of the composer's transactions.[1]

Schubert's wish that the "illustrious name of Scott" should appear in the title was duly observed. The German text which he had used was that of Philip Adam Storck, printed at Essen, 1819—nine years after the appearance of the original poems in Edinburgh. Most unfortunately, Storck's verse and Scott's by no means agree, for whereas the one employs some dozen syllables to the line, the other (the original) has but eight. The result may be imagined. No amount of arranging, though it was attempted, could reconcile the two versions. Six of the pieces, nevertheless, gave both texts. They were issued as opus 52 (on April 5, 1826), with the title "Sieben Gesänge aus Walter Scotts Fräulein vom See," etc.

[1] See the account of the sale of six of the "Winterreise," which Haslinger bought for tenpence a-piece (p. 149).

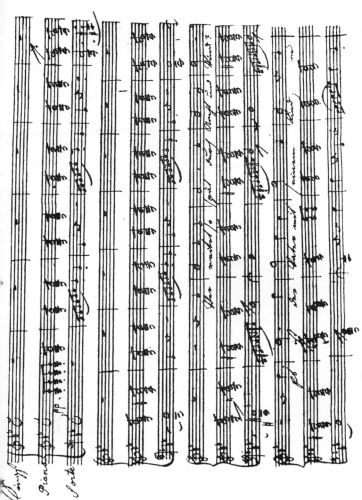

Facsimile of Page from MS. of "The Erl-King"

Scott

1. "Soldier rest" (Ellen's first song), "Lady of the Lake," canto i. stanza 31.

2. "Huntsman rest" (Ellen's second song), "Lady of the Lake," canto i. stanza 32.

3. "Hail to the chief" (set for T.T.B.B.), "Lady of the Lake," canto ii. stanza 19.

4. "He is gone on the mountain" (Coronach) (set for S.S.A.), "Lady of the Lake," canto iii. stanza 16.

5. "The heath this night must be my bed" (Norman's song), "Lady of the Lake," canto iii. stanza 23.

6. "Ave Maria,"[1] "Lady of the Lake," canto iii. stanza 29.

7. "My hawk is tired of perch and hood" (lay of the imprisoned huntsman), "Lady of the Lake," canto vi. 24.

Schubert set three more German versions of Scott's poems as follows :—Annot Lyle's song from the "Legend of Montrose"—Op. 85, No. 1. This was written in 1827 and appears as "Lied der *Anne* Lyle" ("Wärst du bei mir im Lebenstal"). The second song is included in the same opus number, and dates from the same year. This is Norna's song, "For leagues along the watery way"—"Gesang der Norna" ("Micht führt mein Weg"), which is drawn from "The Pirate." Third and last is "The Crusader's Return," from "Ivanhoe"—"Romanze des Richard Löwen-herz" ("Grosser Taten tat der Ritter"). The last song was printed in March 1828, as opus 86, the MS., however, being dated two years earlier.

The story of the origin of "Hark, hark, the lark" has

---

[1] Exception should be made of the "Ave Maria," the music of which can be used (in a slightly adapted form) in conjunction with Scott's verse. The adaptation is made in Augener's edition.

already been told. It is understood that the two other of
Shakespeare's songs set by Schubert followed in the course
of the same evening; and certainly Schubert's habit of
composing music to several songs by the same writer, at
one sitting, seems to favour the probability of its accuracy;
while the inscription—Währing, July 1826—which appears
on the songs, forms another link in the chain of evidence.
The remaining songs are: " Who is Sylvia" (Op. 106, No. 4)
from " The Two Gentlemen of Verona," or, as it appears in
Bauernfeld's version, "Gesang an Sylvia" ("Was ist Sylvia");
and the " Trinklied " (" Bacchus, feister Fürst "), or, as we
know it in the play of " Anthony and Cleopatra," " Come
thou monarch of the vine." The translation of this last
song is by Ferdinand Mayrhofer, and that of " Hark,
hark "—Ständchen (" Horch, horch, die Lerch' ")—above-
mentioned, by A. W. Schlegel. It is a fortunate circum-
stance that, whether by chance or design—for there was
time to profit by the experience of the Scott songs—
German and English words agree in this group of
Shakespeare's lyrics, which therefore can be sung in
Shakespeare's own words.

A few other English songs which had found their way
into German passed through Schubert's hands, and, almost
by virtue of the touch, became music. Thus Colley
Cibber's " Blind Boy " (" O say what is that thing call'd
light ")—which is included in Palgrave's " Golden
Treasury "—was translated by Craigher (author of " Die
junge Nonne ") and became transformed to " Der blinde
Knabe " (" O sagt, ihr Lieben, mir einmal"), appearing with
music as op. 101, under date 1825. There is an allusion
to this song in 1827, when, during the visit of Hiller and
Hummel to Vienna, Vogl and Schubert performed it before

the two visitors. Hummel then, as a token of approval, took the theme of the song, and, to Schubert's great delight, gave a pianoforte extemporisation founded upon it. A song by Pope, done into German by Herder, namely "Verklärung" ("Lebensfunke vom Himmel entglüht"), had quite early attracted Schubert's attention, indeed while he was yet a pupil of the Convict, as is seen from the date of the MS., May 4, 1813. This is none other than the well-known "Vital spark of heavenly flame." There are probably a few further English poems found in translation among the 603 published songs of Schubert; the above, however, are the best known. The sanguinary ballad of "Edward"[1] from Percy's "Reliques"—another of Herder's German paraphrases—was also set by Schubert under the title "Altschottische Ballade" ("Dein Schwert wie ist's vom Blut"), op. 165, No. 5, the composition of which is assigned to November 1827. Brahms, it will be remembered, took the same poem for the "programme" of his Ballade in D minor, for pianoforte, op. 10.

If our native poets have been somewhat unfortunate in the treatment of translators, the original German poems rendered into English have met with scarcely better fortune. Of the seventy poems by Goethe which Schubert set to music, but few have attracted the attention of English poets able to render a truly singable version. I have no intention of casting any slight on the existing translations which English music-publishers have provided. These are not under consideration. Only the *poets'*

[1] It begins,

"Quhy dois zour brand sae drop wi' bluid,
Edward, Edward?"

[No. 5 of Percy's "Reliques," 1765.]

versions of the poets are now in view. Sir Walter Scott's translation of Goethe's "Erl-king" is a good example of what is meant. Although this spirited rendering is widely used, several alterations in the number of syllables are rendered necessary by the poet's not adhering strictly to Goethe's verse. Passing to Carlyle's rendering (in English verse) of the songs from "Wilhelm Meister" (Goethe), these, however much one may wish it, are not singable without serious modifications. It is the more to be regretted, as the metre is practically the same, and a mere knowledge of the music was all that was necessary to make a perfectly harmonious translation. It is with some pleasure that we find Coleridge able to meet all the requirements of poetry and music in the little song of Schiller, everywhere known—I refer to "Das Mädchen's Klage" ("Der Eichwald brauset"), which is not, as far as the writer is aware, given in any of the music-books, and is therefore quoted here :—

> " The cloud doth gather, the greenwood roar,
> The damsel paces along the shore ;
> The billows they tumble with might, with might,
> And she flings out her voice to the darksome night :
> Her bosom is swelling with sorrow.

> " The world it is empty, the heart it will die,
> There's nothing to wish for beneath the sky,
> Thou Holy One call thy child away,
> I've liv'd and lov'd and that was to-day,
> Make ready my grave-clothes to-morrow."

But alas, Coleridge stops after two stanzas, and the original song has four.[1]

[1] Mrs Hemans has left an excellent version of Mignon's song, " Kennst du das Land ? " which is eminently singable, and therefore

Songs composed at Night

Randhartinger has related how the group of songs entitled "Die schöne Müllerin" came to attract Schubert's attention. On an occasion when Schubert called at his house in the Herrengasse—presumably in October 1823— he discovered lying on the table a collection of poems by W. Müller, for which Randhartinger himself had intended to compose some music. Schubert quietly pocketed the little volume, and returning home at five o'clock in the evening, set to work at once on several of the pieces. Randhartinger tells how he was surprised at seeing the book of poems at Schubert's lodgings, where he called the following forenoon. "Do not be angry with me, dear Benedictus" (said Franz), "the poems have so inspired me that I had to compose music to them, and I scarcely slept two hours last night; and now you see the result. I have already seven poems set to music. I hope you will like my songs; will you try them?" Randhartinger duly tried them and was naturally delighted. "I will never touch the book again" (said he); "keep it, as, after Schubert, Benedictus has no right to compose." The same week, it is said, saw the whole series of twenty songs completed.[1]

We may now refer to the music. The period (1823) was one in which the composer's attention was concentrated chiefly upon opera. It would doubtless be a

---

deserves to find a place in association with Schubert's music in the English editions.

[1] It is but right to add that another account says: "The task of writing the set of twenty songs occupied our master at intervals during the summer, and helped to while away the time he spent as a patient in a hospital" (see p. 124).

relief to turn to lyrical composition for a time. The tone of the pieces is for the most part idyllic. It is the exception to meet with the fiery impatience so wonderfully reproduced in " Ungeduld," or the untrammelled freedom displayed in the setting (No. 17) of " Die böse Farbe." A gem—of purest ray—is the " Morgengrüss "—and no less superb in their intimacy are the " Trock'ne Blumen "[1] and " Des Baches Wiegenlied " (Nos. 18 and 20). It may seem invidious to single out these particular numbers ; they, however, are the most striking in a series which cannot boast of equal merit. Others in the collection which seem to follow in point of excellence are numbers 11 and 12—" Mein " and " Pause."[2] It appears that Schubert omitted three numbers from the collection of poems, in addition to the prologue and epilogue, with which Müller had furnished his collection. In their complete form they may be found in the first volume of " Gedichte aus den hinterlassenen Papieren eines reisenden Waldhornisten" (" Poems found among the papers of a travelling Frenchhorn player "), first published at Dessau, in 1821. Liszt transcribed six of the above settings for pianoforte.

Another famous group of songs is that known by the title " Die Winterreise," written in 1827, a year which, according to Kreissle, " may be reckoned among the happiest periods of Schubert's life and progress. Inspired

---

[1] A set of Variations for Flute and Pianoforte (op. 160) employ, as their theme, the air of " Trock'ne Blumen." They are dated January 1824.

[2] Messrs Novello issue the above series with an English translation by Natalia Macfarren. The Augener edition gives another English translation, with a German original printed beneath.

Tenpenny Songs

with a lofty consciousness of his mission as a great art-creator, he put forth more exalted efforts, as we gather from the larger works of this date, and he experienced for the last time the happiness of a free, unfettered enjoyment of nature's beauties and the attraction of simple friendly companions, who met him half-way with entire abandonment of ceremony and conventional restraints." Kreissle apparently alludes to the visit Schubert had made in September, in the company of his friend Jenger, to the Pachlers of Gratz. In acknowledging the kindness of this family, Schubert's letter to Herr Pachler says pretty much the same thing. He specially mentions the freedom from restraint that he enjoyed, and finally observes that "these were the happiest days I have passed for a long time." He had already set the first half of the "Winterreise" songs in the month of February. After the visit to Gratz he set about the remaining twelve, which were completed in October. Franz Lachner, who was a close friend of Schubert's during the last six years of his life, has left on record some interesting facts relating to this series of songs. "Half a dozen of them," says he, "were written in one morning." He does not specify which half-dozen, nor would it profit anyone to know. Lachner states that he took—apparently at Schubert's request—six of these very songs to Haslinger the publisher, who bought them for six Vienna Gulden, or as money then ranked, for a sum total of five shillings. We need not pause to comment on the incredible meanness of the transaction, which will pursue the name of that publisher as long as the incident survives record—in itself sufficient punishment, for if the songs were worth printing at all, they were worth a proper remuneration. The date is not vouchsafed, but the incident in all probability refers to the early summer of 1828, when Schubert proposed to himself another trip to his friends at Gratz. "It is all over with Gratz," writes he, "for money and weather are both against me." The first part of the "Winterreise" had been published by Haslinger in January of this year (1828). The second half was only in proof at the time of Schubert's death. It is said to have been one of his last occupations correcting and revising their publication.

A note of deep melancholy for the most part dominates the music of these pieces, of which the majority are in the minor key, and, in accord with the poetry, deal with sad ideas, if not depression and pessimism. There are several notable exceptions, however, among which No. 1 is prominent. The air here is of a finely passionate character, and a beautiful effect is produced by the last stanza being given in its *major* form. There is nothing better in the whole series than this "Gute Nacht." Another splendidly poetic utterance is the fifth piece, "Der Lindenbaum." It is curiously confirmative of their melancholy mood, to find in this series of songs such a piece as "Frühlingstraum" strongly tinged with dejection. This, however, was imparted to it by Müller[1] the poet, so Schubert was bound to follow where he led. "Die Post" (No. 13) is more robust, and is comparatively remarkably cheerful, though it is none of the poet's contriving that so it turns out; but the bustle and excitement which the

---

[1] Müller's poems, the order of which is completely altered in the musical setting, first appeared in a second volume published at Dessau, 1824. The title is given in the note on "Die schöne Müllerin," p. 148.

Der Leiermann

post called up in the mind of the musician overruled the blank dismay and bitter disappointment which the non-arrival of a letter from the loved one was calculated to produce. "Im Dorfe" is a finely-coloured piece of writing which never fails of effect, if skilfully rendered. One can hear the bark of the watch-dogs and the faint sounds of the sleeping village, and yet enter into the mood of the watcher as he speculates on "Sleep that knits up the ravell'd sleeve of care"; the outburst of music in the final verse suddenly inspires the song with intense poetry, as if the midnight hymn of some distant monastery fell upon the ear of the listener. A solemn little song is No. 21—"Das Wirthshaus"—the words of which read strangely when one remembers they were corrected during Schubert's last days, as he lay in his chamber, weak and ill :—

> " Auf einen Todtenaker hat mich mein Weggebracht,
>   Allhier will ich einkehren, hab' ich bei mir gedacht."

Last of all comes the half playful, half plaintive, "Der Leiermann," which is a wonderfully effective picture of the street-minstrel as he exists *in the Land of Poetry*.

The fourteen songs forming the "Schwanengesang" are always thus grouped together in a series, but there is nothing to show that the composer intended their association ; and as for the title, it was given by Haslinger the publisher. Schubert had not intended to compose any more songs, for in offering his C-major Symphony to the Vienna Musik-Verein he stated (according to Kreissle) that he desired to write no more songs, "now that he was firmly planted in opera and symphony." In August (1828 — his last year) he changed his mind.

Schubert

Schindler's efforts to introduce his music to Beethoven—late, almost too late, as these were—had wrought a deep impression on him, and we find him visiting Schindler and looking over the Beethoven papers, etc., in Schindler's possession. Among these was a bundle of anonymous lyrics—some twenty—which Beethoven had intended to set to music. Naturally these attracted Schubert's attention, and he carried some of them home, returning two days later with three of the poems clothed with song. They are now known to be by Rellstab, and the music appears in Nos. 1, 3 and 5 of the "Schwanengesang"—three of the best songs in the collection. Rellstab is the author of the first seven of the "Schwanengesang," Heine of the next six (Nos. 8-13), and the last is written by Seidl. The six pieces of Heine are the only ones for which Schubert composed music, and the poem of Seidl was the *last* piece Schubert wrote. It is dated October 1828. Schubert died the following month, and the fourteen songs of the "Schwanengesang" series appeared in May 1829. Liszt transcribed the whole series for pianoforte-solo.

The last works of a man of genius always lay claim to an exceptional amount of attention, though they are not of necessity the things he will be remembered by. In so short a life as that of Schubert, the shadow of death falling preternaturally soon, the powers of his mind and imagination were at their very best, if we may judge by the compositions of this final year—among them the "Schwanengesang"—a veritable swan-song, although the title was of Haslinger's bestowal. One can then approach these pieces without any misgiving that human sympathy is awakened rather than a real admiration. All the songs are masterpieces, though some are more pregnant with significance than others. A charming Idyl, entitled "Liebesbotschaft," is placed first. This is distinctly a chamber-song, delicate and restrained in its effects, and of true poetic conception. A widely different impression is created by the second song, "Kriegers Ahnung," a fine dramatic portrayal of the soldier's dream on the eve of battle. Fame has long ere this set her seal to the fourth piece, "Ständchen," which is as widely known and loved as any serenade in the world. Why this should be so, it is not easy to tell. Certainly the conception is remarkably new; but then the air is for the most part in the *minor;* it is difficult of performance, and the poem is by no means an inspiration. It speaks well for popular taste that a composition so beautiful and original should be everywhere admired. "Aufenthalt" (No. 5) is a grand dramatic piece of a class which Schubert himself invented. Its strongly impassioned melody is supported by an accompaniment which literally throbs with suppressed excitement. Another feature of interest is the rhythm, which carries all before it in its powerful sway. It will scarcely escape notice that the fine opening phrase of the accompaniment is afterwards (in the final line) transferred to the voice. "Abschied" (the seventh and last of Rellstab's poems) is set in a remarkably bright and joyous vein. It is the "good-bye" of one who reflects on the happy hours, the smiling faces, and the *good* generally, the splendid memory of which cannot be taken from him. We now come to the six poems of Heine (Nos. 8-13), the best of which is No. 12, "Am Meer," set to a finely emotional melody, simple, but full of feeling and colour. Seidl's "Die Taubenpost" comes last. This is under-

stood to be Schubert's final effort. It breathes of content-
ment, and even of happiness :—

> " Sie wird nicht müd, sie wird nicht matt,
> Der Weg ist stets ihr neu."

A feature of striking beauty is seen in the accompaniment—throughout forming an eloquent commentary on
the text of the melody. The sable king of fears certainly
had no part or lot in the framing of this picture—the last
of its composer's earthly scenes.

Before quitting the subject, attention may be usefully
drawn to some remarkable features in the songs reviewed.

Here, for example, is a remarkable cadence, the effect
of which is as a bitter cry. Perhaps the composer knew
only too well what the burden of sorrow meant, and hence
his sympathy with the fabled Atlas. There is a very
unusual ending to the song " Die Stadt " (No. 11). These
are the two last bars :—

A Bach Phrase

Moderato.

If Ruczizka[1] had been put to it for an explanation of
such an ending—say before the pupils of the Convict—
he would probably have pointed out that the final C
resolves the preceding diminished chord, as it indeed
does both theoretically and harmonically; though the
ear nevertheless retains the sound of that diminished
chord.   In No. 13, "Der Doppelgänger," it is of interest to
note the leading phrase of the accompaniment, reminding
one of Bach's theme in the well-known Fugue in C sharp
minor, No. 4 of the forty-eight.

Sehr langsam.

Schubert employs the same phrase in the Agnus Dei

[1] Ruczizka had to explain a harmonic combination in the "Erl-king."

of the Mass in E flat, and again in the opening of the Allegro of the Overture to *Fierrabras*.

"The theatrical atmosphere" (says Kreissle) "is of so

Opera

peculiar a kind, that many a poor weed may thrive therein while the healthy flower fades and dies." Schubert's strenuous attempts to establish himself in opera proved a dire failure. While barely sixteen years of age he had been drawn to dramatic composition, and in his eighteenth year alone there followed no less than six operatic pieces. The total of eighteen dramatic works was finally reached before the composer's short career was closed. Ten of these are now published, in more or less complete form, together with a supplement of four fragmentary pieces. Performances of six of these have taken place at long intervals. *Die Zwillingsbrüder* (a Singspiel in one act) was performed at the Kärnthnerthor theatre, Vienna, June 14, 1820; and on August 19 of the same year, the three-act melodrama *Die Zauberharfe* was given at the theatre "an-der-Wien," where (in 1823) the four-act drama of *Rosamunde* also obtained a hearing. No other dramatic work of Schubert was produced in his life-time. A few posthumous performances may be added, such as the production under Liszt's direction of *Alfonso und Estrella* (with only small success), at Weimar, in 1855. The Vienna Musik-Verein gave a concert performance of *Der häusliche Krieg* (known also as *Die Verschworenen*) in 1861, a production which was afterwards imitated at Frankfort-on-Maine, where the work had the additional advantages of stage-representation. To this list—which is not intended to be complete—may be added a performance of *Die Vierjährige Posten*, an operetta brought to light in 1897,

Why his Operas failed

at the commemoration in Vienna of the composer's birth.

There is little or no difficulty in assigning reasons for Schubert's failure in dramatic enterprises. The time was not ripe, and the city did not favour German opera. Where Beethoven barely succeeded, Schubert could scarcely hope to win his way. The pleasure-loving Viennese preferred the honeyed strains of Rossini. Even Weber exercised more obvious charms with his romantic creations. Then the influence of important persons— without which no opera-stage is ever at the composer's command—was decidedly lacking in Schubert's case, Vogl being his chief ally.

When a composer's opera fails, the librettist may look for the blame. With one notable exception,[1] Schubert's librettists are far above the average, so that the common excuse for failure will not serve. Goethe is responsible for the book of the three-act opera *Claudine von Villabella*; Körner wrote the libretto of *Die Vierjährige Posten*; and Mayrhofer—a tragic poet of note, and the close personal friend of the composer—supplied the story of *Die beiden Freunde von Salamanka* (an operetta) and the play of *Adrast*. So completely were most of these pieces forgotten that when Liszt, in 1847, enquired of Schober for an opera by Schubert, the reply came that *Alfonso und Estrella*, which Schober had himself compiled, was the only finished opera. As we have already stated, there were six operas available. It is almost pathetic to find that Schubert, undeterred by the total neglect of his dramatic endeavors, was, at the time of his last illness, meditating a new opera in conjunction with Bauernfeld. This work

[1] Helmina von Chezy's *Rosamunde*.

bore the title *Der Graf von Gleichen*, and, according to the librettist, an instrumental sketch by Schubert was in existence. Of this (says Kreissle) " I have not succeeded in finding any traces." There are two operas of this name by other composers, but of Schubert's music, if any was ever conceived, nothing now remains.

" The latest news in Vienna " (wrote Schubert on March 31, 1824) "is that Beethoven intends giving a concert, when we are to have his new symphony, three numbers out of the new Mass and a new overture. God willing, I intend also to give a similar concert next year." Beethoven's concert came off on May 7, and the symphony referred to (the Ninth), was duly given, together with portions of the Mass in D, and the Overture (op. 124). It is doubtful if Schubert attended this concert, as he makes no reference to it; moreover, early in May, he accompanied the Esterhazys to their Hungarian retreat. The intention with regard to a concert of his own was carried into effect four years later. This took place in the Hall of the Musik-Verein, on March 26, 1828. It was the only concert that Schubert ever undertook, and although its success encouraged him to promise himself further undertakings of the kind, his early death prevented their fulfilment. The programme was as follows :—

1. First movement of a new String Quartet   *Schubert*.
   Performed by Messrs Böhm, Holz, Weiss and
   Linke.

2. Four Songs   .   .   .   .   .   *Schubert*.
       (*a*) The Crusade.
       (*b*) The Stars.

His only Concert

(*c*) The Wanderer to the Moon.
(*d*) Fragment from Æschylus.
Sung by Herr Vogl, retired imperial opera-singer,
with accompaniment for pianoforte.

3. Serenade (words by Grillparzer) . . *Schubert*.
Soprano solo and chorus, performed by Mdlle.
Josephine Fröhlich and pupils of the Con-
servatoire.

4. New Trio for pianoforte, violin and 'cello *Schubert*.
Performed by Messrs Boklet, Böhm and Linke.

5. On the Stream (words by Rellstab) . *Schubert*.
Song with accompaniment for horn and pianoforte,
performed by Messrs Tieze and Lewy, junior.

6. Omnipotence (words by Ladislaus Pyrker) *Schubert*.
Song with pianoforte accompaniment. Herr Vogl.

7. Battle Song (words by Klopstock) . *Schubert*.
Double chorus for male voices.

ENTRANCE, 3 florins Viennese.

The concert-room was crowded to overflowing, and a
brilliant success secured for the performances. Another
welcome result was the balance of gain, amounting to
800 Vienna Gulden, or about £32. The new quartet was
probably op. 163, published (in parts) during the year by
Spina; and the trio would be either op. 99 or 100. The
song with horn obbligato is a very beautiful piece which
deserves to be better known. (See B. & H.'s edition,
vol. x. p. 2.) It is dated March 1828, so was possibly
written for the concert.

Schubert

"The best sort of music" (says Coleridge) "is what it should be—sacred; the next best, the military, has fallen to the lot of the devil. Good music never tires me nor sends me to sleep. I feel physically refreshed and strengthened by it, as Milton says he did."[1]

The sacred music of Schubert has many great qualities

Sacred Music which not only make it worthy of the services of the Church for which it was primarily intended, but also entitle it to rank with the great works of Bach, Handel and Beethoven. Schubert's début, as a Church composer, was on the occasion of the production of his Mass in F at the Lichtenthal parish church in 1814. The encouragement he then received at the hands of the choir-master—Michael Holzer (his first teacher)—found recognition in the dedication which the young composer made to his former master in the Mass in C. The latter was evidently a favourite work, and though written in 1816, a new number (the Benedictus) was added as late as 1828. It is curious to note that of the six published Masses, none found their way to the Chapel Royal, Vienna, during the composer's life-time. The neglect is thus explained by Dr Hauer:—"Some time in the year 1827, I was sitting, after an evening's music, with Schubert at the 'Zum Rebhuhn' coffee-house, sipping (confidentially) a cheerful glass of 'Schwarzen,' when my friend said to me; 'Not long since I brought Hofcapellmeister Eybler a Mass, to be performed by the Imperial choir. On hearing my name, Eybler declared he had never heard a composition of mine of any kind. I certainly am not an over-conceited man, but should have thought that the Hofcapellmeister of Vienna must

[1] "Table-talk," July 6, 1833.

Secret Composition

have already heard something of mine. A few weeks afterwards I came again to enquire after the fate of my bantling, when Eybler said the Mass was good, but not composed in the style the Emperor liked. So I took my leave, thinking to myself, I am not fortunate enough, then, to be able to write in the imperial style.'" Beethoven's Masses also failed to attain the imperial standard, which seems to have required a contrapuntal pattern in choral writing—such as the Reutter Masses—which contain short and easy fugal movements.

The profoundest secrecy seems to have attended the composition of Schubert's one oratorio— *Lazarus* — of which (unfortunately) only a fragment remains. Neither Schober nor any other of the close personal friends of the composer knew anything about this important work, which was designed as an Easter cantata, and bears the date February 1820. This is the more remarkable, as Schubert, at the period of its composition, was living with Mayrhofer, in the Wipplingerstrasse. Kreissle, who assisted in unearthing the second part of the MS. in 1861, described the work as "one of Schubert's most significant and characteristic musical poems of a religious kind." The first performance took place, March 27, 1863, in Vienna.

An Oratorio

Schubert was put to many shifts for his writing-materials. At the Convict, Spaun and others found him in music-paper; at Währing we have seen him composing on a bill of fare; our story now discovers him writing music in chalk. His brother Ferdinand was appointed (in 1820) to the office of *Regius Chori* in the church of Altlerchenfelder, where music had fallen into sad disorder. Some

L

161

new pieces were wanted for performance on the coming Easter Day—already close at hand. In this dilemma, he applied to his brother Franz—good at need—who forthwith composed the Antiphons (op. 113), and finding his stock of MS. music-paper exhausted, the compositions—which are for four voices—were set down in black chalk, on coarse, grey wrapping-paper.

The setting of the Twenty-third Psalm, though not strictly speaking a Church composition (as the pianoforte accompaniment shows), is nevertheless a highly devotional work. Like so many of Schubert's most successful pieces, it was called forth for an especial occasion, being written for the sisters Fröhlich. The MS., which bears the date Dec. 1820, contains parts for two trebles and two altos, with the accompaniment as stated.[1]

The Song of Miriam (words by Grillparzer) was set as a cantata for solo, chorus and pianoforte—performed, as we have already seen, at Schubert's concert, in March 1828. It was completed shortly before that date. Franz Lachner afterwards arranged the accompaniment for orchestra, and in the latter form it is now well known.

It was fitting that some part of Schubert's last year should be devoted to the composition of sacred music. We have now to describe his masterpiece in this department. The Mass in E flat will rank with the finest compositions of its class. Its place lies between the Mass C major of Beethoven and that same master's stupendous Mass in D. A deeply inspired tone pervades the Schubert work, which is beautifully scored for voices

---

[1] A *facsimile* page is given in the *Musical Times* of Sept. 1901.

Mass in E flat

and orchestra.   Unconventionality reigns throughout.
Thus in the opening Kyrie, the second portion from the
words "Christe Eleison" is begun *forte*, with the voices
high in their register, and proceeding (crescendo) to
fortissimo effects.   The movement ends as it commenced
with subdued low chords.   The Gloria is a strong
rhythmical piece of writing, leading to a contrasted section
at the words "Domine Deus, Agnus Dei," which is
sung somewhat slower.   The quicker movement returns
at "Quoniam tu solus" and proceeds to a fully developed
fugue—Cum Sancto Spiritu—the general effect of which
is very powerful.   It would have been interesting to
have had Sechter's opinion on this particular part of the
work.   (See p. 74.)   The Credo opens in a subdued
manner, and becomes finely expressive at the "Incarnatus
est" and strongly dramatic in the "Crucifixus."   Another
fugue is developed on the words "Et vitam venturi."
The counterpoint is not exactly that of the schools, but
it is anything but weak, as it has been so often called.   The
tonality—so constantly that of tonic and dominant—
may be thought by some to be monotonous, but the
effect is not so.   Light and shade are duly imparted by
the expression, which is a material part of the whole
design.   The Sanctus is distinguished by bold modulation—always   at   the   composer's   ready   command.
"Hosanna in excelsis" introduces more fugal writing of
a fluent and adequate kind.   A chaste and expressive
subject brings us to the Benedictus, relieved by a fugal
passage given *forte*, and a repetition of the "Hosanna."
Finally there comes the "Agnus Dei," the chief subject
of which is the same as the great theme of Bach's five-
part fugue in C sharp minor.   The beseeching (almost

demanding) tone of this short passage, purposely contrived to be an oft-repeated petition, does not allow of
its regular development into a real fugue, though most
of the constituents are present. This gives way to a
plain but truly fervent " Dona nobis pacem," which leaves
us with a very real impression of the Peace which passeth
all Understanding. Schubert has himself explained the
secret of his power in dealing with sacred words :—" I
think that the reason of this is that I never force myself
into devotion, or compose hymns or prayers unless I am
really overpowered by the feeling; that alone is real,
true devotion."

Schubert cultivated pianoforte-playing chiefly as a
As Pianist means to an end; and though on rare
occasions he played perhaps one of his
Sonatas or Fantasias, he was more often content if
he could play the elaborate accompaniments to his songs,
or maintain sufficient technique to bear a part in the
duets with Gahy, Hüttenbrenner or Jenger. He used
the key-board daily as an aid to composition, testing
passages that were afterwards transferred to paper. He
was also fond of extemporising dance-music, some of
which was immediately written out. His technique was
not considerable, and he relied on expression, and fine
poetic taste, rather than upon the practised equipment
of a virtuoso. There is an interesting expression of
his opinion on pianoforte-playing in one of the letters
of 1825.[1] " I played " (says he) " alone, and not without
success, for some of the listeners assured me that the
keys sang, under my hand, like voices ; which, if it
be true, is a delightful compliment; for I cannot abide

[1] Letter of July 25, written from Steyr, to his parents.

Fantasie in C

that execrable pounding ("vermaledeite Hacken") common even to distinguished players; for it neither pleases the ear, nor moves the heart."

Gahy, who often played duets with Schubert, speaks of his pure, rapid playing, and of the bold conception, and fiery energy alternated with tender feeling—all of which qualities, possessed by "his short, fat friend, raised his (Gahy's) spirits to the highest pitch." When the pianist, Johann Horzalka, heard Schubert play one of his sonatas, he was moved to exclaim, "I admire your playing even more than your composition"—a remark so equivocal that Schubert interpreted it in its least flattering sense.

There is an amusing incident recorded of Schubert's performance of his Fantasia in C major (op. 15)—a work which every student may know is not to be trifled with. Schubert was playing this composition to an audience of friends, among whom were Kupelwieser, Spaun and Gahy. The *A Break-Down* first part of the piece had been successfully tackled, and the middle portion expressively played; the player also survived Part iii. Then, with the impetuous finale, came disaster. He played it at full speed, with ever-increasing energy; but—alas—he was riding for a fall. This soon came, for he suddenly stuck fast in the middle of the movement. The story adds that Schubert rose hastily from his seat, and invoked infernal aid in the following terms, "Let the devil himself play the stuff."

It would seem that neither in his own day nor in ours, have Schubert's pianoforte compositions been thoroughly appreciated, though both pianist and theorist are forced

Schubert

to admit that his best examples (some of which are mentioned later) are second only to the best of Beethoven's. Here is Liszt's view:—

"Our pianists have no notion what beautiful treasures his pianoforte compositions contain. Most players go through them *en passant*, and, observing here and there repetitions, long-drawn passages, and what might appear to be carelessness, forthwith do lay them aside. Like the bird in the air, he lived in music, and sang thereby most heavenly songs."

With his usual fine critical perception, Sir Hubert Parry has written as follows:—

"Schubert's sonatas do not show any operatic traits of the old manner, but there is plenty in them which may be called dramatic in a modern sense. His instincts were of a pre-eminently modern type, and the fertility of his ideas in their superabundance clearly made the self-restraint necessary for sonata-writing a matter of some difficulty. He was tempted to give liberty to the rush of thought which possessed him, and the result is sometimes delightful, but sometimes also bewildering. There are movements and even groups of them which are of the supremest beauty, but hardly any one sonata which is completely satisfactory throughout. His treatment of form is often daring, even to rashness, and yet from the point of view of principle offers but little to remark, though in detail some perfectly magical feats of harmonic progression and strokes of modulation have had a good deal of influence upon great composers of later times.

"As a whole, though illustrating richly many of the tendencies of modern music, the sonatas cannot be taken

Sonata in G

as representing Schubert's powers as a composer of
instrumental music so satisfactorily as his quartets, his
string quintet, and some of his finest symphonies. In
these he often rose almost to the highest point of
musical possibility."

This grand sonata—a fine example of the form applied
to brilliant and spontaneous music, dates from *The G-major*
the year 1826, an eventful though by no *Pianoforte*
means a prolific one. The string quartet *Sonata*
in D minor and the violin rondo (op. 70)
prepared the way for the sonata. Schumann has declared it to be " the most perfect work, both in form and
conception," which Schubert has left us. Doubtless this
should be taken as his opinion with regard to the piano
works only, for the sonata could not possibly challenge
the C-major Symphony in " form and conception." The
autograph reads, " IV. Sonate für Pianoforte allein.
October 1826, Franz Schubert." The publisher (Tobias
Haslinger) was not content with the title, and improved
it into " Fantasie, Andante, Menuetto und Allegretto."
In spite of its absurdity the description clings to the
sonata, and duly appears in Liszt's fine edition (J. G.
Cotta).

From a player's point of view, the sonata demands
great delicacy of tone-production. No serious difficulties
arise, in fact the technique is on the whole quite simple,
yet the gradations of tone, and exquisite lightness of
touch, requisite to make the most of the work, call for
the highest musicianship, and above all for true
poetic conception. Let us examine the work more
closely.

Schubert

From this delicate and fanciful theme (extending to nine bars) the movement proceeds by means of an ingenious "bridge" (B minor and major), which, however, to our surprise, brings a repetition of a portion of the first subject in the initial key (bar 17). The real "bridge" then leads us (bar 23-5) to the second principle theme, a broad singing melody of ten bars (26-36).

A varied presentment of the whole of the second theme follows (bars 37-46). The codetta—a finely coloured piece of writing—leads us direct to a close in the dominant (bar 64). This portion of the movement is then repeated. The "free fantasia" is founded on the first subject, which proceeds from G minor (bar 65) to work to a powerful climax in B flat minor (bar 73). The second subject provides a delicate contrast (bar 77) and gives way (at

"O Tobias!"

bar 82) to a repetition, a minor third higher, of the whole of the "free fantasia" (so far discussed) by way of a huge "step" (82-100). A simple plaintive passage leads us easily and naturally back to the "recapitulation." Here we may note the compression of the original matter of the first principal subject (116-124). Nine bars now serve where twenty-two were originally called for. With such alteration the key of the tonic is maintained and the second subject introduced in formal style in the same key (bar 127). The remainder of the material falls into place in its transposed form, and, at bar 162, the coda proper is introduced with notable effect. This is founded on the opening phrase of the movement and is an exquisite piece of workmanship. The whole movement has occupied no more than 174 bars and is as formal as anything in the whole range of modern sonatas. Well might the erudite "G.,"[1] noticing the publishers' "Fantasie," exclaim, with Beethoven, "O Tobias!"

The second movement—a simple binary or song-form—is a peaceful air dependent upon the expressive powers of the player (bars 1-30).

A marked rhythmical figure (in heavy chords) is then

---

[1] Sir George Grove.

announced, in the key of the relative minor (31-39). The same idea is afterwards presented with a wonderful change from its former harshness to a most enchanting quiet (40-49). Again come those clanging tones (bars 50-58), only to be in turn dispelled by the more pensive mood (59-78), which finally prevails and brings us back to the original song (80). In the recapitulation there is some slight variation of the original material. The rhythmical figure now appears in the key of the tonic-minor (110), and with this change the transposition of the rest of the first portion of the movement is pretty methodically observed until bar 156, when we come back for a brief moment to the first theme in its original key (159-172). A charming little coda of eight bars brings the piece to an end.

The minuet-and-trio is a fresh, characteristic movement, proclaiming the authorship of Schubert in every bar. The trio is finely contrasted, being in the tonic major, as the minuet was in the tonic minor (B). Both parts of the movement are charged with very unusual emotion for the class of piece.

The sonata closes with a grand rondo. This is obviously gipsy music—gay, light-hearted and extremely brilliant. As in the first movement, the player will need the utmost delicacy and niceness of judgment to do it justice.

Gipsy Music

The subject comprises only four bars. This is expanded to 30 or even to 41, when after a sudden break, the first subject resumes. There is a full close in the tonic at bar 54, which serves to introduce the first episode, given in the subdominant :—

The twelve bars (from 56 onwards), beginning as above, provide material for a considerable section of the movement. First, the theme is announced in the upper part, then the bass has a version (bar 69). It passes quickly through A flat, E flat and D flat, only to return (96) to the original key of the subdominant. A few transitional bars (120-3) usher in the first rondo-subject, in its own key (G). Some thirty bars' repeat is here to be noted, with a cleverly designed modulatory passage at bar 156 and onwards. At 167 the rondo again comes round for a brief moment, and closes in the tonic (179). The second important episode follows in the key of E flat.

In its fairy-like passages it matches the first episode. At bar 211 we are led by a crescendo passage to the key of C minor. The theme then announced is grave and impassioned almost as a song of destiny (bars 213-228). This recurs, given *fortissimo* by the bass, which leads gradually to a version of the same theme in C major

Schubert

pianissimo (245). Again comes the tremendous appeal
from the bass (261), which gradually becomes softened
and melts in the ethereal strains of the episode noted
above (bar 279, compare bar 181). We now progress
towards the original rondo-theme, which appears at 321,
and keeps the even tenor of its way for some forty bars
or more. At 367 the coda proper is entered upon, and a
right merry one it is (367-407), ending with a final assertion
of the original statement contained in the little four-bar
subject (408-411). A word may be added on Liszt's very
judicious edition of this sonata. The phrasing is throughout markedly emphasised, and useful suggestions are given
for tone and touch. In a few cases the chords are amplified,
as Schubert was wont to write but thinly for the pianoforte
at times. Nothing is added to the minuet and trio. But
wherever alterations are introduced they are printed
small, and apart from Schubert's own text, which is thus
perfectly respected.

Having so fully considered the Sonata in G (op. 78)—
Op. 53.   "the most perfect in form and conception,"
according to Schumann—very much less space
can be devoted to the others, which, like that in D major (op.
53), would otherwise claim almost equal attention. The
first movement of opus 53 is a powerful piece of work in
which the solo instrument has full play. The vigour of
the writing is remarkable, and only a performer of strongly-
developed finger-power will be able to do justice to the
finely conceived *Allegro Vivace*. There follows a lovely
slow movement—*Con moto*—which takes the form of a
long-drawn and highly expressive song, broken, however, by
a vigorous middle portion. If the piece has a fault, it
must be allowed that its length is somewhat more than

Sonata in A minor

modern average patience is wont to countenance. The scherzo is of determined and original rhythm, made up of strongly devised chords and powerful contrasts; while the trio, a heavenly strain in G major, sets it off to rare advantage. At first sight the final movement seems out of place. The writing appears thin and weak, and the subject-matter far too inadequate for the fine work which has preceded it. But the movement will bear study, and those who take the trouble to master it will not be disappointed. The gipsy element must not be overlooked. Played with extreme delicacy and dexterity it is graceful and supremely charming—especially the middle section (in G), which bespeaks the gaiety of Viennese life, the uncontrollable spirits of youth, the passing fancies of a teeming imagination, or indeed what-you-will of brightness and beauty.

Op. 42—a highly original and characteristic sonata—has been pronounced by some to be Schubert's best. It certainly claims a place with the parallel works in G major and D major, though *A-minor Sonata* inferior to both in technique and in poetic invention. The first movement—moderato in A minor—has fine rhythm and excellent tone-colour, marred to some extent by a thin technical structure which at times is such as we meet with in Mozart. On the other hand, there are passages which, like the whole of the coda, are amazingly strong and massive—even to the point of suggesting an orchestra as a better vehicle for the music's display than a mere pianoforte. The second movement, an expressive air with one or two exquisite variations, an extraordinary example of strength and delicacy in pointed contrast, is nevertheless open to the charge of an imperfect technique. Of the scherzo and trio—a swift and earnest little division of the work—we need not stop to repeat our doubly emphasised view of technical imperfection. Exceptional interest attaches itself to the finale—a spontaneous movement, full of high thoughts and solemn purpose—because it gives a hint of the great theme afterwards employed in the finale of the C-major Symphony.[1]

The simple secret of the inadequacy of Schubert's pianoforte-writing in his sonatas, as compared with the full and finished work of Beethoven, is probably explainable by Franz's half-mastery of the instrument which Beethoven had completely subjugated to his will. The same deficiency is not seen in a comparison of the two masters' string-quartets, and certainly does not exist if the symphonic works be laid side by side. None but a virtuoso ever wrote with a full measure of success for the pianoforte, and it is certain that Schubert fell short of that description.

Space does not allow of a detailed account of the remaining sonatas, which are becoming better known as the popular editions multiply. Those who are interested in the methods of work which belonged to the composer, will read with interest the early sketches and varied copies of several of the well-known sonatas, contained in Breitkopf & Haertel's twenty-first supplement, to which we shall refer later.

Liszt and Schumann were among the first to discover that in the pianoforte compositions of Schubert there was a rich store of pieces of every possible variety and scope, ranging from such important works as the "Wanderer

[1] See bars 181 of the last movement of the Piano Sonata, and compare bars 190 and onwards of the finale of the large C-major Symphony.

Fantasia"[1] (op. 15), written in 1823—one of the finest and most poetic of them all—to the little dance-pieces that are rarely without some special fragrance and delicacy. Some of these works, like the Impromptus (op. 90 and 142), are now widely and deservedly known. The late Sir Charles Halle and Madame Schumann helped to bring them into popular notice, at a time when Schubert's reputation as a composer for the pianoforte was of comparatively small account. The "Moments musicals" (op. 94), together with a mass of short movements grouped in the Ländler, Valses Nobles, Walzer, Ecossaisen, Allemandes, Gallops, etc., indicate a class of work of which we can give but the bare titles. In the pianoforte music for two performers there is much to admire. The variations (op. 10)—presented to Beethoven—form an effective example of this kind. The list could, however, be extended indefinitely; for there are still sonatas (for two players), divertissements, several fine fantasias, and military marches, forming together a whole library of pianoforte-duets delightful to play and to hear. A few further pieces for piano-solo and duet are mentioned at the end of this part of our book.

Most musicians will easily agree with Berlioz that the String-Quartet is the most difficult task a composer can undertake. The best training for such achievements is to familiarise oneself with existing masterpieces by *playing* in

---

[1] Kreissle remarks—oddly enough—of this Fantasia, that "the construction of the first and last movement seems certainly rather uncouth . . . it ignores artistic rules and formulæ, even more than Schubert's other instrumental works." It would have been interesting had we been informed what precise rules and formulæ govern the Fantasia as a musical form.

Schubert

them. A command of vocal counterpoint will not help here. There must be actual and vivid realisation of the written effects. Schubert was a clever viola-player, and could join in rendering the works of Mozart and Haydn with true mastery of their technical difficulties. We need, then, seek no further for the explanation of his wonderful facility in a form of composition admittedly the most difficult of all.[1] As a boy of fifteen Schubert had essayed a work of this class. While he was but sixteen, three further string-quartets were composed. With these, however, we need not concern ourselves. It is convenient to take the nine quartets published by Peters (one of the earliest editions) and rapidly review their leading characteristics.

The first of these (op. 29 in A minor) composed and published in 1824, was the only one issued during Schubert's life-time. It is dedicated to I. Schuppanzigh —one of the Rasoumowsky quartet-players. A few bars of the theme are quoted for purposes of identification.

Allegro ma non troppo.

[1] Schubert's association with Schuppanzigh, Weiss and Linke, three of the players in the famed Rasoumowsky quartet, may be further noted in this connection. In 1824 they took part in a performance of Schubert's Octet, and it is quite possible that their influence counted for much in his later productions for strings.

Beautiful Andante

pp

The character of this movement, at once passionate and graceful, is of undeniable charm. Some points in the opening reveal Schubert's peculiar method of constructing a first movement. Thus after the initial twenty-four bars which lead to a dominant close, the principal subject is given in the *tonic major*, and with very beautiful effect. The so-called "bridge" proceeds anything but directly towards the relative major; yet the music called forth makes one decline to see any necessity why it should. A tonic pedal (in the relative major key) serves as a basis for the second subject, which is sweet and expressive (and not otherwise remarkable); after a brief modulation which no one but Schubert or Beethoven would have thought of, the double bar appears, and the whole material is repeated in the usual way. The interest is maintained to the end, where an exceptionally original coda is introduced.

A beautiful *Andante* movement follows in C major — a very real inspiration — which will always be heard with pleasure; though the construction is of simple design, each part teems with expressive interest. Those who believe Schubert to have possessed but small counterpoint should read, mark and learn bars 54-80. As the *theme* is repeated at this point,

I cannot do better than quote a couple of these bars.

Andante.

For the remaining movements a word must suffice. The minuet and trio is unconventional, in its opening on a dominant pedal; while the final *Allegro Moderato* is full of gaiety, and contains many a quaint touch and original thought which loudly proclaim its composer.

The quartet in E flat (op. 125, No. 1), though written in the same year as the work just discussed, is not so strikingly original. It reminds one of Mozart and Beethoven at the outset.

Allegro moderato.

The whole of the first movement is solidly built, and contains much effective part-writing, which cannot but please players and hearers alike.

Quartet in E

A short scherzo and trio (in E flat and C minor respectively) coming second, remind one of Beethoven's disposition of the four movements, which Schubert has generally followed. The contrast produced by this second movement is excellently contrived. For the third movement, Schubert returns to his original key (E flat). The tone of the opening is decidedly of a religious cast, indeed the first subject would not have been out of place in a Sanctus.

Without change of key, the finale introduces a grand rondo, which is for the most part gay and bright, with an undercurrent of jolly rhythm, which gives way at times to more serious and thoughtful passages, but reasserts itself in the concluding bars.

Of the same year is the Quartet in E (op. 125, No. 2). In this work the composer returns to his own original methods. Brilliance is his aim from the first to the last note. The first movement begins thus :—

Allegro con fuoco.

The andante (in A major) which follows is still in a light vein, but it is melodically so charmingly conceived and so refreshing—if not *naïve*—in its turns and graces, that we are reminded of the methods of Mozart. The

return to the original key—bars 75 and 76—is characteristic enough for quotation :—

The minuetto (*Allegro Vivace*—in E major) is one of
the most original of its kind, with a trio in good contrast
but not otherwise remarkable; while the rondo which
concludes the whole is a well defined formal movement,
which need not detain us.

The posthumous Quartet in D minor (No. 4 in Peters'
edition and 14 in Breitkopf & Haertel's) is a great
masterpiece. It is characterised by intense fire and
energy, deep seriousness, and a formal beauty for which
Schubert is rarely given due credit. The first movement
is of supreme interest. We can only quote the initial
bars.

Wagner Motif

In the second movement—*Andante con moto*, in G minor—Schubert introduces " Der Tod und das Mädchen," the song of Death and the Maiden (op. 7, No. 3), to which he adds five variations. This exquisite theme forms the text of an eloquent discourse, in which chaste and expressive writing distinguish the movement throughout. A vigorous scherzo — the first phrase of which hints at the origin of the *motif* identified with Mime in Wagner's *Siegfried* — with its pendent trio — a truly delicious strain—worthily continue this splendid quartet. The opening of the scherzo is as follows :—

Allegro molto.

A very vigorous and sustained presto movement (in D minor) brings the work to an end. Kreissle mentions that at the first performance of Jan. 29, 1826, this fourth movement was adjudged to be too long, and that Schubert, to oblige his friends, cheerfully cut out a large section. This cannot now be verified, as the autograph score has unfortunately disappeared.

At the end of the Quartet in G major (op. 161) is the date 30/6/26, thus indicating a ripe period of composition. The MS. is understood to have occupied no more than ten days to complete. Like the work last considered, the

Schubert

G-major Quartet is one of the great ones. It has all the vigour of the D-minor (see above), but it does not seem to possess the same variety. The proportions are almost symphonic, and might seem to require a full orchestra in places. The first movement opens with this strain:—

Allegro molto moderato.

The second movement (in E minor) is of elegiac character. An important share falls to the lot of the 'cello, which announces the theme.

There is something of the Beethoven manner in the scherzo, especially in the way in which single instruments take up the lead. From the brisk energy of this number the suave refinement of the trio provides grateful relief. The keys are B minor and G major. One can imagine that the finale would be considered very daring in its day; the subtle admixture of G major and G minor anticipating a similar effect in the opening of Brahms' well-known Symphony in E minor. The general impression of Schubert's finale is almost that of a Tarantella, though it never descends to the flippancy commonly noticeable in such pieces. It is grave, impassioned, and at times of resistless impetuosity.

Early Quartet

[1] Opus 168 will not detain us long. It is quite an early work, and its interest is accordingly not on the same plane as the two previous quartets. The autograph casts an unusual light upon the method in which it was composed. At the head of the first movement is the date of its commencement, namely " 5. Sept. 1814," while at the end we read, " completed in four and a half hours "— certainly a wonderful morning's work for a youth of seventeen. The first violin announces the theme alone, thus :—

On the following day, the autograph shows, the slow movement was begun. This is a graceful, clear-cut and expressive little piece, in the vein of Mozart. It was completed on Sept. 10. The succeeding day was devoted to the composition of a vigorous little minuet (in E flat, with trio in the same key) ; while in three days more, *i.e.* on Sept. 13, 1814, the quartet was completed by the addition of a well-designed but not very original rondo in B flat, which seems modelled to the mood of Beethoven's earliest compositions.

The G-minor Quartet (No. 7 of Peters' edition, and 9 of Breitkopf & Haertel's) dates from a year later than the work just mentioned. It occupied the week March 25 to April 1, 1815. and shows a real advance, especially

[1] This quartet was originally begun in the form of a trio ; after ten lines in that form, it was recommenced and finished as a quartet.

in the first movement, upon its predecessor. The subject promises well :—

The remainder of the movements do not seem to aim so high; for while the andante is a sweet little division, the minuetto (in G minor) a correct and effective number, with the succeeding rondo in the style of papa Haydn, none of these can be regarded as of much importance.

Portions of the Quartet in D major (Peters' No. 8) seem almost too good for the period to which it is assigned (Dec. 1814), did we not know that pieces like " Gretchen am Spinnrade " (op. 2.) were of that year's composition. I give four bars of the opening to ensure identification :—

Quartett-Satz

The andante (in G major) leaves us in no doubt, however, as to the immaturity of the work, and even ends in a lame manner. The minuet (in D) and the trio (in B flat) are fairly interesting; while the final presto (in D major) has many attractive features. What strikes one as a curious merit in nearly all these pieces is the extreme fluency of melody and a no less wonderful mastery of the sonata form. Crudities rarely seem to obtrude themselves.

Another early work, "Quartett-Satz," probably written in 1814, occurs as the final piece in the selection under consideration. The piece is in sonata form and is fairly workman-like and effective, but is of little further consequence, and is only mentioned by way of completeness. Here is the opening subject:—

It is well known that Franz Schubert never visited England. The earliest mention of his music in an English periodical is probably contained in the *Quarterly Musical Magazine and Review* (vol. x. p. 189) of 1828. It reads: "The other young composers who have distinguished themselves at Vienna are MM. Sechter, who is greatest in Fugues, and Schubert, who composes beautiful melodies." In *The*

Music in England

Schubert

Cadeau of 1831—a New-Year's annual—the F-minor melody from the "Moments Musicals" (op. 94, No. 3) makes its first appearance in an English print under the curious description, *Russian Air.* Next year the same publication included the "Erl-king." A separate issue of the same song also dates from 1832, when it was published by Messrs Wessel & Co. (afterwards Ashdown). Five years later, Messrs Ewer & Co. began to bring out songs by Schubert in their "Gems of German Song."

Among the first to popularise the songs in this country were Madame Schroeder-Devrient and Herr Kroff, who visited England between 1832 and 1836.[1]

So many of Schubert's songs now began to make their appearance that a writer in the *Musical World* (1839) is concerned for their origin.

"A deep shade of suspicion, we regret to say, is beginning to be cast over the authenticity of posthumous compositions. The defunct popular composer not only becomes immortal in the poetical sense, but, by a curious felicity which publishers can best explain, actually goes on composing after he is dead. All Paris has been in a state of amazement at the posthumous diligence of the song-writer F. Schubert, who, while one would think his ashes repose in peace at Vienna, is still making eternal new songs, and putting drawing-rooms in commotion."

Comment is now unnecessary, as the catalogues at the end of this book sufficiently explain any "posthumous diligence" imagined of the *Musical World* in 1839.

[1] Herr Kroff is credited with having introduced "The Wanderer," for the first time in this country, at The Classical Quartet Concerts, April 8, 1836.

C-major Symphony

The year 1839 might have become memorable in the history of Schubert's music in England, for then it was that Mendelssohn addressed the Philharmonic Society in London, writing from Leipzig on March 29:—" I hope to be able to send you a very extraordinary and excellent symphony of F. Schubert, the famous composer, which we performed here at our last concert with great applause. I have written to Vienna to get permission to send the work to the Society, and shall forward it immediately if I am allowed to do so."

The parts were duly sent three weeks later. They were copied and a score was made. So much is witnessed by the reply of the Philharmonic Society's secretary (Mr Watts), who explains that it is hoped that the work will be performed next season. Nothing, however, was done until Mendelssohn visited England in 1844 to conduct the Philharmonic Orchestra. Then the symphony was put in rehearsal. Unfortunately the members of the band laughed at the triplets, it is said, of the last movement.[1]

Mendelssohn, in high dudgeon, withdrew the work, and the poor Philharmonic thus wantonly deprived itself of a very considerable honour. After the lapse of twelve long years, and thanks to the sympathetic activity of August Manns, the C-major Symphony was produced, in two sections, at two concerts given in April 1856, at the Crystal Palace.

It attracted but little attention, but the two dauntless admirers of the Vienna master were nothing moved.

---

[1] Habeneck rehearsed the same symphony at Paris in 1842, with the result that the band refused to go on with it after the first movement. What tyrants orchestral players must then have been !

Schubert

The names of Grove and Manns are associated in this production, for though Manns was the one who initiated Grove into Schubert's wonderful work, Grove had been instrumental in getting the conductor duly installed; and in all matters relating to Schubert he proved himself an invaluable ally to the Director of Music. Sir August Manns, alluding to this first production in England, says:—

"I very vividly recollect that after the rehearsal I entered Mr (now Sir) George Grove's office, and stated in the most enthusiastic terms how deep an impression the symphony had made upon me, urging him to come and listen to its performance. He, Sir George Grove, admired, but at the same time pitied my enthusiasm, because the work would never receive the sympathy of a Crystal Palace audience. However, Sir George did come and listen to the performance; and it was from that time that his enthusiasm for Franz Schubert's genius took root, and gradually developed into that active participation in the researches concerning Schubert's compositions which have borne such splendid fruit, and benefited musical art in England and abroad to such a great extent. . . . I have reason to believe that my performance of the C-major Symphony in 1856 was the first in England, although I remember hearing one of the members of my then very small band speak of a rehearsal of it under the late Dr Wylde, when at the close of the first movement the principal horn called out to one of the first violins, 'Tom, have you been able to discover a tune yet?' 'I have not,' was Tom's reply. I quote these remarks made by two of the foremost artists in Costa's band, then the only band in England, in order to show how great was the prejudice at that time against

Facsimile of Waltz by Schubert

(in the Berlin Royal Bibliothek)

any compositions which did not come from the sanctified Haydn, Mozart, Beethoven and Mendelssohn. . . . I feel thankful for having been able to help in the good work which has been accomplished in England during the last forty years." [1]

The story of Sir George Grove's visit to Vienna, in company with Sir Arthur Sullivan, in quest of unpublished MSS., is best told in his own words. A complete account of the successful errand undertaken is given in the Appendix to the English translation of Kreissle's "Life of Schubert." It was in the autumn of 1867, that fired with a noble enthusiasm for the recovery of what remained of Schubert's priceless scores, the two friends set out for the Austrian capital.

Treasure Trove

"So far, success—brilliant success. But I had failed in one chief object of my journey. The *Rosamunde* music was almost dearer to me than the symphonies. Besides the *entr'actes* in B minor and B flat, the 'Ballo, No. 2,' and the 'Ballet Air, No. 9,' which we had already acquired in 1866, we had found at Mr Spina's an *entr'acte* after the second act, and a 'Hirten-Melodie' for clarinets, bassoons and horns; but we still required the accompaniments to the Romance and the two choruses, as well as the total number of pieces and their sequence in the drama. To quit Vienna without these would have been too cruel, and yet neither from Dr Schneider nor Mr Spina, nor in the library of the Musik-Verein—where the admirable librarian, Mr C. F. Pohl, was entirely at our service—had we succeeded in finding a trace of them.

"It was Thursday afternoon, and we proposed to leave

[1] *Musical Times*, February 1897.

on Saturday for Prague. We made a final call on Dr
Schneider, to take leave and repeat our thanks, and also,
as I now firmly believe, guided by a special instinct.
The doctor was civility itself; he again had recourse to
the cupboard, and showed us some treasures that had
escaped us before. I again turned the conversation to
the *Rosamunde* music; he believed that he had at one
time possessed a copy or sketch of it all. Might I go
into the cupboard and look for myself? Certainly, if I
had no objection to being smothered in dust. In I
went; and after some search, during which my companion
kept the Doctor engaged in conversation, I found, at
the bottom of the cupboard, and in its furthest corner,
a bundle of music-books two feet high, carefully tied
round, and black with the undisturbed dust of nearly half
a century. It was like the famous scene at the monastery
of Souriani on the Natron lakes, so well described by
Mr Curzon: 'Here is a box,' exclaimed the two monks,
who were nearly choked with the dust; 'we have found
a box, and a heavy one too.' 'A box,' shouted the
blind abbot, who was standing in the outer darkness of
the oil-cellar—'a box? where is it?' 'Bring it out,
bring out the box. Heaven be praised. We have found
a treasure. Lift up the box. Pull out the box,' shouted
the monks, when we had dragged out the bundle into the
light, and found that it was actually neither more nor
less than what we were in search of. Not Dr Cureton,
when he made his truly romantic discovery of the missing
leaves of the Syriac Eusebius, could have been more
glad or more grateful than I was at this moment. For
these were the part-books of the whole of the music in
Rosamunde, tied up after the second performance in

Instrumental Combinations

December 1823, and probably never disturbed since. Dr Schneider must have been amused at our excitement; but let us hope that he remembered his own days of rapture; at anyrate he overlooked it, and gave us permission to take away with us and copy what we wanted, and I now felt that my mission to Vienna had not been fruitless."

The parts had now to be copied. By writing at their top speed, the two Englishmen, assisted by C. F. Pohl (the well-known German biographer), finally accomplished their work by two in the morning. Report adds that Sullivan and Grove duly celebrated the close of their labours in a game of leap-frog round the room.

Schubert was nothing if not original in his combinations of voices and instruments, or of instruments alone. As early as 1813 he wrote a cantata for three male voices and guitar, in celebration of his father's birthday. The guitar was in some request at that time, a fact which accounts for the several songs in which the instrument plays a part, also for op. 11, where it serves to accompany four voices. Schubert, in the same year, composed the little octet for wind-instruments — "Franz Schuberts Begräbniss-Feyer." There is also the Minuet and Finale for two oboes, two clarinets, two horns and two bassoons; and the "Fünf Minuette und sechs Deutsche" for two horns and strings, another composition of 1813. A much more important work is the Octet (op. 166) for strings, clarinet, horn and bassoon, which, despite its great length—an hour in performance—is a bright and beautiful creation. Smaller pieces may be noted, such as the "Introduction and Variations" (op. 160) for flute and pianoforte, written, it is understood, for Ferdinand Bogner in 1824, or the Sonata for piano and

Schubert

a small harp (Arpeggione) of the same date. Some of the songs too have an obbligato ; for example, " Auf dem Strom " for voice, horn and pianoforte, and " Der Hirt auf dem Felsen " for voice, clarinet and pianoforte. Such pieces have some bearing on the larger combinations, which in the instrumental department naturally find their full expression in the symphony. Nor must we lose sight of such a work as the Quintet in C, for strings—a broad and beautiful composition, recalling the mood of Beethoven, though full of Schubert's own individuality. Passing to the Overtures, these, with the exception of *Fierrabras* and *Rosamunde* — both fine achievements —may be generally pronounced as of less importance than the corresponding works of Beethoven, though they still have an honoured place in Schubert's repertory of compositions, recommending themselves for brightness, brilliancy, lightness of touch, and allied qualities, rather than for the profound and intellectual expression in which the former master's utterances excel.

The first symphony is dated Oct. 28, 1813, being composed while Schubert was still a pupil at
First Symphony in D
the Convict school. It is in the orthodox four movements, the first being somewhat long drawn out (having 533 bars, not counting repeats). Kreissle states that the work was written for the name-day of Dr Lang, who, in 1813, was the Convict Director.

The score reads as follows :—2 violins, viola, 2 oboes, 2 clarinets, 2 bassoons, 2 horns, 2 trumpets, drum, 'cello and bass.[1]

[1] It is not improbable that the Convict Orchestra is exactly indicated in the plan of the score.

First Symphony

[*Introduction.*]   *Adagio.*

Allegro vivace.

Andante.

Schubert

The second symphony followed its predecessor at an interval of little over a year, and the MS. bears the dates Dec. 10, 1814, March 24, 1815. An additional flute is employed in the score, the other instruments remain unchanged. Schubert had left the Convict and was now an elementary teacher in his father's school and a private pupil of Salieri. The symphony is a real advance on No. 1 and possesses more individuality, while the instrumentation is both freer and surer

Second Symphony in B flat

Second Symphony

Schubert

Andante.

Menuetto. Allegro vivace.

Presto vivace.

Schubert proceeded cautiously in his symphonic writing,
for his third work, written in 1815 (the year of
Third the " Erl-king ") shows but little daring com-
Symphony pared with that he put forth in his song-
in D writing. No doubt the Convict orchestra
was the only one which he could as yet command, but it

Third Symphony

is doubtful if such a consideration would count for much.
Beethoven had already produced eight of his symphonies,
most of which Schubert had heard, and in some, had
played. If it surprises one, however, to find Schubert's
third effort still immature, still unindividual, we must turn
to the 144 songs or the five operatic pieces which the
same year brought forth and marvel at the genius which
could produce with such rapidity so many splendid
compositions.

Schubert

Allegretto.
Strings.

Menuetto. Vivace.

Presto vivace. (Strings.)

198

"Tragic" Symphony

The autograph score of the *Tragic Symphony* is in the possession of Herr Nicolaus Dumba of Vienna. It is dated April 1816. The description "tragic" is the composer's own. Kreissle mentions that the second movement of this symphony was given at a concert in Vienna, December 1860. Grove believed the original score to be lost, and obtained a copy of Ferdinand Schubert's transcript, then in the possession of Dr Schneider. The symphony was produced under August Manns' direction on Feb. 27, 1868, at the Crystal Palace. The score is as follows:—2 violins, viola, 2 flutes, 2 oboes, 2 clarinets, 2 bassoons, 4 horns, 2 trumpets, drums, 'cello and bass.

Fourth Symphony in C minor

Schubert

A fifth work is known as "the symphony without trumpets and drums." It is scored for 2 violins, viola, flute, 2 oboes, 2 bassoons, 2 horns, 'cello and bass.

"Without Trumpets and Drums"

Kreissle speaks of its being designed for the Society of Amateurs, for whom Schubert was in the habit of composing—a Society which had grown from a string-quartet (at the elder Schubert's house) into a small orchestra, capable of performing Haydn's symphonies, etc. The autograph of the fifth symphony—preserved in the Royal Library, Berlin—is dated Sept. 1816.

Fifth Symphony in B flat

Schubert

Like the preceding work, the sixth symphony was com-

Sixth Sym-
phony
C major

posed for Schubert's Amateur Society, which, in the spring of 1818, had just removed to its new quarters at Otto Hatwig's house in the Gundelhof. The work was first publicly performed Dec. 12, 1828, in the Redouten-Saal, at the

Sixth Symphony

second Gesellschafts-concert, and repeated March 12, 1829, in the Landständischen Saal. Forty years later the symphony found its way to the Crystal Palace (Nov. 21, 1868). The work marks a transitional period in Schubert's symphonic style. He is just emerging from the influences of Mozart, Haydn and Beethoven. The autograph score, in possession of Herr Dumba, shows the work to have been completed Feb. 1818. Clarinets, trumpets and drums are now added, the score being as follows :—2 violins, viola, 2 flutes, 2 oboes, 2 clarinets, 2 bassoons, 2 horns, 2 trumpets, drums, 'cello and bass.

Schubert

The autograph sketch of a symphony in E minor is so graphically described by the late Sir George Grove, into whose possession it came, that liberty is taken to quote some of his remarks thereupon. "This, like the symphony in B

Sketch of a Symphony

minor, is incomplete, though its incompleteness is entirely
of a different nature. I made enquiries of various members
of Mendelssohn's family, but without success. However,
I persevered, and was at length rewarded by receiving
from Mr Paul Mendelssohn of Berlin, the brother of the
composer, the original MS. sketch which I had so
anxiously desired. Judge of my astonishment and delight when on undoing the parcel I found a whole symphony in forty-four sheets. It is one of the most interesting and singular works to be found in all the musical art.
The introduction and a portion of the allegro are fully
scored and completed; but at the 110th bar (the end
of a page) Schubert appears to have grown impatient of
this regular proceeding, and from that point to the end
of the symphony he has made merely memoranda. But
these memoranda are perfectly orderly and intelligible.
Every bar is drawn in through the entire work; the *tempi*
and names of the instruments are fully written at the
beginning of each movement; the very double bars and
flourishes are gravely added at the end of each, and "Fine"
at the conclusion of the whole; and Schubert evidently
regarded the work as completed."

Schubert

Mr J. F. Barnett scored and completed the above sketch, and the work was brought to a hearing at the Crystal Palace on May 5, 1883. Messrs Breitkopf & Haertel, somewhat inexplicably, ignore the existence of this unfinished symphony.

In his last year, and with barely eight months of life before him, Schubert entered upon the composition of the great C-major symphony. It is by common consent regarded as his supreme achievement, and if long and sustained compositions are the highest test of genius, Schubert has here shown himself worthy to rank with Beethoven and Mozart as a master of the greatest musical form. Freshness, fertility, melodic invention, splendid pulsating rhythms—these are some of the obvious characteristics which inform this noble conception. The orchestration is picturesque to a remarkable degree, and while much of it was experimental in its day, almost the whole has emerged scathless from the fiery test of practical performance. Orchestral players under Habeneck in Paris, or Mendelssohn in London, could ill afford their laugh at the use of the wind instruments in this work. Little did they know that it was their own incapacity that prompted it, and that their successors would vie with one another in repairing the fault.

C-major Symphony

The general design of the symphony is in conformity with classic tradition, as we now know it. Had the work been produced in the year of its composition (1828), it would not improbably have been classed with the foremost of Beethoven's purely instrumental compositions.[1]   A

---

[1] The distinction made allows of the "Choral" symphony being left out of the comparison.

C-major Symphony

lovely theme, given in unison by the two horn-players, serves to open the movement.

Andante.

Corni in C. *p*

The introduction is by no means a merely ornamental preface, but as is shown by its reproduction in the form of a peroration at the very climax of interest, it is in reality one of the essential features of the composition. This introductory passage (of 77 bars) grows in interest and excitement until it enters upon the theme of the main movement, as follows :—

Allegro ma non troppo.

(Oboes.)
(Clarinets.)

(Bassoons.)

(Strings and Trumpet.)   (Horns.)

The subject is a stirring one, and gives a right joyous opening to the symphony. It may be observed that the ordinary "bridge" is dispensed with, and the second subject introduced (at bar 134) without more assistance than is derivable from a simple modulation of two chords; —given in the first bar of the following example.

Schubert

This part of the movement becomes highly expressive depending on the wood-wind instruments, which set forth the leading ideas, to an accompaniment of violins and lower strings. It is curious to observe the trend of the modulations. Having passed through E minor, with some rapid changes of key-colour, the codetta is wholly in G—a most eloquent passage. From here the composer takes us back to the usual re-statement of the whole of the movement so far given—excluding of course the introduction. The piece has so far occupied 253 bars. An unusually short development serves as the "free fantasia"—102 bars only, and of this, one-half is derived from the second bar of the introduction

(see bars 304-355). Then follows an orderly recapitulation which could scarcely have pleased the followers of Haydn, though it is clear and systematic in its form. For now the second subject enters in C minor, is re-stated in A minor, and in due course reaches C major again, where most of the previous material falls into place readily

Grand Slow Movement

enough. A grand coda—*Piu-moto*, from bar 570—leads
to the conclusion, which brings in the theme of the introduction already alluded to. This is given *fortissimo*, in
place of the original announcement of the two horns
piano. The score covers no less than 685 bars.

For the second movement we have a lovely *Andante
con moto* in A minor. There is a brief prelude formed
of the accompaniment, and then the theme
enters as follows, announced by the first
oboe, and accompanied by the strings :— *Second
Movement*

The whole of this movement is in Schubert's very best
manner. It bears the stamp of an extraordinary individuality, and is full of beautiful emotion and fine poetic
effect. The alternation of major and minor—a prominent
characteristic of Schubert's later works—is here seen to its
best advantage. It will also be observed how fiery is the
contrast of the first episode (bar 30) and how gentle the
return (at bar 44). A third theme in F major appears at
bar 93. Passing mention may be made of the use of the
brass—especially the trombones—which in Schubert's
hands become as expressive as any flute. Another feature
is the charming passage leading to a recapitulation (148-
160) by means of a most expressive utterance from the

two horns. Many notable alterations occur in the repeat, which, though it passes through A major, leads back again and ends in the tonic minor, as it began.

In the scherzo (*Allegro Vivace* in C major) Schubert handles Beethoven's weapons with all apparent skill and ease. The form alone is eloquent of Beethoven, the inner spirit is wholly Franz's. Gaiety and sadness are most curiously blended throughout this movement. Which predominates, it is hard to say.

Scherzo. (Strings.)

The opening—a part of which is quoted above—is certainly intended humorously; but the trio, expressively played, might easily draw tears. Attention may be directed (in passing) to the connection between the two sections; where the horns, repeating the note E, are gradually strengthened by clarinets and tenor trombone, and finally by bassoons and alto and bass trombone, and the trio enters in A major. But we must pass to the last and perhaps the greatest of the four movements.

Almost startling is the opening theme—as if a loud cry had been uttered. The rhythm, too, which follows immediately afterwards, is disquietening, and prepares the mind for a troubled mood.

High Tragedy

Long-drawn emotional passages succeed each other—
generally delivered by the expressive wind-instruments—
and always accompanied by the hurrying triplets of the
strings. The dramatic feeling intensifies at times to a
pitch of high tragedy. Indeed the music might be a
veritable ride to the abyss (see bars 114-117); but no!
the human will is the controlling power, and no tricks of
Mephistopheles will here pass muster. After a terrific
emphasis of the dominant, and a brief silence (of two
bars only), the second principal subject is ushered in.

Schubert

(Violins and Violas simile.)

This wonderful theme, which seems almost to throb like a great heart in its singular rhythm, and surrounded as it is by a strenuous and never-ceasing undercurrent or nervous energy, dominates the greater part of the movement. And even when the melody of the theme is no longer present, the rhythm is there. As, for example:—

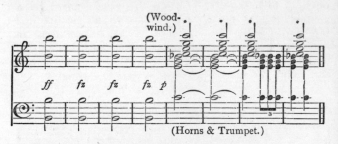

(Woodwind.)

(Horns & Trumpet.)

A notable use to which Schubert put his great theme is seen at bar 202, where the oboes, clarinets and bassoons whisper it forth; the effect of which, after the rough manly strain which preceded it, is much as if the melody had been taken up by the angels, and heard but faintly by muddy-vestured mortals. The first portion of

Colossal Proportions

this *finale* having reached a most glorious climax (bar 334), the tone grows less and less, until one almost has the feeling of standing in some vast cathedral, while the pealing organ gradually fades into silence. It is only for a brief moment, however, for we are hurried back to action, as the whole of this section is repeated.

The "free fantasia" brings with it a large measure of contrast. Delicate song-like passages float upon the broad stream of sound, which never for an instant loses its impetuosity. Even in the quietest moments the rhythm is maintained. A fine point is made of the development of a *pianissimo* into a *fortissimo* (bars 438-472), by means of a rising sequence, which brings in its train a strident utterance of the great second theme (or its main features), from the trombones and horns. Much ingenious development follows, chiefly on a pedal-note (G) which appears in bar 520. This is maintained until the entry upon the "Recapitulation," which, as a veritable stroke of genius, is now commenced in E flat, in place of the original key (C). The material is presented with some grand extensions,[1] and, it may be added, the second subject is given in its orthodox key, that is C. A powerful coda completes the movement, which, in our view, is certainly one of the greatest ever written. Schubert in this work seems to us to have sounded the whole gamut of human passion. It is the whole drama of life summed up in a symphony. Nor are its tragic elements over-

---

[1] The colossal proportions of the finale are well seen from the comparison of its sections ; thus the first part to the double bar occupies 386 bars ; the fantasia takes another 217, and the recapitulation covers 556 more. This makes a grand total of 1159 bars for the last movement only.

Schubert

looked. Those who hear the noble work worthily interpreted, will find little difficulty in agreeing with Beethoven when he exclaimed, "Truly Schubert has the divine fire in him."

The following expression of opinion by one of the most distinguished of European conductors loses nothing of its weight through being rendered with enthusiasm—an enthusiasm born of close intimacy with the work of which he writes :—

Weingart-
ner on
Schubert
"He was the lyric musician κατ᾽ ἐξοχήν. Whatever he wrote, the most serene as well as the most tragic work, seems as it were imbued with that infinitely soft, melodic element, which always lets us perceive his figure as if through tears of gentle emotion. A blissful warmth emanates from his music. Only think of the great Symphony in C major. . . . I cannot conceive how it is that there are still people so ill-humoured as to think this symphony too long, nay, even to ask for cuts to be made in it. I am not of their opinion, and I own that whenever I hear this work well conducted, or when I conduct it myself, I always experience the most happy sensations, and am absolutely intoxicated with music. It produces on me the effect as of flight through a bright ether."[1]

It is difficult perhaps to realise that Schubert never saw the sea; never lent an ear to that wonderful voice which since the foundations of the earth were laid has chanted its ancient ditty, whenever Dame Nature was in the mood to make melody in her heart. I have never yet heard Schubert's beautiful Tone-poem—the B-minor

[1] Felix Weingartner (in the *Contemporary Review* of Feb. 1899).

Unfinished Symphony

Symphony—without being put in mind of the salt-flavoured breeze, the splendid underlying pulsation of its waves, and the freedom and expanse which a wilderness of waters conveys to the mind. It is not for a moment suggested that anything of the kind was in Schubert's mind's-eye, since the emotion which his tone-poem breathes might have been called into being by widely different objects (or causes), or indeed its true source might—nay, probably would—have baffled its human agent to define.

A three-fold subject may be a technical misnomer, but it is the description which best fits the opening subject-matter of this movement. The first section of this three-fold subject (to retain the appellation) is shown in the eight bars quoted above. These have all the significance of an introduction, and surely one of the simplest ever designed. That they are not a mere introductory feature is afterwards proved by the phrase being treated as an important and integral part of the leading theme. The second part of the three-fold theme-material is seen in bars 9-10 announced by all the strings :—

Schubert

pp

Pizz.

It is plainly in the nature of an accompaniment (and a very beautiful one) to a song. But the complete subject does not unfold itself until we reach bar 13, when the oboes and clarinets—in unison—give utterance to the melody which was in waiting :—

Beneath this appears the stringed passage (slightly modified) quoted immediately above. Attention may be directed to the delicate gleam of colour which the horns and bassoons cast on the picture a brief moment later :—

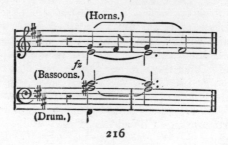

(Horns.)

fz
(Bassoons.)

(Drum.)

Unusual Key

Thought succeeds thought with ever increasing interest and excitement (bar 26), until a powerful climax is wrought (bar 38) and the key of the tonic is reached. Here we meet with a simple little modulation—quite magical in its neatness and beauty—

(Horns and Bassoons.)

which serves to introduce the second subject. So natural is the transition that anyone might hear the movement many times without observing the unusual key to which we have been led—namely, G major, or the first flat key from the tonic :—

(Clar.) *pp*

(Violas.)

(Celli.) *pp*

(C. Bass.) *pizz.*

Here again the accompaniment (bars 42-4) precedes the air ; but being identical with that which accompanies the melody quoted, I do not separate them. The strain (first delivered by the 'cellos) is a haunting one, such as the poet had imaged when he tells us :—

> "This music crept by me upon the waters,
> Allaying both their fury and my passion."

A fuller statement follows, where the upper strings take up the song in place of the mellow-voiced 'cellos. The blank bar (No. 62) suggests a sudden break in the blissful dream ; we are once more face to face with stern realities.[1]

This second theme readily lends itself to imitation and other devices—such as the employment of sections of the main melody for the purposes of episode, etc.—and of these Schubert is not slow to avail himself. Indeed throughout the whole work he seems to be unusually economical of his material, and little or nothing is introduced which does not afterwards unfold many further beauties. We may pass to the codetta, formed of a portion of the second subject, and employed in imitation, as the illustration of our remark. The modulation which induces the repeat (bars 104-110) is a model of directness ; nor is it overlooked in the development.

The free fantasia is truly wonderful. One may hear such mystic sounds in some desolate place where the tide breaks complainingly over the low-lying rocks. It is as a song of forgotten ages ; it touches on the mystery of life and death, the yearning of man, the futility of despair. The mood changes, and Hope (with its trumpet-call) regains its hold upon us.

[1] A slight miscalculation in Schubert's score may be noticed in bars 63-6, where the wood-wind fail to sufficiently assert their phrases. which are the real continuation of the melody in augmentation.

Melody from Fairyland

The quotation shows how important the first section of the first principal subject has now become. Throughout this part of the work the texture is rich in device, and even from a mere technical point of view is of exceedingly fine workmanship. A noteworthy effect is the gradual repression of feeling until a calmer mind is reached (see bar 118). Observe also the use made of bars 20 and 21, which in an extended form reappear, to lead in the recapitulation (113-118).

The course of the recapitulation is marked by freshly-discovered beauties which are disclosed by a treatment both rich and varied. D major is the chosen key for the reassertion of the second subject (158), which occurs as naturally in this key as its announcement formerly did in another no less unusual. From D to B is but a short step, and at bar 212 the coda begins (in the latter key). Here we have a grand extension of the material which formerly served as a codetta (bar 94). As we near the end we are again reminded of the music of many waters —"the murmurs and scents of the infinite sea"—and the last few chords come like the strokes of a hammer, wielded by some invisible hand—and to each stroke a word— but such a word as no *mortal* ear may discover.

Melody such as is here must have come from fairyland,

Schubert

or from some enchanted country which composers would fain visit could they bring away such strains. There seems

Andante of the Unfinished Symphony

scarce any analogy for the inspiration of this movement; we may look in vain for anything at all resembling it in the works of Mozart or Beethoven. The strange blending of peace and passion — and the almost religious atmosphere of the whole, find a counterpart in the well-known passage in the "Merchant of Venice":—

> " How sweet the moonlight sleeps upon this bank !
> Here will we sit and let the sounds of music
> Creep in our ears ; soft stillness and the night
> Become the touches of sweet harmony.
> See, Jessica, how all the floor of heaven
> Is thick inlaid with patines of bright gold ;
> There's not the smallest orb which thou behold'st
> But in his motion like an angel sings,
> Still quiring to the young-eyed cherubins ;
> Such harmony is in immortal souls ;
> But whilst this muddy vesture of decay
> Doth grossly close us in, we cannot hear it."

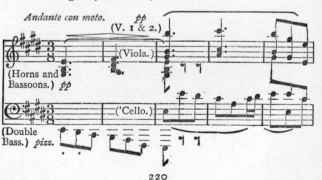

Bridge of Single Sounds

Extremely delicate contrasts of horns and bassoons (with a pizzicato bass), and violins, violas and 'cellos, mark the opening of this delicious movement. A break from this quiet vein occurs at bar 33, where the trombones and trumpets utter a broad theme in strong contrast to the stringed octaves :—

Repeated in sequential steps, the passage acquires considerable force and character; then it "dwindles and blends like a peace out of pain," and flutes, clarinets and bassoons take up the original tender air (see bar 45). The device of introducing a new theme from sustained single sounds (which keep the ear in an expectant attitude) is here employed with remarkable success (60-3) :—

The second principal theme (see above) thus makes its appearance in the relative minor (C sharp minor). Who could believe that this plaintive melody—faintly breathed by clarinet, oboe or flute—should shortly appear clad in thunder—pealed forth by the full orchestra? (bar 96). A new and delightful feature of the continuation of the movement is the duet between 'cellos and basses on the one part and the first and second violins on the other (bar 113 and forwards). The return from C to E (bars 134-142) is a most poetic device, with oboe, flute, horn and clarinet gently calling to one another, while the strings slowly glide to the appointed key (E major). In the repetition, much of the material is untouched; the second theme, however, now appears in A minor, in place of C sharp minor. An especially beautiful and prolonged coda closes the movement.

In concluding these remarks it may be questioned whether the impression conveyed by the title—"Unfinished"—is realised to any extent by the hearer of this symphony. The unity of the four-movement type of symphony (or sonata) is probably an illusion of habit, which works like Beethoven's Sonata in E minor (op. 90) or that in F sharp (op. 78)—another two-movement sonata—were intended to illustrate.

Portrait of Schubert

(from a lithograph made in 1846 by J. Kriehuber)

Final Supplement

In their new critical and complete edition of Schubert's works, Messrs Breitkopf & Haertel publish a large number of pieces which have not before seen print. *Breitkopf & Haertel's Final Supplement* Among the widely miscellaneous assortment offered, some numbers have the mere interest of curiosity, others are incomplete—breaking off quite suddenly—while a smaller number are available for purposes of performance or practice. For example, let us take the publishers' Series XXI.—a supplement—containing piano-pieces, a few early scores and some late choral music. With the incomplete movements we are scarcely concerned, unless it be to express regret that the setting of Goethe's " Gesang der Geister über den Wassern " (for four male voices and piano)— which promised such great things—was not carried to completion.[1] First to catch the eye is a Concertstück (or concerto, as it is sometimes called) for violin, with an accompaniment for a small orchestra, comprising trumpets, drums and strings, written in 1816. There is a short introduction (*Adagio*), followed by a bright *Allegro* in D major, reminiscent, it is true, of Haydn. The orchestral accompaniments are not the least interesting feature of a work which, though it cannot add to Schubert's great reputation, might nevertheless be usefully added to the repertory of the violin-player. A short string-trio in B flat (in four brief movements), for violin, viola and 'cello, will prove an attraction to performers who are in want of a fresh, easy work. The trio, which is modelled on Mozart, is dated Sept. 1817, and contains many an individual touch which none but Schubert would have contrived. Two excellent pianoforte-duets are given in the same

[1] Three finished versions are published (see op. 167, etc.).

volume—a characteristic overture in G, and Schubert's own arrangement of the overture to *Fierrabras* — a splendid composition of its class.

The Sonata in D flat, though unfortunately short of a few bars towards the end of the last movement, is of almost unique interest, in that it gives us an example of a whole sonata planned in one key, and finally published in another. For this D-flat sonata is none other but that which appears in the printed editions as op. 122 in the key of E flat. In all probability, Schubert transposed it to the latter key to please the publishers with its easier appearance—a course often adopted with the published songs—for there can be no doubt that the sonata sounds better in *D flat*.

A "Tantum ergo" for chorus and orchestra (dated 1828) cannot but be of interest, on account of its composition occurring in Schubert's last year. The same remark applies to an Offertorium—"Intende voci orationis meae"—which is not only of 1828, but bears the addition of the month—namely, October—which shows that the work was among the very latest pieces Schubert wrote. It is a characteristic work, full of effect, and in every way suited for performance in the service of the Church, for which it was intended. The score is somewhat unusual, and contains parts for the following instruments and voices :— Oboe solo, two clarinets, two bassoons, two horns, three trombones, the usual string-parts, solo tenor, and mixed chorus.

No attempt has been made at completeness in the foregoing pages, for a glance at the list of Schubert's compositions (Appendix " B ") will show that this is beyond the limits of a volume such as the present. So rich is the legacy of beautiful work, that one may be excused hesitation in pointing to the masterpieces, where these are so plentiful. Turn where we may—to symphony or sonata, to opera or oratorio, or to the chamber music, with its marvellous array of songs—at each step we are greeted by some lovely treasure which one is inclined to praise as of highest excellence, until by looking further another engrossing work meets our glance, and we are in doubt as to which should be most valued. It is Schubert's proud boast—a posthumous one, it is true, for pride held no place in his life, that he has enriched every department of music with a masterpiece.

Time, that compresses most men's work with rigorous hand, will deal gently with much of the master's best and most perfect utterances, which will descend on the stream of the years fresh and undefiled, a pure legacy to Schubert's heirs—those who love music throughout the wide world.

On Jan. 31, 1897, the birth-centenary of Schubert was celebrated at Vienna by a series of performances extending over a week. At the Imperial opera-house, performances were given of *Der häusliche Krieg* and the Singspiel *Die vierjährige Posten*. The first named work had been produced in 1871. The *Rosamunde* overture, played at the commencement, made an excellent impression. The *Posten* had been reinforced by a few numbers from other of Schubert's dramatic works. It also won much applause. At the Lichtenthal church—once the scene of Franz's earliest triumph in Church music—the Mass in F was given by the Schubertbund and the ladies' choir. At the first grand concert, Richter directed performances of the "Unfinished" Symphony, the

Centenary Celebrations

Appendix A

BIBLIOGRAPHY

THE Schubert bibliography is neither attractive nor voluminous, and compares very unfavourably with that of Beethoven. The materials are slight, and even of these, the best fail to carry that weight which a thoroughly sound historical narrative must demand. Few letters are preserved—scarcely more than thirty-two, and though an editor would be more than mortal if he were not humbly thankful that Schubert's correspondence did not equal that of his brother in art—Tschaikowsky, whose 4112 letters should surely create a sort of corresponding record—even he could wish for more than a meagre thirty-two. Schubert's diary deserved a better fate than that allotted it. It has already been related how a mercenary dealer sold it piece-meal. A portion of the few remaining leaves we have included in our pages. Schubert's manner of life was too simple and retired to attract much attention. It seems only too likely that few, if any, of his friends knew what a great man he was. Vogl could not have known it, or he would not have laid a finger on his songs, whereas he altered many of them ; Mayrhofer speaks of his own poems as a source of inspiration, and does not seem to have realised how little these mattered in comparison with the settings, which will hand them down to all posterity. Bauernfeld appears to have been a sponge. Two men there are, however, who stand out as made of the stuff that goes to make a friend—namely, Spaun and Schober. Both were practical men, and each as far as ever he was able helped the impractical Schubert : Spaun from his earliest years ; Schober with continuous and affec-

tionate regard.   Schubert had a firm friend in his brother
Ferdinand, whose four short essays call for first notice.

Ferdinand Schubert's Essays.   These appeared in Nos. 33-36
(April 23-May 3, 1839) of the *Neue Zeitschrift für Musik*, and
supply many useful and authentic details of the musician's life.
Ferdinand's knowledge of his brother's career was chiefly
valuable through its casting a light on his home and school
life, his industrious art-achievements, and his general success
in the music world.   It scarcely touches the social side of his
relations with men and things.   Ferdinand was the custodian
of his brother's MSS., and his list of the compositions, though
not complete, was invaluable to those who first laboured in the
same field.

Mayrhofer's " Erinnerungen," which appeared in Feb. 23,
1829, as a contribution to the *Neues Archiv für Geschichte,
Literatur und Kunst* (Vienna), is valuable because the writer
had lived with Schubert for a couple of years, and was always
more or less in touch with him.

Bauernfeld's several essays supply useful information upon
points untouched by the other writers.   Bauernfeld, Schwindt
and Schubert lived together in common (about the period
1826), and one of the essays referred to (that in the Vienna
Presse of April 17, 1869) serves well to display the unfortunate
results to Schubert of such Utopian schemes.

Ueber Franz Schubert. Bauernfeld, *Wiener Zeitschrift*,
June 9-13, 1829.

Articles, quoting 6 letters, etc. Bauernfeld, *Freie Presse*
(Vienna), April 17-21, 1869.

The articles were reprinted in the Leipsic *Signale* in Nov.
15-28, 1869, and in Bauernfeld's " Gesammelte Schriften," vol.
xii., Vienna, 1873.

Schindler's contributions to Schubert's bibliography are as
follows :—

Bäuerle's Wiener Theaterzeitung (an article in the number
for May 3, 1831).

This is valuable, because the writer describes what he
actually witnessed.

Niederrheinischer Musikzeitung (for 1857) also contains
articles by Schindler, bearing on the subject.

Appendix A

Four Letters, Two Poems and a Dream were printed by Robert Schumann in his *Neue Zeitschrift für Musik*, Feb. 1-5, 1839.

It may be added that all the biographies of Beethoven contain passing references to Schubert—whose personal contact with the great master was, however, but slight.

The following list further illustrates the sources whence information concerning Schubert may be seen in its original form :—

Diary. Sofie Müller, Vienna, 1832.

Unvergessenes. Frau von Chézy, Leipsic, 1858.

Erinnerungen. W. von Chézy, Schaffhausen, 1863.

Künstlerleben. Ferdinand Hiller, Cologne, 1880. This contains a paper entitled "Vienna fifty-two years ago," which describes the visit Hiller paid to Beethoven and Schubert in 1827, when he was travelling in company with his master—Hummel.

F. Schubert, sa Vie, etc. H. Barbedette, Paris, 1866.

Articles on Schubert scattered in the writings of La Mara (Marie Lipsius), Otto Gumprecht, etc.

Biographisches Lexicon. Wurzbach (part xxxii. pp. 30-110). Vienna, 1876.

Actenmässige Darstellung der Ausgrabung und Wiederbeisetzung der irdischen Reste von Beethoven und Schubert. Vienna, 1863.

Vom Wiener Männergesangverein. Festschrift zur Enthüllung des Schubert Denkmales am 15 Mai, 1872.

The above contains a sketch of Schubert's life, an account of the unveiling of the statue in the Stadt Park, and much information in brief compass.

Kreissle von Hellborn, Heinrich (Doctor Juris), may be regarded as Schubert's principal biographer, as indeed he was the first. Kreissle was born in 1803, and in course of time became "Imperial finance secretary" at Vienna, and a director of the Gesellschaft der Musikfreunde. His first attempt at a Schubert biography was in the form of a small octavo, printed in 1861, at Vienna, under the title, "F. Schubert, eine biografische Skizze von Heinrich von Kreissle," which prepared the way for his larger work on the same subject. The

Schubert

latter was issued by Gerold of Vienna, in octavo, 1865. Both these works form the basis from which more modern writers build up their narrative. They are distinct, the former containing some material which does not re-appear in the larger volume. In spite of this, the later volume must be taken as superseding the earlier. It is more than three times as long and is naturally a more mature presentment of the subject. Following the custom of German biographers, Kreissle gives pretty full accounts of all the characters met with in the course of his story. There is perhaps more excuse for this than usual, for the materials are unusually slight which directly concern the principal character. The biographer must in such cases lay hold upon and gather up every straw which may afterwards prove of use when he comes to weave his narrative. This is what Kreissle has done, and whatever the reader may think of it, there is no question but that future biographers will be heartily obliged. The following passage seems to explain Kreissle's point of view :—" None can deny that, if a number of letters, diaries and other memoranda, ranging over a long period of the author's life, can be connected together as a whole, such things are admirably adapted to widen and intensify our knowledge of the character and life of the writer in question. . . . But very few of Schubert's letters have up to this time become known. It may be because he was not fond of letter-writing (of this, however, no proof is forthcoming) ; or, again, his letters may have been lost or kept back, from a false shame and aversion to their being seen by other eyes than those for whom they were originally intended. . . . Whether Franz kept memoranda ranging over a long period, I have not been able to discover. Neither these short notices nor the letters are calculated by the intrinsic worth of their contents to arrest in any great degree the interest of the reader ; for Schubert was never wont to wear his heart upon his sleeve, even for the inspection of his most trusted friends. Still, slender as the resources are which illustrate but meagrely the existence of Schubert, the biographer must be permitted to avail himself of every help he can lay hold on, be it seemingly never so trivial, and give the originals without curtailing a syllable, for

Appendix A

these authentic records invariably throw streaks of light on the face of the individual whose portrait we are painting, let alone the thought that small episodes of this kind break in agreeably on the monotonous process of reckoning Schubert's compositions—a feature which will form the chief element in the history of the composer's career."

So keeping all this in view, Kreissle puts together a most interesting study, built up from slender grounds, but casting a steady light on the composer and his friends. True, the letters from the music-publishers are too much in evidence; but they at least serve to show why Schubert remained in comparative want during his last years. A list of the composer's works fittingly closes this biography. The English translation is now to be considered.

Arthur Duke Coleridge, M.A., translated (in 1868) Kreissle's "Life of Schubert," which was issued in two octavo volumes by Longmans, in 1869, with a dedication to Madame Jenny Lind Goldschmidt. As the work is now out of print, it may be noticed here, apart from the original just dealt with. "We are now"—says the translator, under date 1868—"beginning to realise the importance of his (Schubert's) music; and if (as many believe) a great future be in store for Schubert in this country, let us acknowledge our obligations to the joint exertions of my friend Mr George Grove, and that admirable musician Mr Manns, the conductor of the Crystal Palace Concerts. Mr Charles Halle's efforts have also powerfully aided the cause of Schubert's popularity; and Mr Arthur Chappell, the director of the Monday Popular Concerts, has been indefatigable in bringing forward his Quartets, Quintets, Octet, and others of his splendid chamber compositions." Mr Coleridge completed the chief part of his work without knowing of Wilberforce's epitomised translation. A feature of the book, which is an addition to the work as drawn from Kreissle, will be found in the Appendix "by George Grove, Esq." This part of the book contains a useful thematic catalogue of Schubert's Nine Symphonies. The nine are made up by including the sketch (afterwards finished by J. F. Barnett) which came into Grove's possession through Mr Paul Mendelssohn.

Schubert

I quote one breezy paragraph, which occurs on the final page :
—" Good God, it makes one's blood boil to think of so fine
and rare a genius, one of the ten or twelve topmost men in
the world, in want of even the common necessaries of life.
Failure, disappointment, depreciation, and suchlike shocks
and wounds of the heart and soul, these are the necessary
accompaniments of a fine intellect and a sensitive heart ; but
to want the ordinary comforts and amenities of life, *to want
bread*, it is too dreadful to think of. And yet such troubles
have been the lot of all the great men from David downwards ;
only Schubert's was peculiarly hard, for he had all the
struggles of youth and none of the repose of age."

Sir George Grove's article " Schubert" in his " Dictionary
of Music and Musicians" (vol. iii. p. 319) is, as would be expected from so able a writer, a masterly account of the life
and works of the composer. Sir George has always the true
instinct of a biographer, and though he is much handicapped
by the limits imposed by a " dictionary," he has produced an
excellent record of the life and works of Schubert. Grove had
the inestimable advantage of being early on the scene. The
years 1866-7 saw him at Vienna, busy collecting material which
afterwards became public property. He had to face all the
difficulties of a pioneer. The patient and accurate research
which he brought to bear on the subjects alike of Beethoven
and Schubert, no less than the graphic pen which he had at
ready command, combine to place these two articles first, in
point of value, of the Dictionary. Nevertheless Grove had a
weakness. He was not enough of a musician to be sure of
his ground when tackling a technical point. For example,
Grove (referring to Schubert) does not hesitate to set down
such a statement as this : " His vocal fugues are notoriously
weak, and the symphonies rarely show those piquant fugatos
which are so delightful in Beethoven and Mendelssohn." In
another place we read : "counterpoint he was deficient in, but
the power of writing whatever he wanted he had absolutely
at his fingers' ends." The last-quoted sentence, though founded
on a misconception, is, in part, perfectly true. Schubert certainly had the "power of writing whatever he wanted," but
just as certainly was he *not* deficient in counterpoint. I have

234

Appendix A

not space to go into the matter at length, but it is worth pointing out that no quartet-writer, to be successful, can be deficient in counterpoint. The fugues of Schubert are not his best work. The fugue form probably had few attractions for him. Those he has left are (*mirabile dictu*) not so much short of science as of inspiration. Take, for example, the fugue for piano-duet (op. 152), written in Schubert's last year—about the period he thought of taking some contrapuntal lessons from Sechter, as the tradition is—an excellent little piece for players of moderate ability, which is happily now available in Breitkopf's edition (price 1 mark). Here, the fugue-subject is somewhat commonplace, but the counterpoint is skilful enough. Modulation (as Grove truly says, always a strong feature with Schubert) makes its appearance towards the end, with marked effect. But each repetition of the subject only emphasises its monotony. I think we are right in asserting Schubert did not like the fugue as a form of expression for his own utterances. Counterpoint is a very different thing. No instrumental work can exist without it, though most people have in mind the counterpoint of the schools, the counterpoint of choral-writing, or the counterpoint of Cherubini, Fux and the rest. What is counterpoint? There are two answers. One is that it is everything else but the melody. The other answer is that it *is* melody. Both methods were tried by Schubert. His little fugue cited comes in the first category; the greater part of his music comes under the second. The truth is that Schubert was one of the greatest contrapuntists who ever lived. He could inspire his counterpoint, as old John Sebastian knew so well how to do. It is unnecessary to pursue the subject of Schubert's counterpoint further, though the opinion contested is mischievous. There is such a healthy, manly tone in Sir George Grove's estimate of Schubert, that one could wish to be able always to agree with him. Whether Grove knew counterpoint or not when he saw it, he undoubtedly recognised a *man* as soon as anyone, and his two articles on Beethoven and Schubert—the conjunction is a happy one—have served and will continue to help the English-speaking world to a better and nobler view of the personality of these two extraordinary beings. Schubert would seem to have been especially belittled by his eccentrici-

Schubert

ties in preferring simple and even common surroundings. The simple and common things of life have more poetry in them than can have the imagined superior. The gold of the dandelion is finer than the finest burnished reality. It touches on a truer thought—beauty for its own sake, while the reality has to be handled carefully. "Auri sacra fames" (says the poet of old), "quid non mortalia pectora cogis"; and although all temptation is usually out of the poet's way, he is, none the less, speaking the profoundest sense. Men like Schubert tried to live a simple poetic life. The realities to such people are found in the ideas of simplicity and naturalness. Class distinction doesn't exist for them, and they try (usually with hopeless results) to fulfil an unfettered destiny which the force of their own genius would seek to impose. Beethoven was much of Schubert's mind, but his own powerful character prevented him from ever scorning the aids to independence. A patron was a necessary evil; he commanded one. A pension was an unavoidable necessity; he accepted it. Poor Franz Schubert was fighting all his life, with the weapons of heaven's own forging, for a victory over difficulties which a plough or a spade sometimes achieves. Songs of his, sold for tenpence apiece, were worth a king's ransom. Grove has not neglected this side of the picture, and all Schubert-lovers will be indebted to him, as indeed is the composer's own memory. Sir George's tribute is well summed up in his remark, "There never was one like him, and there never will be another."

Franz Schubert—a musical Biography by Edward Wilberforce (W. H. Allen & Co., 1866)—is an eminently readable little book. Founded, as the author tells us, upon Kreissle's larger work, it gives a real glimpse of the composer and his habits. Wilberforce had the advantages and disadvantages of being early on the scene. Kreissle had published his large "Life" in 1865, while the smaller one had already appeared in 1861. The translation of Mr Duke Coleridge was not printed until 1869. Wilberforce brings a sympathetic pen to deal with his subject, but he would seem to be occasionally without critical perception of much value. Thus we read on page 72 (speaking of the "Rossini-fever" of 1823), that "the effect it had on Beethoven himself is much to be regretted; he refused to see Rossini, called him a scene-painter, and admitted grudgingly that he would have been a good composer if his master had flogged him more." Then occurs the passage which, in our view, is absurd, thus : "Schubert, however, had even more cause to complain. With a facility second only to Rossini's (as he had shown by the composition of his overtures in the Italian style), a power of melody, hardly second to him, and a natural turn for the opera, he found himself entirely excluded." We have, of course, had opportunities since 1866 for a more correct view of the relative importance of Schubert and Rossini, so that the facility "only second to Rossini's" and "a power of melody hardly second to him" will merely make a modern musician smile. Without agreeing with those who view Rossini as a charlatan, one can admire the exquisite ridicule of his French biographer, who exclaimed, "Non, vous n'avez pas le feu céleste. You bargain for asparagus." Not the least interesting feature of Wilberforce's book is the essay on "Musical Biography" which is given in an appendix. It is full of sound sense.

Franz Schubert. Reissmann, Berlin, 1873. This excellent little book has fallen out of print, like several other of the books mentioned in our list. Reissmann's selection of examples was unusually attractive, and included five pieces then printed for the first time, and a facsimile page. The illustrations give twelve pages of the Quintet-Overture, and among other things that charming little piece for pianoforte for performance during the recitation of Pratobevera's poem "Die Falke."

The Great Tone Poets, by Frederick J. Crowest (Bentley, 1874), includes a chapter on Franz Schubert.

Life of Schubert (a sketch comprising 100 pp. German text), by A. Niggli, 1880, Breitkopf & Haertel, is well worth reading.

Schubert, by H. F. Frost (edited by Francis Hueffer in the "Great Musicians" series, Sampson Low, 1881), like the work above-mentioned, is a marvel of completeness, seeing only 120 pp. are offered.

Franz Schubert, a sketch by Ernst Pauer, is prefixed to Messrs Augener's edition of Schubert's Pianoforte Sonatas. The story is well told and well illustrated.

Schubert

Beiträge, Dr Max Friedländer, Berlin, 1883, contains much admirable material.

Naumann's " History of Music " (Cassell, 1886) includes a short paper on Schubert, and three *facsimiles*.

The Musical Times of 1886 (Jan. to Sept.) contains a short and well-written account of the master's career.

The Art-Ballad, by Albert B. Bach (W. Blackwood, 1890), gives an interesting study of Schubert and Löwe, a clever comparison, which helps towards a better understanding of each.

Makers of Music, by Mr A. Farquharson Sharp (W. Reeves, 1901), contains a careful and critical estimate of Schubert's life and work.

Old Scores and New Readings, by John F. Runciman (Unicorn Press, London, 1901), proves clearly enough that the writer had unbounded admiration for his Schubert.

Article in **Encyclopædia Britannica**, vol. xxi. p. 458.

Article in **Chambers's Encyclopædia**, by Mr Harry Whitehead.

Schubert's Masses. E. Prout, *Musical Record*, 1871, and *Concordia*, 1875. An important series of critical articles by this distinguished musician and writer. Schubert's instrumentation, it may be added, is commented upon in the same writer's " Instrumentation " primer (Novello) and " The Orchestra " (Augener). Authoritative information on such matters is the more necessary when writers like Berlioz pass over Schubert's use of the orchestra.

The Musical Record of Feb. 1, 1897, contains an excellent article on Franz Schubert.

The Musical Times contains:—

> Schubertiana, Aug. 1893.
> Franz Schubert, Jan. 1897.
> Schubert's Music in England, Feb. 1897.
> Schubert and British Poets, Oct. 1901.
> Schubert's 23rd Psalm, Sept. 1901 (with a facsimile page).

The Oxford History of Music. Vol. v. The Viennese Period. By W. H. Hadow. 1904.

Appendix B

LIST OF SCHUBERT'S WORKS

FOUNDED UPON BREITKOPF & HAERTEL'S COMPLETE EDITION, AND COMPARED WITH NOTTEBOHM'S THEMATIC CATALOGUE

OPUS NO.	COMPOSITION	INSTRUMENTS, ETC.	KEY	DATE
1	Song ("Erlkönig")	Tenor and pianoforte	G minor	1815
2	Spinning Song	Soprano and pianoforte	D minor	October 19, 1814
3	4 Songs	Tenor and pianoforte	Various	1814-16
4	3 Songs (including "The Wanderer")			1815-20
5	5 Songs	Tenor and pianoforte	Various	1815-16
6	2 Songs and a duet ("Antigone")		Various	1816-17
7	3 Songs	Soprano and pianoforte		1817
8	4 Songs	Tenor and pianoforte		1817-20
9	Erster Walzer	Pianoforte solo, also as duets		Published 1822
10	Variations	Pianoforte duet	E minor	1822

Schubert

Opus No.	Composition	Instruments, etc.	Key	Date
11	3 Quartets	Male voices and pianoforte		1819 (?)
12	3 Songs ("Wilhelm Meister")	Tenor and pianoforte	A minor	1815-16
13	3 Songs	Tenor and baritone and pianoforte		1817
14	2 Songs ("Suleika," etc.)	Mezzo and pianoforte	B minor and A♭	1821
15	Fantasia	Pianoforte solo	C major	February 1823
16	2 Quartets	Male voices and pianoforte		
17	4 Quartets ("Jünglingswonne," etc.)			Published 1823
18	Waltzes, etc.	Pianoforte solo		1820-3
19	3 Songs	Bass and pianoforte		1815-1817
20	3 Songs	Tenor and pianoforte		1817-1821
21	3 Songs	Bass and pianoforte	E♭ and D minor	1817
22	2 Songs	Baritone and pianoforte		1823
23	4 Songs	Tenor and baritone		1822
24	2 Songs	Baritone and tenor		1817
25	20 Songs ("Die schöne Müllerin")	Tenor and pianoforte		1823
26	*Rosamunde* (Drama in four acts)	Voices and orchestra		1823
27	3 Marches	Pianoforte duet	B minor, C and D	

28	Der Gondelfahrer	Male quartet and pianoforte		1824
29	Quartet	Strings	A minor	1824
30	Sonata	Pianoforte duet	B♭	May 1824
31	Song ("Suleika" II.)	Mezzo	B♭	1821
32	Song ("Forelle") (Breitkopf prints four copies)	Tenor and pianoforte	D♭	1817
33	Dances and Eccossaises	Pianoforte		1824
34	Overture	Pianoforte duet	F	1824 (?)
35	Variations	Pianoforte	A♭	1824
36	2 Songs	Tenor and mezzo		1819-20
37	2 Songs	Mezzo and tenor		1817-1823
38	Ballad ("Der Liedler")	Soprano and pianoforte	A minor and A♭	July 1815
39	Song ("Sehnsucht")	Bass and pianoforte	B minor and E	1819 (?)
40	6 Marches	Pianoforte duet		
41	Song ("Einsame")	Mezzo	G	1825
42	Sonata	Pianoforte	A minor	1825
43	2 Songs	Mezzo		1825
44	Song	Tenor and pianoforte	E♭	1816-17
45	Tantum Ergo ("Totus in corde")	4 voices and orchestra	C major	1822
46	Offertorium (I.)			
47	Offertorium (II.) ("Salve Regina")			
48	Mass	Soli, chorus and orchestra	C	1818
49	Galop and Eccossaises	Pianoforte solo		
50	Valses sentimentales	Pianoforte solo	Various	January 1826 (?)
51	3 Marches	Pianoforte duet		

Q

Opus No.	Composition	Instruments, etc.	Key	Date
52	7 Songs ("Lady of the Lake")			1825
53	Sonata	Pianoforte solo	D major	1825
54	Divertissement à l'Hongroise	Pianoforte duet	G minor	1824
55	Funeral March (Emperor of Russia)	Pianoforte duet		December 1825
56	3 Songs	Tenor and pianoforte		1822
57	3 Songs	Tenor and pianoforte		1815
58	3 Songs	Tenor and pianoforte		1814-16
59	4 Songs	Mezzo and pianoforte		1822-3
60	2 Songs	Bass and pianoforte	B minor and A	1823
61	6 Polonaises	Pianoforte duet		
62	4 Songs ("Wilhelm Meister")	Mezzo and pianoforte		1816-26
63	Divertissement†	Pianoforte duet	E minor	
64	3 Quartets	Male voices (unaccompanied)		1816-22
65	3 Songs	Baritone and pianoforte		
66	Heroic March (for ceremony of anointing Nicholas I.)	Pianoforte duet	A minor	1826
67	Eccossais	Pianoforte solo		
68	Song ("Wachtelschlag")	Mezzo and pianoforte	A	1822

Appendix B

No.	Title	Scoring	Key	Date
69	Alfonso und Estrella (Opera 3 acts)	Soli, chorus and orchestra		1821-2
70	Rondo	Violin and pianoforte	B minor	1826
71	Song ("Drang in die Ferne")	Tenor and pianoforte	A minor	1823
72	Song ("Auf dem Wasser")	Baritone and pianoforte	A♭	1823
73	Song ("Rose")	Mezzo and pianoforte	C minor	1822
74	Trio	Male voices		
75	4 Polonaises	Pianoforte duet		1823
76	Fierrabras (Opera 3 acts)	Soli, chorus and orchestra		
77	12 Valses nobles	Pianoforte solo		Published January 1827
78	Sonata	Pianoforte solo	G major	October 1826
79	2 Songs	Tenor and pianoforte		1825
80	3 Songs	Baritone, tenor and Mezzo		1826
81	2 Songs ("Alinde"; "An die Laute")	Tenor and pianoforte		1816
82	Variations (theme by Hérold)	Pianoforte duet	G major	February 1827
	Introduction and Variations	Pianoforte	B♭	Published December 1827
83	3 Songs (Metastasio's words)	Baritone and pianoforte		1827
84	Air varied (French theme)	Pianoforte duet	B minor	
	Rondo brillante	Pianoforte duet	E minor	
85	2 Songs (Annot Lyle; Norma)	Alto and pianoforte		1827

Opus No.	Composition	Instruments, etc.	Key	Date
86	Song ("Richard Löwenherz")	High baritone	B minor	March 1826
87	3 Songs			Written between 1812-21
88	4 Songs	Tenor and mezzo		1817-26
89	24 Songs ("Winterreise")	Tenor and pianoforte		1827
90	4 Impromptus	Pianoforte solo		1828
91	Grätz Waltzes	Pianoforte solo		1827
92	3 Songs	Tenor and bass		1815-22
93	2 Songs	Tenor and pianoforte		1825
94	Moments Musicals	Pianoforte solo		Published 1828
95	4 Songs	Mezzo and pianoforte		1826
96	4 Songs ("Die Sterne" etc.)	Tenor and baritone		1828
97	Song ("Glaube")	Mezzo	E♭	1824
98	3 Songs	Tenor and Pianoforte	B♭	1816-17
99	Trio	Pianoforte, violin and 'cello		October 1827
100	Trio	Pianoforte, violin and 'cello	E♭	November 1827
101	Song (Cibber's "Blind Boy")	Soprano	B♭	1825
102	Quintet	Male voices		
103	Fantasia	Pianoforte duet	F minor	

No.	Title	Instrumentation	Key	Date
104	Trio ("Der Hochzeitsbraten")	Soprano, tenor, bass and pianoforte		1827
105	Vocal Quartet and 3 Songs			1826-8
106	4 Songs ("Who is Sylvia," etc.)	Tenor and pianoforte		1826-7
107	Rondo	Pianoforte duet	A	July 1828
108	3 Songs	Mezzo and tenor		1815-26
109	3 Songs	Alto, bass and mezzo and pianoforte		1815-16
110	Song ("Kampf")	Bass and pianoforte	D minor	November 1817
111	3 Songs	Tenor, mezzo, alto and pianoforte		1815-16
112	3 Choral pieces	Mixed voices and pianoforte accompaniment		1815
113	Antiphons	4 voices unaccompanied		1819
114	Quintet	Pianoforte and strings	A major	1815-27
115	3 Songs	Tenor and pianoforte		February 27, 1815
116	Song ("Erwartung")	Tenor and pianoforte	B♭	February 1815
117	Song ("Sänger")	Tenor	D major	1815
118	6 Songs			
119	Song ("Auf dem Strom")	Tenor (with horn obb.)	E major	March 1828
120	Sonata	Pianoforte solo	A major	1825
121	2 Characteristic Marches	Pianoforte duet		
122	Sonata	Pianoforte solo	E♭ (another version in D♭ —incomplete)	1817
123	Song ("Viola")	Tenor	A♭	March 1823
124	2 Songs (Florio and Delphine)	Tenor and pianoforte		September 1825

Opus No.	Composition	Instruments, etc.	Key	Date
125	2 Quartets	Strings	E♭ and E	
126	Song ("Ein Fräulein")	Tenor and pianoforte	Begins G minor, ends E minor	
127	20 Waltzes	Pianoforte solo		September 1816
128	Cantata (for J. Spendou)	Soli, chorus and orchestra		October 1827
129	Song (with Clarinet obb.)	Soprano and pianoforte	B♭	
130	Song (Echo)	Tenor	B♭	1826
131	3 Songs			1812-15
132	23rd Psalm	Female voices and pianoforte (also for male voices)		1828
133	Chorus ("Gott in der Natur")	Female voices and pianoforte		August 1822
134	Nachthelle	Tenor solo, chorus and pianoforte		1826
135	Ständchen (Grillparzer's words)	Alto solo, chorus and pianoforte (also for female voices)		1827
136	Miriam's Song (Oratorio)	Solo, chorus and pianoforte		March 1828
137	3 Sonatas	Violin and pianoforte	D, A minor and G minor	December 1816
138	Rondo	Pianoforte duet	D major	

Appendix B

139	2 Quartets	Male voices and pianoforte		1824 and 1827
140	Sonata	Pianoforte duet (for orchestra, arranged by Joachim)	C major	1824
141	Mass	Solo, chorus and orchestra	B♭	1815
142	4 Impromptus	Pianoforte		December 1827
143	Sonata	Pianoforte	A minor	February 1823
144	Allegro ("Lebensstürme")	Pianoforte duet	A minor	May 1828
145	Adagio and Rondo	Pianoforte solo		1817
146	Quartet	Mixed voices and pianoforte	E♭	
147	Sonata	Pianoforte solo	B major	August 1817
148	Nocturne	Pianoforte, violin and 'cello	E♭	
149	Salve Regina	4 Voices		
150	Graduale (Benedictus)	Chorus and orchestra		
151	Schlachtlied	8 Male voices (also a version with pianoforte accompaniment)		
152	Fugue	Pianoforte duet	E minor	1828
153	Offertorium(Salve Regina)	Solo, chorus and orchestra		January 1824
154	Hymn to the Holy Ghost	Soli and male chorus		March 1826
155	Trinklied	Male chorus		
156	Nachtmusik (Serenade)	Male chorus and orchestra		
157	Constitutionslied			February 1822

Opus No.	Composition	Instruments, etc.	Key	Date
158	Cantata ("Frühlings-morgen")	Soprano, alto, tenor bass and pianoforte	C	1827
159	Fantasie	Violin and pianoforte		
160	Introduction and Variations	Pianoforte and flute	E minor	January 1824
161	Quartet	Strings	G	June 1826
162	Sonata	Pianoforte and violin	A	August 1817
163	Quintet	Strings (2 'celli)		1817
164	Sonata	Pianoforte	A minor	1815-19
165	5 Songs	Tenor and Soprano	F	March 1824
166	Octet	2 violins, viola, cello, contrabass, clarinet, horn and bassoon		
167	Gesang der Geister	8 Male voices and string accompaniment		1820
168	Quartet	Strings	B♭	1814
169	Der Wintertag	4 voices		
170	Overture (Italian style)	Orchestra	C major	November 1817
171	12 Ländler	For 2 and 4 hands pianoforte		
172	6 Songs	Soprano and Tenor		1815-20
173	6 Songs	Tenor and mezzo		1815-21

Appendix B

Teufels Lustschloss	Operetta 3 acts	Book by A. von Kotzebue	1814
Vierjährige Posten	Singspiel 1 act	Book by T. Körner	May 1815
Fernando	Singspiel 1 act	Book by A. Stadler	July 1815
Claudine v. Villabella (fragment)	3 acts	Book by Goethe	July 26, 1815
Spiegelritter	Operetta 3 acts (fragment)	Book by Kotzebue	1815
Adrast	Opera (fragment)	Book by Mayrhofer	1815
Freunde v. Salamanka	Operetta 2 acts	Mayrhofer	December 31, 1815
Die Bürgschaft	Opera 3 acts (fragment)	After Schiller	May 1816
Die Zwillingsbrüder	Vaudeville 1 act	Hofmann	January 1819
Zauberharfe	Melodrama 3 acts	Book by Hoffmann	1819
Sakuntala	Opera 3 acts (sketch)	Book by J. F. Neumann	October 1820
Verschworenen ("Häusliche Krieg")	Operetta 1 act	Castelli	April 1823
Graf v. Gleichen	Opera 3 acts (sketch)	Bauernfeld	1827
Die Salzbergwerke	Opera (sketch)		
Der Minnesänger	Singspiel (lost)		
Mass (No. 1)	Solo, chorus and orchestra	F	1814
Mass (No. 2)	Solo, chorus and orchestra	G	1815

Schubert

Composition	Instruments, etc.	Key	Date
Mass No. 5	Solo, chorus and orchestra	A♭	1819-22
Mass (No. 6)	Solo, chorus and orchestra	E♭	1828
Deutsche Messe	4 voices and wind-instruments	F	1826
Lazarus (fragment of an oratorio)	Solo, chorus and orchestra		February 1820
Quartet	Strings	B♭	1812
,,	,,	C major	1812
,,	,,	B♭ major	1812
,,	,,	C major	1813
,,	,,	B♭	1813
,,	,,	D major	1813
,,	,,	D major	1814
,,	,,	G minor	1815
,,	,,	C minor	1820
Quartet-movement	,,	D minor	1825
Quartet	,,	B♭	(1816?)
Trio	Violin, viola and 'cello	D major	October 28, 1813
Symphony (1)	Small orchestra	B♭ major	1814-15
,, (2)	,,	D major	May 24, 1815
,, (3)	,,	C minor	April 1816
,, (4) ("Tragic")	"Without trumpets and drums"	B♭	September 1816
,, (5)	"Without trombones"		
Symphony (6)		C major	February 1818

Appendix B

Work	Instrumentation	Key	Date
Symphony (7)	Full Orchestra	C major	March 1828
("Unfinished") (8)	" "	B minor	October 30, 1822
Teufels als Hydraulicus (Overture)	" "	D	June 1812
Overture	" " "	Bb	September 1816
Overture	" " "	D	
Overture ("Italian style")	" " "	D	May 1817
Overture	Orchestra	E minor	1819
5 Minuets and 6 trios	Orchestra		November 19, 1813
5 Deutsche and 7 trios	Orchestra		1813
Minuet and finale	Wind-instruments	F	
Trauermusik	Wind-instruments		
Children's March	Piano duet	G major	October 12, 1827
Four Ländler	Piano duet	D major	
Overture	Pianoforte duet	Various	July 1824
Allegro and andante	Pianoforte duet	C and A minor	
Fantasia	Pianoforte duet	Series IX., Nos. 30-2, B. & H.	1810
Fantasia	Pianoforte duet		1811
Fantasia	Pianoforte duet		1813
Sonata	Arpeggione or cello, and pianoforte	A minor	November 1824
Sonata	Pianoforte	E	1815
Sonata	Pianoforte	C major	1815
Sonata	Pianoforte	Ab	1817
Sonata	Pianoforte	E minor	1817
Sonata	Pianoforte	C minor	September 26, 1828
Sonata	Pianoforte	A major	1828
Sonata	Pianoforte	Bb	1828
Variations	Pianoforte	F major	1812

Schubert

Composition	Instruments, etc.	Key	Date
Variations (Hütten-brenner's theme)	Pianoforte	A minor	August 1817
Variations (Diabelli's theme)	Pianoforte	C minor	March 1821
Andante	Pianoforte		1812
Klavierstück	Pianoforte	A	
Adagio	Pianoforte	E	
Allegretto	Pianoforte	C minor	1827
3 Klavierstücke			
5 Klavierstücke			
2 Scherzos	Pianoforte	B flat and D flat	1817
March	Pianoforte	E	
Ländler, Deutsche, etc.	Pianoforte		
Dance movements "Grät-zer Galopp," etc.	Pianoforte		September 1827
Latin hymns "Stabat Mater," etc.	4 voices and accompaniment	G minor and F minor	1815 and 1816
Gesang der Geister	8 voices (see also op. 167)		
Sehnsucht	5 voices		
Wer ist gross?	Chorus and orchestra		
Beiträge (for Salieri)	Chorus (unaccompanied)		June 1816
Cantata (Father's name-day)	Chorus and orchestra		September 27, 1815
An die Sonne	Chorus and pianoforte		
Lebenslust	Chorus and pianoforte		
Cantata (I. Kiesewetter)	Chorus and pianoforte		

Angels' song	Chorus (Faust)		July 1828
Psalm 92	Chorus (unaccompanied)		
Overture	Small orchestra	B♭	September 1816
Overture	Full orchestra	D minor	May 1817
Concertstück (Concerto)	Violin and orchestra	D major	December 1816
Rondo	Violin and string-quartet	A major	June 1816
Trio	Violin, viola and 'cello	B♭	September 1816
Overture	Pianoforte duet	G minor	October 1819
"Fierrabras"	Overture pianoforte duet	F minor	
Sonatas (many fragments)	Pianoforte		
Tantum ergo	Chorus and orchestra	E♭	1828
Offertorum	Tenor, chorus and orchestra	B♭	October 28
Terzette	3 male voices		1813

Note.— Among the pieces without opus number there are some 300 songs.   Space does not admit of our giving a complete list.   Messrs Breitkopf & Haertel print an alphabetical catalogue.

Appendix C

1797. Franz Schubert born.
1800-4. Taught music by his father.
1804-6. Franz becomes a pupil of Holzer.
1807. Appointed soprano at Lichtenthal parish church.
1808. Entered Imperial Convict School.
1809. Napoleon signed treaty of peace at Vienna.
1810. Date of Schubert's "Phantasie" (4 hands).
1811. Date of String-quartet and "Hagar's Klage."
1812. Schubert's mother died.
1813. Schubert leaves the Convict.
1814. Became elementary teacher in his father's school.
1815. Wrote the "Erl-king."
1816. Salieri's jubilee.
1817. Rossini in Vienna.
1818. Schubert became teacher to Count Esterhazy.
1819. Schubert visits upper Austria.
1820. Two operettas produced this year.
1821. The "Erl-king" published.
1822. Schubert meets Weber.
1823. Schubert wrote "Fierrabras" and "Rosamunde."
1824. Love affair at Zelész.
1825. Five months holiday with Vogl.
1826. Lived with Bauernfeld and Schwindt.
1827. Visited Beethoven's sick-bed.
1828. Wrote Symphony in C. Died November 19.

Appendix D

Schubert Personalia and Memoranda

Barbaja (Domenico), b. Milan 1778. First a waiter, afterwards circus-proprietor and finally the most popular of operatic managers. From 1821-5 he was manager of the two chief houses in Vienna—the Kärnthnerthor theatre and the An der Wien, where he introduced Rossini and Weber. Schubert was neglected. Among other of his numerous theatrical undertakings, Barbaja managed the San Carlo (Naples) and La Scala (Milan).

Bauernfeld (Eduard), b. at Vienna 1804. Studied Law during time of his acquaintance with Schubert. Was employed in the Diplomatic service 1826-1848. Shared rooms in common with Schubert and Schwindt in 1826. Contributed several papers of reminiscences of Schubert.

Beethoven (Ludwig van), 1770-1827. Schubert and Beethoven only became really acquainted during Beethoven's last illness. Schubert is said (by Kreissle) to have been one of the thirty-eight "torch-bearers" at Beethoven's funeral.

Boieldieu (Francois Adrien), b. at Rouen 1775 ; d. 1834 near Paris. One of the most distinguished of the French comic opera composers. "La Dame blanche" is his finest work.

Castelli (Ignaz Friedrich), b. at Vienna 1781 ; d. 1854. German dramatist ; wrote books for Weigl's "Swiss family," Schubert's "Verschworenen," and adapted "Les Huguenots" (Meyerbeer). Founder and editor of "Allgemeiner musikalischer Anzeiger." (1829-40).

Schubert

Cherubini (Maria Luigi Carlo Zenobi Salvatore), b. at Florence 1760; d. 1842. His "Medée" and "Deux Journées" still keep their hold on the German public. Beethoven termed him "the most admirable of living composers."

Chézy (Wilhelmine—or Helmine—Christine von), *née* von Klencke, b. 1783 at Berlin, married de Chézy the orientalist. She is the librettist of Schubert's "Rosamunde" and Weber's "Euryanthe." Her "Unvergessenes" (Leipsic 1858) and the "Erinnerungen" of her son W. von Chézy (Schaffhausen 1863) contain much gossip concerning Schubert.

Claudius (Matthias), 1740-1815. German poet, and author of many popular songs, which appear under the collective title of "The Wandsbeck Messenger." Schubert set eleven of his lyrics.

Craigher (Jac. Nic.). Author of the fine ballad "Die junge Nonne" and translator of Colley Cibber's "Blind boy"— Der blinde Knabe. (1825).

Cureton, William D. D. (1808-1864). Orientalist, b. at Westbury, Shropshire. Became Assistant-keeper of MSS., British Museum. Rector of St Margaret's, Westminster, and Canon of Westminster. Created F.R.S. He found at the Monastery St Mary Deipara (in the desert of Nitria) near Cairo, the Epistles of St Ignatius to St Polycarp, Ephesians, and the Romans in ancient Syriac. These he edited with English translation, and notes.

Diabelli (Anton), 1781-1858. Composer of pianoforte music of an easy kind, and of church music popular in its day. Beethoven took a waltz of Diabelli's as the theme for the thirty-three variations (op. 120). Diabelli joined Peter Cappi in 1812 as a music publisher. It became Diabelli & Co. in 1824. The firm absorbed the following well-known businesses :—Artaria, Weigl, Berka, Leidesdorf, Pennauer, Traeg, and (later) Mecchetti. In 1852 it changed to C. A. Spina and in 1872 to F. Schreiber. under which name it was carried on by Mr A Cranz, who purchased it in 1876. The old firm of Diabelli published for Schubert, Czerny, Strauss and Lanner, Marpurg, Sechter, and Reicha.

Appendix D

Dietrichstein (Count Josef Carl). Curator of the Convict School, when Schubert was a pupil.

Dietrichstein (Count Moritz) had charge of the Vienna Court music. Called by Beethoven "Hofmusikgraf." In 1821 wrote a testimonial for Schubert, in which he shows penetration speaking of "Schubert's particular genius for dramatic music"—an opinion new at the time. "The Erl-king" is dedicated to him.

Doppler (Josef). Foreman and chief manager of C. A. Spina's publishing business in Vienna. Played the bassoon in the orchestra that grew up from the Schubert household quartet. Was present at the christening ceremony of Schubert, of whom he has left on record many valuable personal reminiscences. "I shall never forget the droll shock" (says Grove) "which I received on asking Doppler (in 1867) if he knew Schubert. 'Know him,' was the reply; 'I was present at his baptism.'"

Dräxler (Philipp). A Vienna official who wrote the libretto of Schubert's cantata "Prometheus" (1816) which was lost in 1828. The work (a favourite with its composer) is for solo, chorus, and orchestra.

Duport the Manager (or administrator) of the Kärnthnerthor theatre, Vienna, in 1826, when Schubert applied for the post of Conductor.

Ebner (Leopold). One of the contemporary scholars at the Convict with Schubert.

Esterhazy (Count Johann Carl). Head of a musical family which included the Countess and Caroline (both altos) and Marie, the possessor of an exquisite high soprano voice. Schubert taught the several members (at two gulden a lesson) both in Vienna and at Zelész (Hungary). He was further regarded as a friend.

Eybler (Josef), b . 1764 ; d. 1846. A pupil of Albrechtsberger, was successively appointed "regius chori" (Carmelite church, Vienna) Imperial music-teacher and in 1825 full Capell-meister.

Ewer & Co. A firm of music publishers established by John J. Ewer in 1820, at Bow Churchyard, London. Merged in Novello, Ewer & Co., 1867. The original Ewer & Co., were almost the only foreign music importers of their day.

Fouqué (Friedrich Heinrich Karl, Baron de la Motte), 1777-1843. Popular German author. Schubert set Fouque's "Gebet," at the request of Countess Esterhazy, as a vocal quartet, in the course of one day. (Op. 139.) Five of the Lieder are by this writer.

Friedländer (Dr Max), b. 1852. Baritone singer edited new collections of Schubert's songs with Peters. Author of "Beitrage" (1883), etc.

Fries (Reichsgraf Moritz von). An influential supporter of Schubert's, to whom he dedicated his op.2, "Gretchen am Spinnrade," receiving (as is noted in a letter of 1822) the sum of twenty ducats, "a fact" (says he) "which suits me extremely well."

Fröhlich. There were four sisters of this name. Nanette, 1793, a pupil of Hummel, taught singing in the Vienna Conservatoire. She induced Schubert to set Psalm xxiii. and Miriam's Song, among other pieces. (2) Barbara married Ferdinand Bogner an eminent flute-player. She was a good contralto. (3) Josefine became a distinguished concert-singer, d. 1878. (4) Katharina ("Kathi"), 1800-79, was the intimate friend of Grillparzer, the great Austrian poet, who resided with the sisters most of his life.

Führer (Robert), b. at Prague, 1807. Organist and composer. He won a good reputation as a composer. In 1846 he very foolishly published Schubert's Mass in G (with Marco Berra of Prague) as his own composition—a fraud by which he bids fair to be chiefly remembered; so true it is that

> "The evil that men do lives after them;
> The good is oft interred with their bones."

Führer died in great distress in a Vienna hospital in 1861.

Gahy (Josef). An amateur pianist of considerable skill who played duets with Schubert (arrangements of the latter's works and the symphonies of Beethoven), d. 1864.

Gänsbacher (Johann), 1788-1844. Pupil of Vogler—with Weber

Appendix D

and Meyerbeer. Became Capellmeister of Vienna Cathedral in 1823, and held the appointment until his death.

Gläser (Franz), 1792-1861. Operatic composer. Became Capellmeister of the Leopoldstadt theatre, in 1826, afterwards proceeding to Berlin and Copenhagen, where he had similar appointments.

Gluck (Christoph Willibald Ritter von), 1714-1787. Wrote much in conjunction with Metastasio. His best works are the " Orféo" and " Iphigenia in Tauris " and "Alceste"—operas which still hold their own. Marie Antoinette was at one time a pupil of Gluck.

Goethe (Johann Wolfgang von), 1749-1832. The supreme importance of Goethe to the song-renaissance which Schubert brought about is well shown by the fact that Schubert set no less than 70 of the poet's songs alone. 1797 was Goethe's great ballad year ; the musician's was 1815. The earliest pieces of Goethe which were set to music seem to have been twenty little songs, with pretty music by Bernard Theodor Breitkopf—of the publishing family, entitled " Jungenlieder" (1769). Zelter set over 100 of Goethe's poems, Reichardt some 60. The "Erlking" has obtained 39 distinct settings.

Grillparzer (Franz), 1791-1872. Dramatist and poet, born at Vienna. " Sappho" is one of his best works. He also wrote " Der Spielmann"—a story of a musician's life. His dramatic works revived by Heinrich Laube at the Court Theatre, Vienna, in 1849 suddenly made him the most popular writer in Germany. Grillparzer wrote Schubert's epitaph.

Grob (Therese), b. 1800. Daughter of a Vienna silk-factor. She belonged to a musical family with which Schubert was on very friendly terms. She possessed a fine high soprano voice, and sang in the first performance of Schubert's Mass in F. Schubert also wrote a "Tantum ergo" and a "Salve Regina" for her.

Grove (Sir George), b. at Clapham, 1820. Civil Engineer ; for fifteen years editor of *Macmillan's Magazine* ; Secretary Crystal Palace, 1852. Editor of " Dictionary of Music and

Schubert

Musicians" (1879-89) director R.C.M. 1883—knighted the same year—retired 1894 ; d. May 1901.

Gyrowetz (Adalbert), 1763-1850. A Bohemian law student, and afterwards composer and "Operncapellmeister" at Vienna. Enjoyed much popularity, and retired on a pension.

Harrach (Count). Hofmusikgraf, with whom the candidates (of which Schubert was one) had to deal, when competing for Vice-Hofcapellmeistership in 1826.

Haslinger (Tobias), b. 1787 (in Upper Austria), d. at Vienna, 1842. Chief of a well-known music firm which gained distinction through being in touch with Beethoven and Schubert.

Hauer (Dr Josef). Pupil of the Convict School in 1816. In later life Schubert invited him to join in studying Handel's works.

Haydn (Joseph), 1732-1809. The great composer.

Haydn (Michael), 1737-1806. Brother of preceding and an estimable church composer.

Herbeck (Johann), 1831-1877. Court Capellmeister at Vienna, Director of the Court opera, etc.

Himmel (Friedrich Heinrich), b. 1765. Succeeded Reichardt as Court-Capellmeister at Berlin 1794. Died at Berlin 1814.

Hofmann, Secretary of the Kärnthnerthor theatre, wrote two librettos for Schubert ; namely "Die Zwillingsbrüder" (produced June 14, 1820) and "Die Zauberharfe" (produced Aug. 19, 1820).

Hölty, Ludwig, Heinrich, Christoph (1748-1776). One of the most popular German poets, and a principal founder of the famous poetical brotherhood known as the "Hainbund." Hölty is represented by twenty-two songs of Schubert's setting.

Holz (Karl), 1798-1858. Violinist. In 1824 became a member of Schuppanzigh's Quartet.

Holzapfel (Anton). The oldest of Schubert's school-friends at the Convict. A good tenor singer and 'cello player. He (like Randhartinger) is credited with being the pupil who first sang the "Erl-king" at the Convict.

Holzer, Michael. Choirmaster of the Lichtenthal parish church

Appendix D

(Vienna) and first teacher of music to Schubert, whom he long outlived.

Hummel (Johann Nepomuk), b. at Pressburg, 1778; d. at Weimar, 1837. Pianist and composer. Pupil of Haydn and Salieri. Capellmeister to Prince Esterhazy (1804-11).

Hüttenbrenner (Anton), b. 1794. A prolific composer, editor, etc.

Hüttenbrenner (Heinrich), wrote words of "Der Jungling" (op. 8. no. 1).

Hüttenbrenner (Josef). The third brother, an amateur who served Schubert with great fidelity, making duet-arrangements, correcting proofs, and looking after his business arrangements.

Isouard (Nicolo), 1775-1818, b. at Malta. A clever operatic composer. Of his thirty-three operas written in sixteen years, one, in an English version (by Mr Santley), reached London.

Jäger. A singer who on February 28, 1819, sang Schubert's "Schäfers Klagelied," (perhaps) his first piece publicly performed. The concert was given by Jaëll.

Jaëll (Eduard). A violinist who gave a concert at the "Römische Kaiser," Vienna, where Jäger sang a Schubert song, for the first time in public.

Jenger (Johann Baptist), b. at Breisgau. Held a military appointment at Gratz. Became a great friend of Schubert with whom he often played duets, taking the bass ; d. at Vienna, 1855.

Kenner (Josef). School friend of Schubert at the Convict, before 1816. Several of his verses were set to music by the composer.

Kiesewetter (Irene, afterwards Mad. Prokesch v. Osten) daughter of Schubert's friend the "Hofrath." Schubert wrote an Italian cantata, "Alla bella Irene," December 26, 1827.

Kinsky (Princess). A note, under date 1827, shows that Schubert visited at her house.

Kleindl. A schoolmate of Schubert at the Convict. He became Rath of the supreme court of Vienna.

Klopstock (Friedrich Gottlieb), 1724-1803. German poet.

Schubert

Author of "The Messiah," an epic poem. Schubert set nineteen of his poems.

Körner (Karl, Theodor), 1791-1813, b. at Dresden. Through his parents, was intimate with Goethe and Schiller. In 1813 he wrote Der vierjährige Posten, afterwards set as a Singspiel in one act by Schubert (1815). The poems *Leyer und Schwert*, sung to old national melodies round the camp-fires at night, made Lutzow's Free-corps (of which Körner was a member) an enthusiastic band of soldiers, almost irresistible in their ardour. Shot by a chance bullet, while pursuing the French, between Gadebusch and Schwerin. (August 26, 1813.) Schubert wrote the music for sixteen of Körner's poems.

Körner. The singing master at the Convict in 1808, and doubtless the same who held the appointment of Court Tenor until 1826, when we read of his beginning to fail.

Kotzebue (August Friedrich Ferdinand von), 1761-1819, b. at Weimar. Dramatist. Obtained an appointment at St Petersburg. Arrested and sent to Siberia in 1800. A comedy secured his return, when he received the directorship of the German theatre at St Petersburg. Schubert set several of his operatic books.

Kozeluch (Leopold), 1754-1811. Bohemian composer of some thirty symphonies. There is a story of Kozeluch remarking to Mozart, when trying through a new quartet by Haydn, "I should not have written that so." "Neither should I," answered Mozart—"and do you know why; because the thought could never by any chance have occurred to either of us." Mozart made an enemy.

Krebs (Karl Augustus). Conductor of the Court Theatre, Vienna, until 1826, when he removed to Hamburg. Father of Miss Marie Krebs, the pianist.

Kreissle von Hellborn (Heinrich), 1803-1869. Schubert's principal biographer. His two books are noticed in Appendix "A." Kreissle became a Doctor in Laws, and Imperial Finance Secretary, Vienna. He was also one of the managing members of the "Gesellschaft der Musik-freunde." His books have been reproduced in

Appendix D

English and French, and form the groundwork of all Schubert biography.

Kreutzer, 1782-1849. Became Hof-theater-Capellmeister, under Barbaja's management. Afterwards succeeded to the post of Capellmeister to the Josefstadt theatre. Finally removed to Cologne, and Riga, where he died.

Krommer, 1759-1831. Composer of Military music, symphonies, and (strange to say) of quartets and quintets for flutes. Schubert, as a student at the Convict, used to laugh at his symphonies, preferring those of Kozeluch.

Kupelwieser (Leopold), b. at Pisting, Austria, 1796. Became professor and Imperial Rath at the Kunstakademie, Vienna ; d. in 1862. He was a great friend of Schubert. Kupelwieser's sketch of Schubert was engraved for Kreissle's frontispiece to the biography.

Kupelwieser (Josef), brother of preceding. Compiler of Schubert's opera-book for " Fierrabras."

Lablache, Luigi (1794-1858), b. at Naples. His mother was Irish. Perhaps the finest bass ever known, his voice covered two octaves from E-flat below the stave and upwards. Sang as a child at Haydn's funeral. Sang in Mozart's Requiem at Beethoven's funeral, and also acted as one of the torch-bearers, in company with Schubert. To Lablache, Schubert dedicated his three settings of Metastasio's (Italian) songs. These were written in 1827, and form opus 83.

Lachner (Franz), 1804-1890. A pupil of Stadler and Sechter. Became an inseparable companion of Schubert in the latter's last few years. Apart from his own compositions he is remembered for having orchestrated Schubert's " Song of Miriam."

Lascny. Herr Lascny, an Hungarian landowner, and his wife, an accomplished singer, kept open house to Schubert and his friends. Here Lablache was to be heard (he took second bass in Schubert's " Gondelfahrer ") ; here too, Hummel extemporised on Schubert's " Der blinde Knabe."

Lang (Dr Innocenz), Director of the Convict School during Schubert's pupilage. The first symphony (Schubert) was

Schubert

written for the name-day festival of Dr Lang, being performed by the pupils in 1813.

Leidesdorf (Max Josef), 1785-1840. A picture-dealer and music-seller of Vienna. Intimate with Beethoven, who refers to him as "Dorf des Leides," (village of sorrow), and afterwards with Schubert. (See Diabelli). Leidesdorf finally established himself in Florence.

Leitner (Gottfried Ritter von). Poet. Met the Pachlers in 1825, where Schubert became acquainted with him, setting eight of his poems to music.

Lenz (Wilhelm). Biographer of Beethoven. He is responsible for the view that Beethoven and Schubert were purposely kept apart by the misrepresentations of mutual acquaintance.

Lincke (Joseph), eminent 'cello-player and composer (1783-1837) was a member of the Rasoumowsky quartet and played under Beethoven's supervision.

Liszt (Franz), 1811-1886, produced Schubert's "Alfonso und Estrella," at Weimar, June 24, 1854. He transcribed no fewer than fifty-seven of Schubert's songs, and by his arrangements no less than his playing, bore a large part in establishing Schubert's reputation.

Manns (August Friedrich), b. at Stolzenburg, North Germany, March 12, 1825. Came to England 1854, for opening of Crystal Palace. Became conductor of the Crystal Palace Orchestra in 1855. Manns encouraged the production of native composition in an unprecedented manner. He has conducted seven triennial Handel Festivals. Received the honour of knighthood in 1903. One of the foremost to make Schubert's works known in England.

Mayrhofer (Johann), 1787-1836. Austrian poet and a close friend of Schubert, who set forty-seven of his songs and two opera-librettos to music. Mayrhofer and he lived together for some years. After the musician's death, Mayrhofer, who was employed as an officer of the Austrian censorship, suffered from deep melancholy, and ended by throwing himself in the Danube.

Méhul (Etienne Henri), 1763-1817, produced twenty-four operas

Appendix D

in seventeen years. The famous "Chant du Départ" is Méhul's composition.

Mendelssohn (Felix Mendelssohn Bartholdy), 1809-1847. Mendelssohn produced for the first time Schubert's great Symphony in C-major, at the Leipzig Gewandhaus concerts, on March 21, 1839.

Merveldt Foundation provided free scholarships, with board and education, for scholars of the Convict who, having passed the proper examinations, were recommended for the same. Schubert, acting on Theodor Körner's advice, refused to enter the examinations.

Metastasio the assumed name of Pietro Trapassi (1698-1782). Italian poet, librettist and translator of the "Iliad." Metastasio was a great friend of Farinelli the famous singer. He lived in Vienna for some years (in 1830). Eleven poems were set by Schubert.

Milder (Anna), 1785-1838, born at Constantinople. Married Hauptmann, a jeweller. Cherubini wrote his "Faniska" and Beethoven his "Fidelio" for her voice. Milder sang to Goethe in 1823 some settings which moved the poet— probably including some of Schubert's songs. "Hirt auf dem Felsen" was specially written for Milder-Hauptmann.

Mozart (Wolfgang Amadeus), 1756-1791. The great composer.

Mosel (Ignaz Franz), 1772-1844. A Vienna diplomatist and clever amateur composer. In 1821 he was vice-director of the Royal opera house.

Müller (Sofie). A famous actress, who came to Vienna in 1824. Jenger, Vogl and Schubert often visited her in 1825. Madame Müller sang "Die junge Nonne" at sight, at one of these meetings. Her diary was published. She died in 1830.

Müller (Wilhelm), 1794-1827, b. at Dessau. Father of Max Müller the Philologist. Wilhelm served as a volunteer in the Prussian army through the battles of Lutzen, Bautzen etc., and the occupation of the Netherlands. Schubert set forty-five of his songs to music.

Napoleon (Buonaparte), 1769-1821. Vienna twice fell into Napoleon's hands, namely in 1805 and in 1809. During the latter year he took up his residence in Vienna, where magnificent reviews daily took place. There he celebrated his birthday (August 15th, 1809). Deposed (1814-15).

Neefe (Hermann). Scene-painter, son of Gottlieb Neefe, Beethoven's teacher in Bonn.

Neumann (Professor Johann Phillip), writer of the book for the opera "Sakuntala" (1820) and compiler of the words of the "Deutsche Mass."

Niemeyer (A. H.), b. at Halle. Professor of theology and afterwards Chancellor of the Hochschule in Halle. His sacred poem "The Feast of the Resurrection" supplies the words for Schubert's oratorio "Lazarus." D. 1828.

Nourrit (Adolphe), tenor singer, b. at Paris, 1802. Sang much in Rossini's operas. Popularised Schubert's songs in France. Committed suicide in 1839. The "Erl-king" and "Die Junge Nonne" were among his songs.

Pachler (Dr Carl) advocate at Gratz. His wife, remarkable for her musical ability and beauty, attracted much society to their house. Schubert, Teltscher and Schönstein commonly stayed with the family.

Palffy (Count Ferdinand von). Proprietor of the Imperial theatre "An der Wien."

Parry (Sir Charles Hubert Hastings, Bart.), b. 1848. Distinguished English composer. Professor of Music, Oxford University; Director of The Royal College of Music. His books and papers on music are of the highest order of merit.

Paumgartner (Silvester), a person of importance at Steyr in 1819. Vogl and Schubert more than once quartered themselves on the good-natured citizen, who died in 1841.

Philharmonic Society (London), founded 1813. Schubert though taken up by Mendelssohn in 1839—was not represented at the Philharmonic, until 1867, when W. G. Cusins conducted the B-minor Symphony. Distinguished visitors of the past have included Cherubini, Spohr, Weber, Mendelssohn, Wagner and all the principal performers.

Piazza (Lucca). A costumier of the Theatre an der Wien, in 1820.

Pichler (Caroline). Schubert set three of her poems to music.

Pinterics (Carl). Private secretary (to Count Palffy) and an

Appendix D

accomplished pianoforte player.   Friend of Schubert and
Beethoven.

Pohl (Carl Ferdinand), b. at Darmstadt, 1819. Biographer of
Mozart and Haydn. D. at Vienna, 1887.

Probst. A publisher in Leipsic (predecessor of Senff) who
served both Schubert and Beethoven.

Pyrker (Ladislaus), Patriarch of Venice. Much esteemed as a
poet. Schubert set his "Die Allmacht," and dedicated
"Der Wanderer" and other pieces to him. Schubert
mentions with gratitude having received a gift of 12
ducats (£6) from the Patriarch in 1822.

Quarterly Musical Magazine and Review. The first English
journal devoting itself to music. Projected and edited by
Richard M. Bacon, a Norwich man, who carried his paper
successfully forward for some ten years. Beethoven was
treated with suspicion, while Schubert was not sufficiently
important to attract much notice.

Randhartinger (Benedict), 1802-1893. A fellow student with
Schubert at the Stadtconvikt during the year 1812-13.
He had a good tenor voice, and in 1832 sang in the court
chapel. Thirty years later he became conductor at the
same church.

Rasoumowsky (Andreas Kyrillovitsch), 1752-1816 (?), son of a
Russian peasant. In 1815 attained the rank of prince.
His famous string quartet (which is also known as the
Beethoven quartet) was founded in 1808 with Schuppanzigh,
Rasoumowsky, Weiss and Lincke. The Prince pensioned
the three players in 1815, and Schuppanzigh (with Sina as
his second player) continued the quartet-playing for many
years afterwards.

Reichardt (Johann Friedrich) b. at Königsberg, 1752.
Appointed in 1776 as Capellmeister and court-composer
to Frederick the Great, at Berlin. Visited England in
1785. Dismissed from his Berlin appointment 1794.
Reichardt was an able critic and writer on music ; his
programme-annotations are in all probability *the first*.
Some of his settings of Goethe's songs, sixty of which are
printed, are deservedly held in respect.

Rellstab (Heinrich Friedrich Ludvig), 1799-1860. Trained as a

Schubert

musician; but devoted himself to literature. Wrote for Schubert and Mendelssohn.

Richter (Jean Paul), 1763-1825. The poet was greatly attracted by Schubert's genius, and (says Kreissle) "found in his declining years of blind old age, a consolation in Schubert's Lieder, and asked for the 'Erl-king' a few hours only before his death."

Rinna (Dr von), Court Physician at Vienna in 1828, who advised Schubert in his last illness to remove to the Wieden suburb of the city. (Ferdinand's new quarters.)

Rochlitz (Freidrich von) came to Vienna in 1822, in order to see Beethoven. He met Schubert during this visit; and in 1827 we find him approaching the latter with a view to his setting the poem "Der erste Ton," which was never done.

Roller. Master of the machinery at the imperial theatre an-der-Wien, in 1820.

Rosetti (Francesco Antonio), the assumed name of Franz Anton Rössler (1750-1792), Court Capellmeister at Schwerin. He composed 19 symphonies, and many quartets, concertos and oratorios.

Rossini (Gioacchino Antonio), 1792-1868. Schubert rightly described this remarkable person as a "rare genius." Others, such as Beethoven, disliked his music, while Berlioz would have cheerfully burnt the fifty Rossini-operas. Time reconciles violent opinions.

Ruczizca (Wenzel), 1758-1823. Violinist at the Hofburg theatre, Vienna. Court organist in 1793. He first put into shape the famous Rakoczy march. Schubert studied harmony and composition with Ruczizca, before taking regular lessons from Salieri.

St Anna School, where Schubert studied, 1813-14, to qualify as a teacher for his father's school. Ferdinand ten years later became master, and, in 1851, Director of the St Anna School, Vienna.

Salieri (Antonio), 1750-1825. As composer and theorist Salieri was an important personage in his time. Settled in Vienna as early as 1766. Became Court Capellmeister

Appendix D

and composer in 1788. Both Beethoven and Schubert were proud to declare themselves his pupils. At his jubilee (Vienna, 1816) a cantata of Schubert's, specially composed, was produced under the composer's direction. Gluck was an early patron of Salieri, who is said to have intrigued against Mozart, but to have also befriended his son.

Schaufl (Jacob), received (in 1816) on the recommendation of Salieri the appointment of principal teacher at the Normal Institute of Music, in Laibach, for which Schubert had offered himself.

Schechner (Nanette), born at Munich, 1806, and became one of the first singers in Germany. A pupil of Weber. Sang much in Italian opera, and afterwards in German. A rival of Sonntag. Quitted the stage in 1835. Married Herr Waagen in 1832. Died in 1860. Her part in the transaction which lost Schubert the conductorship of the Kärnthnerthor theatre does not seem to be in any degree blameworthy, though the results were unfortunate.

Schellmann. On two occasions Schubert visited the Schellmanns, resident at Steyr (Upper Austria). Dr Schellmann's family numbered five daughters, and in the same house, on the upper floor, were the District-treasurer and his three daughters. The party is alluded to by Schubert as "the eight Schellmann girls."

Schiller (John Christoph Friedrich), 1759-1805. Schubert set forty-two of Schiller's poems.

Schlegel (Friedrich), 1772-1829. Famous chiefly as an historian of literature. Married a daugher of Moses Mendelssohn. Schlegel's son became a celebrated painter.

Schlegel (August Wilhelm von), brother of the preceding German poet, critic and translator. His Shakespeare translations—were afterwards revised and continued by Tieck.

Schneider (Dr Eduard), Schubert's MSS. came into the hands of Dr Schneider, nephew of the composer, who practised as a barrister, living in the Tuchlauben, Vienna. (1867).

Schober (Franz von), b. in Sweden, 1798, famous as an Austrian poet. Became one of Schubert's most intimate friends.

Schubert

Schober wrote the libretto of "Alfonso und Estrella" and fifteen poems which Schubert set to music.

Schroeder-Devrient (Wilhelmine), 1804-1860. A dramatic soprano of extraordinary reputation in her day; took leading rôles in operas of Mozart, Beethoven, Weber and Wagner.

Schubert (Ferdinand), an elder brother of Franz, born 1794. Joined his father as assistant-teacher, and finally Director of the Normal School of St Anna, Vienna. Some church music by Ferdinand is printed, but his school-books, some twelve of which came into use, and his connection with the Bell-Lancastrian teaching method gained him prominence. Died 1859.

Schubert (Franz, the elder), son of a Moravian peasant. Came to Vienna, 1784; he kept school in the Himmelfortgrund. Afterwards appointed to the Rossau parish school.

Schubert (Ignaz), the eldest son of the preceding, was also a school master. His letters show him much attached to his brother the composer, and something of a sceptic, much averse to his teaching business. D. 1844.

Schubert (Therese), sister of the composer. Married Matthias Schneider, a professor at the Imperial Institute of Orphans (Vienna).

Schulz (Johann Abraham Peter), 1747-1800. An early German song-writer who forms an important link in the chain of song composers who led up to Schubert.

Schuppanzigh (Ignaz) b. at Vienna, 1776. Founder of the famous Rasoumowsky Quartet (q. v.) d. 1830.

Schwindt (Moritz von) 1804-1871. A painter of the Romantic school, born at Vienna. A close friend of Schubert, some of whose songs he illustrated. Executed designs in conjunction with Schnorr for the stained glass windows of Glasgow Cathedral. In 1857 Schwindt visited England to officially report to King Louis on the Manchester art-treasures.

Scott (Sir Walter), 1771-1832. Scott's connection with Schubert is two-fold; several of his poems were set (in translation) to music—such as the famous "Ave Maria;" the poet also rendered the "Erl-king" in English.

Appendix D

Sechter (Simon), 1788-1867. A famous theorist and professor of Counterpoint, with whom Schubert intended to study, in his last year. Sechter's pupils included Thalberg, Bruckner Nottebohm, Vieuxtemps, Pauer and Pohl.

Sehnsucht ('Longing' or 'Yearning') a song occurring in Book IV., chapter XI. of Goethe's "Wilhelm Meister." It begins "Nur wer die Sehnsucht kennt." Beethoven set it four times for voice and piano. Schubert has left some six settings—songs and versions for five men's voices, and as a duet for Mignon and the Harper. It was the last-named form that Goethe indicated in Wilhelm Meister.

Senn (Johann Michael), 1795-1857. A soldier and poet who studied at the Convict, whence he was ejected in 1815 for taking part in an *émeute*, Senn being the ringleader. Two of his lyrics are set by Schubert in op. 23 (nos. 2 and 3) ; both striking songs.

Seyfried (Ignaz Ritter von), 1776-1841, a pupil of Mozart, and native of Vienna. Wrote several dramatic pieces for the Vienna theatre, of which he was director, while also holding a position as Capellmeister.

Singspiel, would now be termed Operetta. The music was not of first importance in the early *Singspiele*. Neefe and Reichardt were among the improvers of this peculiarly German form.

Sonnleithner (Dr Ignaz Elder von) Rath, Advocate and Professor in Vienna. During years 1815-24 held regular meetings at his house where Schubert's music was much cultivated.

Sonnleithner (Leopold), son of the preceding, was intimate with Schubert from his earliest schooldays. He and his father (with two others) were sponsors for the publication of the "Erl-king" in 1821.

Spaun (Joseph Freihier von), 1788-1865. One of Schubert's earliest friends ; pupil of the "Convict," where he studied Law and Music. Author of the words of song "Jungling und der Tod," set by Schubert. He also helped to preserve his MSS. and Biographical material.

Schubert

Spendou (Josef). A doctor of Divinity, Privy-Councillor, Royal Commissioner for Schools, and chief superintendent, Vienna (1816). Schubert wrote a cantata in his honour (op. 128).

Spina (Carl Anton), successor to Diabelli, Vienna publisher. (1852). Original publisher of many of Schubert's works, and a great enthusiast.

Spontini (Gasparo Luigi Pacifico), 1774-1851. A considerable operatic composer—"La Vestale" being perhaps his best known work.

Stadler (Albert), b. at Steyr, 1794. Studied music with Weigl and Wawra. Met Schubert at the Convict, where he went to study law. An industrious composer, and intimate friend of Schubert.

Sullivan (Sir Arthur Seymour), b. 1842, at London. Mendelssohn scholar 1856, Principal of National Training School for Music (the forerunner of R.C.M.) 1876-81. Prolific composer of comic operas and much serious music ("Golden Legend," Leeds, 1886). D. Nov. 1901.

Széchényi. Hungarian writer, two of whose songs ("Abgeblühte Linde" and "Flug der Zeit") Schubert set to music in 1817.

Teyber (Anton), 1754-1822. A composer of chamber music in Vienna.

Tieze. One of the Schubert vocal quartet-party with Umlauff, in 1821. The composer often accompanied his songs for Tieze, who at the time was in the front rank of solo or concerted singers.

Troyer (Count Ferdinand). A distinguished amateur clarinettist, by whose order Schubert's Octet (op. 166) came to be written. (1824).

Umlauff (Michael), 1781-1842, a native of Vienna. Became Weigl's colleague at the Opera-house. Beethoven had a good opinion of him. Umlauff also knew Schubert. Schuppanzigh and Umlauff were the chiefs of the Akademien, founded by Beethoven in 1824, where the "Mass in D" and the "Ninth Symphony" were first produced.

Vogl (Johann Michael), b. at Steyr, 1768. Became a great operatic singer. After being pensioned off in 1822, he took to Lieder singing, and, although thirty years older than Schubert, became his companion and friend. Vogl died on November 19, 1840, on the twelfth anniversary of Schubert's death.

Watteroth (Professor Watteroth von Dräxler) a distinguished Vienna official, for whose name-day festival (in 1816) Schubert wrote the cantata " Prometheus " ; his first composition for money.

Weber (Carl Maria von), 1786-1826. Weber visited Vienna in 1823 to conduct his " Euryanthe."

Weigl (Josef), 1766-1846, a prolific Hungarian composer. " Die Schweizerfamilie," produced at Vienna, 1809. Weigl succeeded Salieri, as Hoftheater - Capellmeister, 1790.

Weingartner (Paul Felix), b. 1863 at Zara (Dalmatia). Studied at Leipzig. Court Capellmeister at Berlin 1891, and at Munich 1894. Eminent composer and distinguished conductor.

Weiss (Franz), 1788-1830. Played the viola in the Rasoumowsky Quartet.

Weissenwolf (Countess Sofie von) 1794-1847. Writing July 25, 1825, Schubert says, " At Steyreck, we put up at the Countess Weissenwolf's—a great worshipper of my littleness ; she has all my songs, many of which she sings beautifully."

Witásek (Johann Nepomuk), August 1771-1839. A Bohemian who wrote dance music and much popular classical music. Became President of the Society for the Improvement of Church Music. Died at Prague.

Würfel, b. 1791, at Planim, Bohemia. Became Professor of Music at Warsaw, 1815, and in 1826 was elected Capellmeister of the Court theatre, Vienna. Wrote several operas, including the well-known " Rübezahl."

Zelter (Carl Friedrich), 1758-1832, the famous Berlin composer. A friend of Goethe—one hundred of whose songs he set to music.

Zierer (Franz), Professor of the Vienna Conservatorium and member of the court opera band in 1826.

Schubert

Zumsteeg (Johann Rudolf), 1760-1802. Composer of operas and songs. He was much encouraged by the poet Schiller. In 1792 he became Capellmeister to the Duke of Würtemberg. Schubert appears to have taken him for a model in his first efforts in musical composition.

Index

Schubert

Index

---

[1] A complete list of Schubert's known letters is here given. Where no page is set down no quotations have been made.

Schubert

Index

Index

PRINTED BY
TURNBULL AND SPEARS,
EDINBURGH